RONALD RIBMAN is a native New Yorker and was educated at the University of Pittsburgh where he received a Ph.D. in English literature. *Cold Storage*, his eighth play, enjoyed a highly acclaimed run on Broadway and won the New York Dramatists Guild Award. He is perhaps best known as the author of the Obie Award-winning *The Journey of the Fifth Horse* and *Harry, Noon and Night*, both of which starred Dustin Hoffman. These and two other plays, *The Ceremony of Innocence* and *Fingernails Blue as Flowers*, were initially presented at the American Place Theater. He is also the author of *Passing Through from Exotic Places*, *A Break in the Skin*, and *The Poison Tree*, which starred Cleavon Little and was produced at Broadway's Ambassador Theatre in 1976. Mr. Ribman's *The Journey of the Fifth Horse* and *The Ceremony of Innocence* have been seen on public television, and his *The Final War of Olly Winter* was nominated for an Emmy Award. He has been a Fellow of the Rockefeller Foundation, the Guggenheim Foundation, and the National Endowment for the Arts. In 1975 he received the Rockefeller Foundation Award "in recognition of his sustained contribution to American theater."

FIVE PLAYS BY
RONALD RIBMAN

 A BARD BOOK/PUBLISHED BY AVON BOOKS

AVON BOOKS
A division of
The Hearst Corporation
959 Eighth Avenue
New York, New York 10019

Harry, Noon and Night copyright © 1967 by Ronald Ribman
The Journey of the Fifth Horse copyright © 1967 by Ronald Ribman
The Ceremony of Innocence copyright © 1968 by Ronald Ribman
The Poison Tree copyright © 1977 by Ronald Ribman
Cold Storage copyright © 1976 by Ronald Ribman
Published by arrangement with the author.

Library of Congress Catalog Card Number: 78-58907
ISBN: 0-380-40006-5

First Bard Printing, September, 1978

BARD TRADEMARK REG. U.S. PAT. OFF. AND IN OTHER COUNTRIES, MARCA REGISTRADA, HECHO EN U.S.A.

Printed in the U.S.A.

CONTENTS

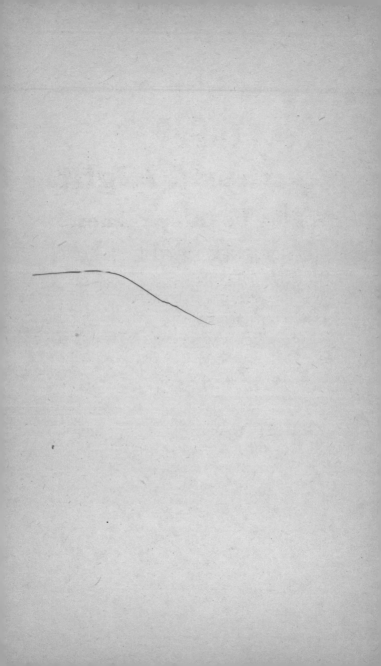

Harry, Noon and Night

A Play in Three Scenes

For Arthur and Rosemary Hagadus
and Charles Crow

They said, "You have a blue guitar,
You do not play things as they are."
The man replied, "Things as they are
Are changed upon the blue guitar."

—Wallace Stevens

The first performance of *Harry, Noon and Night* was given on March 17, 1965, at the American Place Theatre in New York City. It was directed by George Morrison. Scenery, lighting, and costumes were by Robert Mitchell.

THE ORIGINAL CAST
(*In Order of Appearance*)

HARRY . . . . *Joel Grey*
SOLDIER . . . . *Richard Schaal*
PROSTITUTE . . . . *Lynn Bernay*
ARCHER . . . . *Gerald S. O'Loughlin*
IMMANUEL . . . . *Dustin Hoffman*
HERMAN (*Offstage voice*)
HERMAN'S WIFE . . . . *Lotte Stavisky*
POLICEMAN . . . . *Bruce Glover*

SCENE I

Harry entertains a soldier from Nashville. The Dolly Bar: late afternoon.

SCENE II

Immanuel entertains a visitor from Ohio. Harry and Immanuel's room: the same afternoon.

2

SCENE III

To divide what is thine from what is mine. Harry and Immanuel's room: ten-thirty that night.

TIME: *December 1955*
PLACE: *Munich, Germany*

SCENE I

Harry entertains a soldier from Nashville

PLACE: *The Dolly Bar in Munich, Germany.*

TIME: *December 1955, late one afternoon.*

SCENE: *A small round table and three chairs. On the table are several beer bottles, glasses, and ashtrays littered with cigarette butts. Upstage left is a very scraggly Christmas tree, interlaced with small electric light bulbs and beaten-up ornaments. Offstage, a jukebox is playing "Hark, the Herald Angels Sing."*

ON RISE: HARRY *and a* SOLDIER *are sitting on opposite sides of the table. Between them and facing the audience is a young, attractive German* PROSTITUTE. HARRY, *about twenty-five, is industriously writing in a child's notebook. The* SOLDIER, *several years younger, is kissing the* GIRL'S *neck. Throughout the scene, the* PROSTITUTE *is mechanical in her movements, as if nothing that goes on has anything to do with her. She smokes, drinks, looks about for future customers, advertises her body, keeps time to melodies heard and unheard. She moves to her own rhythm.* HARRY *and the* SOLDIER *regard her more as an object than as a human being. Whenever it pleases them they fondle her. They run their hands over her legs, her breasts, and they never miss a beat in their conversation. As* HARRY *continues writing, the* GIRL *puts her arms around the* SOLDIER *and begins warming him up, literally crawling all over him.*

4

While the music plays, the SOLDIER *and the* PROSTI-
TUTE *continue this lovemaking. When the music stops,*
HARRY *speaks. He does so without looking up as he
continues writing.*

HARRY: Do you have to do that? [*Neither the* SOLDIER
nor the GIRL *seems to have heard.* HARRY *writes a bit
more. This time when he speaks, it is startlingly
loud.*] Do you?

SOLDIER: [*As if coming out of a trance*] Huh? What's
the matter?

HARRY: [*Imitating his words and facial expression*]
Huh? What? Huh?

SOLDIER: What's the matter, man?

HARRY: [*Sharply*] This is what's the matter, man. [*He
slowly pulls the* GIRL *over to him and begins kissing
the* GIRL'*s throat and running his hands over her
body. She begins to respond to him just as she had
to the* SOLDIER. *The* SOLDIER *is plainly embarrassed.*]
Do you have to do that?

SOLDIER: I thought you wanted to write awhile.

HARRY: How am I supposed to write? Here . . . [*Shoves
book and pencil at him.*] You write. [HARRY *goes
into a noisy parody of the* SOLDIER'*s lovemaking technique. The* SOLDIER, *dumbfounded, stares at the
book and pencil.*] Go on, write!

SOLDIER: What?

HARRY: Anything. The pledge to the flag. Dixieland.
[SOLDIER *just sits there while* HARRY *continues to
mock his lovemaking technique. The noises grow
more and more passionate and animalistic.*] Can't be
done, can it? [SOLDIER *mumbles something.* HARRY
cups his hand to his ear.] Eh? Eh? What's that?

SOLDIER: No.

HARRY: [*Stops his necking parody.*] You bet your ass
it can't be done. [SOLDIER *is nervously trying to light
a cigarette.*] You think I'm blind? I mean you sit
there running your tongue along her neck, blowing

into her ear, and she's wiggling her breasts all around and snaking up against you and all them goddamn sucking sounds and hot breathing. What am I supposed to do? Ignore it? [*The* SOLDIER *is thoroughly chastened.* HARRY *stares at him and then looks back at his notes.*] Where was I?

SOLDIER: The blue braid in my hat.

HARRY: [*Puts the notebook and pencil down in disgust.*] I don't know. I lost my whole train of thought.

SOLDIER: I think you wanted me to tell you about the braid.

HARRY: That's not the point. I lose track of one thing I forget about everything. That's the kind of mind I got. One interruption and I can't remember beans. I'm the only one in my family like that.

SOLDIER: [*He has grown even more uncomfortable.*] I'm pretty sure we were up to the braid.

HARRY: [*Stares off into the blue and then suddenly shouts.*] Let's go with the jukebox. Play something with Christ in it. Let's put Christ back in Germany. What do you think we're here for? [*He pulls the* SOLDIER *toward him and loudly whispers.*] This is confidential. [*Winks.*] Entre nous, you know what I mean? Why, with a palaceful of queens, do you wanna have at it with just this princess? [SOLDIER *shrugs, extending his palms up.* HARRY *tries again as if eliciting a great secret.*] Come on. What's the story? [SOLDIER *shrugs in the same fashion.* HARRY *becomes annoyed and imitates* SOLDIER's *motions.*] What's that mean? What's it, a code or something?

SOLDIER: No, man. [HARRY *nudges him in a secretive way.*]

HARRY: What's the story?

SOLDIER: You're not going to put this in the article, are you? If my mother read . . .

HARRY: [*Loudly*] Whoa! Whoa! [*Then confidentially*] This is for me, off the record. What we writers call entre nous. It goes in my files and they can't be subpoenaed. [SOLDIER *nods head.*] You see, *American Farm and Garden* is for mothers. In a hundred years there hasn't been one article in *American Farm and Garden* about soldiers getting laid. The American mother doesn't want to read about it. We wanna keep America clean. You're for that, aren't you?

SOLDIER: Yeah.

HARRY: [*Rests back content. There is a moment of silence.*] Well?

SOLDIER: Huh?

HARRY: Why do you want to have at it with this one in particular?

SOLDIER: I don't know.

HARRY: Of course you know. What's the story? [SOLDIER *sits there nervously fidgeting.*] You find her witty, clever?

SOLDIER: She doesn't speak English.

HARRY: Her personality. You like her personality? [SOLDIER *shrugs noncommittally.* HARRY *slices through the pretense. Grabs the* GIRL's *breasts.*] The va-va-vooms. Is it the va-va-vooms?

SOLDIER: [*Shyly*] I don't know.

HARRY: You know! You know!

SOLDIER: It's kind of funny to explain. [*He hopes* HARRY *will let it go at this.* HARRY *just keeps staring at him.*] It changes from week to week. [HARRY *continues to stare.*] It changes. Sometimes I like a girl . . . [SOLDIER *indicates with his hands that sometimes he likes a girl with big breasts. He is too embarrassed to put it bluntly, but* HARRY *won't let him get away with it. He mimics the* SOLDIER's *gesture.*]

HARRY: What's this? [SOLDIER *is quiet.*] Big va-va-vooms? [SOLDIER *nods.*]

SOLDIER: Sometimes it's other parts.

HARRY: What other parts?

SOLDIER: Other parts.

HARRY: The legs? [SOLDIER *still shakes head.*] Well, what the hell you on this week? Hair? Arms? Toes?

Crotch? [HARRY *suddenly stands the* GIRL *up, whirls her around. Finally her back faces the audience.* GIRL *smooths out dress along her buttocks. They stare silently for a moment while the* GIRL *emphasizes that asset.*] That's what you're on this week. Right? Right? [SOLDIER *doesn't say anything, but you can see* HARRY *is right.* HARRY *turns to* GIRL.] Here, put it in the jukebox. I wanna hear something with Jesus in it. [*Gives her money. She walks offstage wiggling all the way. Before she leaves, the* SOLDIER *nervously calls after.*]

SOLDIER: You come back right after. You understand? *Versteh?* Here! [*She goes offstage.*]

HARRY: Okay, let's get back to work. You were on the blue cord. [SOLDIER *is still looking after the* GIRL.] Look, I only got so much time. If you don't want the money for paradise, just let me know and I'll get somebody else to interview.

SOLDIER: No, man, I need that money bad. I've been waiting for her since Thanksgiving.

HARRY: Okay, then. Let's go with the blue string.

SOLDIER: You shouldn't have sent her to the jukebox. They ain't reliable like the girls back home. Somebody's gonna pick her up. [*Looks after the* GIRL. *Turns to* HARRY.] Maybe I oughtta . . . [*Indicates he wants to go after her.* HARRY *gives him a nasty look and the* SOLDIER *realizes he'd better continue.*] The blue cord in the hat is for the infantry. And the blue braid here . . . [*Points to a cord running through the epaulet of the shoulder.*] . . . also means infantry. This crest . . . [SOLDIER *leans across the table so* HARRY *can get a closer look at the crest on the epaulet.*] . . . is the battalion crest, "Courage Conquers." Can you see that?

HARRY: [*Squints at it, keeps revolving it around presumably to catch the light, pulls at the epaulet.*] What the hell's that supposed to mean? Conquers what?

SOLDIER: It's the battalion crest.

HARRY: But what the hell does it mean?

SOLDIER: It doesn't mean anything. It's just the battalion crest. Every battalion has its own motto, see? [*Looks around for the* GIRL.]

HARRY: Every battalion got a different motto?

SOLDIER: Yeah. [*Still looking. Then, practically in anguish*] I don't hear the jukebox.

HARRY: Like what?

SOLDIER: Huh?

HARRY: Like what? Like what? What other mottoes?

SOLDIER: Man, I don't know. You don't go around memorizing those things.

HARRY: Listen, you said you were gonna be honest and open with me. That's the American way. Don't be a clown.

SOLDIER: I am being honest and open. You don't go around memorizing . . .

HARRY: Wait a minute. [*Starts digging around in his pockets. He mumbles.*] Honest and open, huh.

SOLDIER: Man, I *know* what I signed.

HARRY: Just a minute. [*Keeps searching*]

SOLDIER: But I remember what I . . .

HARRY: Can you wait just that minute? Just that minute? [*Pulling out a piece of paper*] Here, read it. [SOLDIER *wearily takes it and stares at it.*] Out loud.

SOLDIER: [*Reading as fast as possible*] "I do solemnly swear to Harry to tell the truth, the whole truth, and nothing but the truth to Harry so help me God." I am telling the truth, Harry. Lemme think. [*Raises his hand to get a second's peace.* HARRY *doesn't give it to him.*]

HARRY: That's the American way. Every magazine writer in America has to get his information sources to sign that pledge of truth. It's the only way we have of knowing that what we're told is the truth, the whole truth, and nothing but the truth. Nothing can be printed unless that pledge is signed. If I were interviewing the President of the United States he'd have to sign the pledge. You know that? Even the President!

SOLDIER: [*Thinks for a moment.*] "Men of Blood," that's one motto for the 356th Airborne. "To the Death" is another. That's all I can remember.

HARRY: There was a soldier in here last week whose battalion crest said, "Sur le Pont d'Avignon." What outfit's that?

SOLDIER: Said what?

HARRY: "Sur le Pont d'Avignon."

SOLDIER: I never heard of that outfit. [HARRY *stares at him in disbelief.*] I never heard of that outfit!

HARRY: Okay. Just don't clown around with me. What's that check mark on your sleeve?

SOLDIER: [*In surprise, pointing to his PFC chevron*] This? [HARRY *nods*] Man, how can you be writing an article about army life and know so little?

HARRY: That's why I'm talking to you. What do you think I'm paying you money for? You want the money or don't you want the money? [*Pause that is almost a contest of wills.* SOLDIER *gives in by nodding his head.*] All right. What's the story with those check marks?

SOLDIER: They're chevrons. They tell rank. I'm a PFC, that's a private first class. [SOLDIER *is looking around; then suddenly*] Oh, man, you know what she's doing? She went out for a quickie.

HARRY: The ones with two check marks are privates second class?

SOLDIER: They're corporals. You don't know the kind of women they got around here. Shut your eyes for a second and they're on their back with three other guys, humping away like there was no tomorrow.

HARRY: The ones without stripes are privates second class?

SOLDIER: They're just privates.

HARRY: [*Exasperated*] Then who's a private second class?

SOLDIER: [*More exasperated*] There ain't no private second class.

HARRY: [*Most exasperated*] Then what the hell do they have to have private first classes for?

SOLDIER: Man, you got this thing all confused. I don't know where to begin. [*Switches topic. Starts mumbling about the* GIRL.] They don't give a damn about who they sleep with. If a gorilla bust outa the zoo they'd sleep with him. You know that? Just as long as he had the money. That's all.

HARRY: What's that horse manure on your chest?

SOLDIER: Aw, don't call it that, man. It's ribbons and decorations. . . . Christ! Right out for a quickie. [*Slaps hands together and slides them off each other, and then starts nodding his head up and down.*]

HARRY: What's that one?

SOLDIER: The National Defense Ribbon. You get that when you're in the service four months.

HARRY: You mean they give you a ribbon just because you've been sucking around for four months?

SOLDIER: It's for active duty. It's got nothing to do with sucking around.

HARRY: Listen, I'm taking this down. If you're feeding me a load of horsefeathers . . . [*He starts searching for the oath.* SOLDIER *grabs his hand.*]

SOLDIER: Oh, man, not the oath thing again. I'm giving it to you straight arrow.

HARRY: Okay. I'm relying on you. I can't write an article that's full of cow crap. You feed me cow crap and they'll fire me. I got a kid that's stone blind depending on me. He sits in a roachy apartment all day depending on me.

SOLDIER: Oh, sweet Jesus.

HARRY: Not too many people know about it.

SOLDIER: What's the name of that magazine?

HARRY: *American Farm and Garden*.

SOLDIER: [*Nods head*] Well, I'm giving you the truth.

HARRY: What's that one for?

SOLDIER: The European Occupation Medal. You get that for being here during the time of occupation.

HARRY: Occupying what?

SOLDIER: Germany.

HARRY: Are you sure about that? My brother Archer was here when they were fighting hand to hand in the streets and I don't recall him getting any occupying medals.

SOLDIER: When was that?

HARRY: Nineteen forty-four.

SOLDIER: Well, they weren't occupying then. They were still fighting, see?

HARRY: Archer was in the Air Force. Got a Congressional Medal for strafing. He kept strafing and strafing. That was his specialty. He could keep strafing and strafing at things until they crumbled. [*Lapses into self-thought.*]

SOLDIER: Well, that would explain it. You gotta be in the Army to get an occupation medal. The Air Force flies over. You gotta be on the ground.

HARRY: [*Snaps out of it.*] Are you sure about this being the Army of Occupation?

SOLDIER: Sure I'm sure about it. What do you think they got all these soldiers here for? This is the Army of Occupation.

HARRY: I'm writing that down, so if you're feeding me a wagonload of mule shit . . .

SOLDIER: Go on, put my name down. It's the truth. My name's Humphrey Hill.

HARRY: Okay, I'm gonna do that. I'm quoting you.

SOLDIER: Go ahead. [HARRY *starts writing. The* GIRL *returns and sits down. The* SOLDIER *stares at her, trying to make up his mind if she went out with another* SOLDIER. *She begins adjusting herself: her dress, her hair, her makeup.*] She's all mussed up!

HARRY: You spell Hill with an *i* or an *e*?

SOLDIER: [*Impatiently spells it out.*] H-I-L-L. Look how mussed up she is. [HARRY *goes back to his writ-*

ing. SOLDIER *begins a detailed inspection of the* GIRL.]
The lipstick's smeared. The mascara's running. The
zipper is open halfway down her back. [*Sticks his
head under the table.*] One of the garters is un-
hooked! Man, I tell you, you send them off to juke-
boxes and they're down on their backs, arms and
legs flailing all over. They have no morals. One second and rummmmmm. [*Makes sound of a racing
car zooming by. To* GIRL] You sleep with people one
at a time, not in groups. [*Sticks his hand inside front
of blouse.*] Oh, man, they tore the strap. Oh, man.
[*He is real sorrowful, as if his own private property
has been damaged. He keeps trying to fix the strap,
while he moans.*] Oh, man, let's meet tomorrow and
finish this. Give me the forty marks now and I'll meet
you tomorrow, anywhere you say. Be a buddy, it's
Christmas.

HARRY: Can't. Not enough time.

SOLDIER: Please, man.

HARRY: I gotta finish the article today. I'm booked on
the track-four night express to the Dachau circus.
Fourteen dancing bears, seven singing kangaroos, and
Moko . . . Moko, the crying clown. [*The* SOLDIER *just
stares at him. Then the* SOLDIER *continues to fix the
strap.* HARRY *looks up.*] What's that ribbon for?

SOLDIER: Huh?

HARRY: Will you leave her boombos alone for a second?

SOLDIER: I'm listening.

HARRY: You're running your hands up and down her
boombos. You're playing footsie. You had your hand
on her belly a minute ago. You're doing everything
but listening. [SOLDIER *is chastened.*] Now what is
that purple and white piece of rag?

SOLDIER: This? It's blue.

(HARRY *grabs the row of decorations on the* SOLDIER'S
chest and pulls them toward himself. He stares at

*them from all angles, as if he can't make up his mind
what color it is.*)

HARRY: You're right. Is that the Navy Cross?

SOLDIER: It's the Italian Campaign Medal! I'm in the
Army! The battalion I'm in, the 370th Armored Infantry, fought in Italy during the Second World War
and they gave this medal to the battalion to com-
memorate that action.

HARRY: You were fighting in the Second World War?

SOLDIER: Not me, personally. I was a kid then.

HARRY: Then what the hell you doing sucking up
medals for battles you never fought in.

SOLDIER: I don't have to have fought in the Italian
campaign. They gave the medal to the entire battalion
and now everybody in the battalion wears it.

HARRY: Everybody? [SOLDIER *nods his head.*] You mean
the whole sucking battalion is going around with
World War II medals for battles they never been in?
What kind of sheep dip you feeding me? You expect
me to believe that? You really expect me to believe . . . This is going into a mothers' magazine. It
has to be accurate. Let me tell you something. Do
you know who the editors of *American Farm and
Garden* are? Three women. Two sisters and a mother.
Each one is a worse bitch than the other. They have
chin whiskers, all three of them, and they catch me
in one mistake, that's it, out . . . oh, you, tee, out.
My kid is stone blind!

SOLDIER: I'm telling the truth. Man, I don't know what
to do with you. I swear I'm telling you the truth.

HARRY: You're sure?

SOLDIER: Yeah.

HARRY: You swear? [*He starts digging around for the
pledge. The* SOLDIER *reaches out and holds his arm.*]

SOLDIER: Please, man, I already swore.

HARRY: Because I'm quoting you. I got your name
down here. [*Shows him the book.*] Angler.

SOLDIER: My name is Hill! Lemme see that. [HARRY *holds on to book but lets him see it. Studies quote.*] You got that quote wrong. I didn't say that. [HARRY *snatches book back and looks at it.*]

HARRY: Are you Hill or Angler?

SOLDIER: Hill. I told you before. Don't you remember? You asked if it was spelled with an *i* or an *e*.

HARRY: You didn't say the military around here was just sucking up the taxpayer's money?

SOLDIER: No, man, no! I never said that. You got the quotes mixed up between me and this Angler guy.

HARRY: You deny you said that?

SOLDIER: Yeah. I deny it.

HARRY: Okay, I'll take your word. I'm relying on you. I'm crossing it out. I'm giving you another chance. [*Starts crossing out.*]

SOLDIER: [*Shaking head*] Man, they should've given you another assignment. Something else.

HARRY: Why do you say that? Don't you think I'm competent?

SOLDIER: It's not that.

HARRY: I've written lots of articles on the military. You ever hear of *The Brothers Karamazov?* [SOLDIER *shakes head.*] I wrote that. *Wuthering Heights?* [SOLDIER *shakes head.*] I wrote that, too.

SOLDIER: You ever been in the Army?

HARRY: What makes you ask that? Do I look like a draft dodger to you?

SOLDIER: I was just asking.

HARRY: I wanted to go. They wouldn't take me. I got syphilis. I stood in the goddamn rain in front of the draft board for two hours and they wouldn't take me. Whole town came down to see me off. Even my brother who won the Congressional Medal for strafing came around. He and his old buddies borrowed a brace of P-51's and strafed over the draft board while I was waiting in the rain. Whole town turned out. The doctor from the draft board read the medical report out on the street. My mother passed out from embarrassment.

SOLDIER: You gotta watch who you sleep around with.

HARRY: I did. I did. I watched all the time.

SOLDIER: Didn't you know she had syphilis?

HARRY: Huh? What are you talking about?

SOLDIER: The girl you slept with.

HARRY: What's girls got to do with this?

SOLDIER: Man, some girl gave it to you.

HARRY: The syphilis?

SOLDIER: That's where you got it from.

HARRY: What are you talking about? I got it from a caterpillar. It was on a toilet seat and bit me. [SOLDIER *shaking his head violently.*] Whatta ya shaking your head?

SOLDIER: Listen, man, I don't know where you've been getting your medical information from, but they been feeding you a pack of lies. I bet you ain't got syphilis at all.

HARRY: Whatta ya talking about? The goddamn fang marks. You wanna see them?

SOLDIER: It ain't possible to get syphilis from a caterpillar.

HARRY: The thing was right on a toilet seat. [SOLDIER *just sits there shaking his head.*] Will you stop that? Will you?

SOLDIER: It ain't possible. Listen, man, they're too small to have sexual relations with. [HARRY *stares at him.* SOLDIER *changes topic. Points to ribbon.*] You wanna know what this one's for?

HARRY: I wanted to serve. You better believe it. I woulda done anything to get behind Old Glory. I wanted to be a fighter pilot.

SOLDIER: This is the Good Conduct Ribbon.

HARRY: You ever had syphilis?

SOLDIER: I told you I was a Baptist.

(HARRY *begins writing furiously. The jukebox blares*

out "The Stars and Stripes Forever." The GIRL *begins shaking all over and running her hands over the* SOLDIER. *She pulls the* SOLDIER *to his feet and they dance sexually, provocatively. The* GIRL *is blatantly advertising her wares to the* SOLDIER. *After a few moments of writing,* HARRY *looks up.*)

HARRY: What the hell's happening here? [*He gets up, grabs the* SOLDIER *and starts pulling him away. The* GIRL *keeps gyrating obscenely. It gets to be a kind of tug of war between* HARRY, *who tugs, and the* GIRL, *who makes open invitation.*] Who gave the signal for this? What's wrong with her body?

SOLDIER: [*Almost stunned*] Oh, man, it's the music. I'm with it. I'm with it.

HARRY: That's "The Stars and Stripes" you're profaning. "The Stars and Stripes"!

SOLDIER: Man, let me have the money. I'm movin'. I'm movin'.

HARRY: Don't dance that way in your country's uniform.

SOLDIER: Oh, man, oh, man.

HARRY: You're sullying your country. What about America? Is this what the Pilgrims died for? Is it? Why doesn't someone think about America once in a while? Think about that. [*Pulls* SOLDIER *away from* GIRL.] Leave go. This is a public place. Don't look at her. Come on. Don't look at her. What about your mother back in Nashville? Think about that. Don't look at her.

SOLDIER: Oh, man. I wanna get outa here. [HARRY *manages to separate them. He pulls the* SOLDIER *back to the chair. The* GIRL *continues with her dance. The* SOLDIER *tries to look.* HARRY *tries to stop him.*]

HARRY: Remember your motto—"Courage Conquers"! Don't sully that too. What's that bottle cap crud on your collar?

SOLDIER: Insignia. I wanna get out of here.

HARRY: What does the U.S. stand for? Uncle Sam?

SOLDIER: U.S.! U.S.! Man, gimme the money, will ya? It's hours before the night express goes. Lemme rip off a quick piece and then I'll give you the rest of the article. That's all I want, a quick piece.

HARRY: Not enough time.

SOLDIER: Ten minutes. Throw her right down on the bed. Ten minutes. [*Music ends with a kind of boompt.* GIRL *stops in middle of her movement.* SOLDIER *stares wildly about him. She returns to the table. Becomes impassive. Lights cigarette and blows smoke.*] Look at that. They're all pairing off and leaving. Two and two, two and two. Eight minutes. I won't even throw the covers back.

HARRY: What's the blue disk?

SOLDIER: That's infantry blue. I told you before. The color of the infantry is blue! Two by two. It's biblical. It's Noah.

HARRY: [*Looks at his watch.*] What time is it?

SOLDIER: [*Looking at his own watch*] Four o'clock.

HARRY: I'm going to adjust my watch to yours. Is that the exact time? [SOLDIER *nods his head.*] My watch says seven o'clock. You sure it's not seven? I've got a train to catch.

SOLDIER: I set it by the radio.

HARRY: Well, that's the right time, then. The radio clocks are never wrong. They set them by electromagnetic waves. Why's the color of the infantry blue?

SOLDIER: Oh, man. What do you mean, why? That's just the way things are. You gotta take things the way they are. Infantry is blue, artillery is red, armor is yellow. That's why I'm wearing a blue scarf. Everything is blue in the infantry. You see that guy over there?

HARRY: The one picking his nose?

SOLDIER: Nobody's picking his nose. The one over there.

HARRY: Way over there?

SOLDIER: Yeah. You see the scarf he's wearing?

HARRY: The orange one?

SOLDIER: It's yellow, man. Well, that's armor. And that guy over there . . .

HARRY: Where?

SOLDIER: Over there.

HARRY: Doing the dirty boogy?

SOLDIER: There ain't nobody doing the dirty boogy. Man, you see everything all wrong.

HARRY: What about him?

SOLDIER: He's in artillery. He's got a red scarf. Every branch got its individual color.

HARRY: How about branch socks?

SOLDIER: Jesus! Jesus H. Christ! You said you only wanted a few answers, but there's no end. You gonna go on and on and on.

HARRY: All the questions are written down here. [*Pointing to his papers.*] Everything's organized. Every question is figured out in advance by electronic computers. Nothing's just made up. I got it down in columns.

SOLDIER: There's no branch socks. All the socks are brown.

HARRY: Everything's in columns. Why don't you have branch socks?

SOLDIER: Because they don't do things that way.

HARRY: Why not? You got blue scarfs and blue braids and blue john paper. Why not blue socks?

SOLDIER: They just don't do things that way. What are you talking about . . . blue toilet paper?

HARRY: How about blue underwear? You forgot about that.

SOLDIER: There's no blue underwear. They got regular white underwear.

HARRY: Well, how do they divide up what's supposed to be blue and what's not?

SOLDIER: [*Throws his arms up in the air.*] They must figure that out at higher headquarters. I don't know.

HARRY: [*Getting excited*] Now we're really getting somewhere. This is going to be a real scoop, maybe even a
lead article. [*Makes a point of writing this down.*]
"They figure that out at higher headquarters." Who's
"they"?

SOLDIER: Huh?

HARRY: Who's the "they" that figure it out? [SOLDIER
raises his hands over his head again.] What is that
supposed to be, Morse code? [HARRY *imitates him
by raising his hands over his head and shaking them.*]

SOLDIER: I don't know who "they" are, man. The
leaders.

HARRY: I can't just put down "the leaders." I gotta
have names. [*Suddenly*] The Secretary of Health,
Education, and Welfare is one, isn't he? [SOLDIER
shrugs.] Okay, we'll get back to that later. I'm gonna
put that in Column A. This may be a scoop.

SOLDIER: Oh, man. Maybe we can do it after you come
back from the Dachau circus. How about that?

HARRY: [*Said very seriously*] I won't be coming back.
Once I go I'm gone. [*Pause. Then* HARRY *jumps back
into character.*] What time is it now?

SOLDIER: Five after four.

HARRY: [*Stares mutely at his watch.*] I got five to four.
My watch is going backwards. It's no good. I never
have the time. I told you about those bitches at the
magazine. They keep me moving. I stay in one place
a second too long and I get a cablegram. Last Thursday I thought I saw one of them looking for me. The
worst bitch of all, the managing editor. I wasn't in
the town a day. Listen, let me tell you. I haven't
stopped moving for years. Three days in Thule, fourteen hours in Cairo, seventeen minutes between ships
in Aden, and all the time I know they're keeping
track of me. They have this big plotting board in
the main office of *American Farm and Garden*. You
know where that is? [SOLDIER *shakes his head.*] Well,
the general public doesn't know about it. It's in

Westerville, Ohio. All the outside men like me are dots on that board. They know where we are every second. If we're a second too long in any place, the dot on the plotting board lights up and the field man is dispatched. If I don't get on that train tonight, my dot's gonna light up.

SOLDIER: So what? The hell with them. [*He absent-mindedly begins fondling the girl, but his eyes are on* HARRY. *He's absorbed in the story.*]

HARRY: "So what," eh? Three lit-up dots in any one year and it's a black mark in the record files, and that's that. You can't erase it, and you can't wash it out, they never forget and they never forgive. Bitches all of them. They play us off, one against the other. That's the worst part of it. Every year for Christmas, you know what they do? [SOLDIER *shakes head. He almost casually, while listening, fondles* GIRL's *breast.*] They cut one of us from the staff. Any one. We never know. They get us all together in the main room on Christmas Eve and then they cut one of us from the staff. I got this stone-blind kid, but it won't make any difference to them. Bitches. So I gotta get everything straight. I can't put down any old horse manure. If I don't get a scoop, what's gonna happen to my kid? He's blind as a bat. You know what it's like to live in a world where you can't tell one color from another? [*As if suddenly coming to, notices the* SOLDIER's *hands on the* GIRL's *breast. Dryly*] Will you cut that out? Will you? [*Goes back to his writing.*] Now you think they got a half-dozen guys on the upper-echelon levels dividing them up?

SOLDIER: Dividing what up?

HARRY: The colors! [SOLDIER *shrugs.*] Okay. I'm quoting you. Would it surprise you if I knew who some of these men are?

SOLDIER: No, man.

HARRY: You see that guy picking his nose? [SOLDIER *turns around and looks offstage.*]

SOLDIER: Who? The guy with the beret?

HARRY: Not the guy with the beret. The guy picking his nose.

SOLDIER: He's got a red scarf?

HARRY: Not the red scarf. The guy picking his nose.

SOLDIER: I don't see anybody picking his nose.

HARRY: [*Violently, and rising out of his seat to point*] Him! Him!

SOLDIER: [*Staring as hard as he can*] Yeah. He's leaning up against the jukebox, right?

HARRY: That's the guy who was doing the dirty boogy. I'm talking about the one picking his nose.

SOLDIER: Yeah. I see him now. It's the smoke in here. What about him?

HARRY: You sure you see him?

SOLDIER: Yeah, I see him now. What about him?

HARRY: He's one of the guys who decides about the division of color. [SOLDIER *looks at* HARRY *disbelievingly*.] He's in the Color Division Section.

SOLDIER: Man, I don't . . .

HARRY: See the way he's rubbing his hand up and down that soldier's back. Whatta ya think he's doing that for? He's checking on the color temperature of his uniform. Every color's got a different heat level.

SOLDIER: [*Staring off real hard*] Is he picking his nose, now? The smoke in here is fierce.

HARRY: [*Violently twists the* SOLDIER'*s head in the direction he wants him to look.*] Him! Over there. Goddamn it, what the hell's wrong with you? Him! Now he's patting his little brother on the head. The kid with the cigarette.

SOLDIER: There's no kids allowed in here.

HARRY: Pretty soon he'll whop the kid for smoking. That's the way he operates. Move in close, smiling, and then, whop with his snotty hands. [*Pause while they stare offstage.* GIRL *starts waving at other customers.*] Whop! [*Shouts.*] That's a way to go! That's a way! Don't give anyone a chance! [*To* SOLDIER] Ask him to join us.

SOLDIER: What for?

HARRY: So we can find out once and for all why things are divided up the way they are.

SOLDIER: Man, she's gonna leave me.

HARRY: No she won't.

SOLDIER: [*Striking down her hands*] Don't wave.

HARRY: [*Grabs the front of her blouse.*] I'll hold her.

SOLDIER: I can't just walk up to the guy and ask him to come over.

HARRY: Sure you can.

SOLDIER: [*Confidentially*] It's what the queers do.

HARRY: And find out what the kid is doing in here smoking a cigarette. Did you ever see such an evil-looking little bastard? Look at him. Wouldn't you like to whop him too?

SOLDIER: They don't allow kids in here. Maybe it's a midget.

HARRY: Well, for Christ's sake, find out.

SOLDIER: Man, why don't you find out?

HARRY: On account of my lungs. I can't get into places where they got too much smoke.

SOLDIER: [*Unwillingly gets up.*] You hold on to her good.

HARRY: I got her by the leg and breast.

SOLDIER: Don't go away, baby.

HARRY: I got her. Watch out for his snotty hands. [SOLDIER *walks offstage.* HARRY *shouts after.*] Keep outa range of the nose! [*The* SOLDIER *is evidently looking back because* HARRY *keeps waving directions with his arms. While* HARRY *is violently engaged in giving directions, he talks. The* GIRL *begins working him over.*] That's what I should've been. A strafer. Get everything in a burst. Right through the heart. Watch things crumble up under my guns. Piece by piece, like powder. Get 'em even in the hospitals. Hide in the corner, I crumble up the wall. Piece by piece. Let 'em have it with a fifty right in the ladies' room. Crumble up like powder. No hiding place. [*Rising from chair, shouts to* SOLDIER.] Not the guy doing the dirty boogy! The nosepicker! Him! Him! [*Violently slaps* GIRL. *She falls to floor, as he utters a cry of anguish. Turns in direction of* SOLDIER, *wildly shouting and gesturing.*] Him! Him!

CURTAIN

SCENE II

Immanuel entertains a visitor from Ohio

PLACE: HARRY *and* IMMANUEL'*s room.*

TIME: *The same afternoon.*

SCENE: *The room is a combination kitchen, bedroom, living room and studio. The kitchen area—sink, shelves, cupboards, coal stove—is on the left side of the room. On the upstage side of the kitchen is a toilet, a small partitioned cubicle jutting into the room. It is the old pull-chain-type toilet and the water box is clearly visible above the partition. The door is open. Somewhat below and right of center is a bed, with the headpost facing and a few feet away from the right wall. Near the foot of the bed is a small walking-cane chair of 1939 World's Fair vintage. A table, littered with assorted articles, separates the cane chair from a comfortable upholstered chair. Downstage right wall has a curtained window. Various paintings, finished and unfinished, are strewn around the room, particularly along the right wall. On the upstage wall, in line with the bed, is a dresser. Between the bed and dresser, on the right wall, is a stand-up closet. A clothesline stretches from the wall on the upstage side of the bed to the upstage wall on the right side of the dresser. In the general vicinity is an open ironing board. A metal stand holding several potted plants is on the left side of the dresser. The entrance door is upstage, left of center. Near the entrance is a phonograph; the lid is open.*

ON RISE: IMMANUEL, *an ascetic-looking individual in his middle twenties, is cleaning a fish on a small table, downstage left. He cleans with a great deal of precision and a definite degree of relish. The feeling we get is that this fish is more than a fish, perhaps an old enemy being disposed of.* IMMANUEL *keeps mumbling to himself in German. Occasionally, a single word or phrase becomes audible. The mumbling is directed toward the fish. The audible words are such as: bones, blood, head, scales.* IMMANUEL's *movements are quick, nervous, insectile. He is wearing an old robe with a shedding fur collar that might be cat fur.* ARCHER, *a big heavy-set person approaching his forties, wearing an expensive-looking topcoat, carrying a rolled-up copy of the* Saturday Evening Post, *is poking around the room examining the contents. He has the involuntary habit of scratching at his nose, and in the general vicinity of his nose.*

ARCHER: As a matter of fact, Harry forgot to mention that the street sign is just a twisted pole. It looks like somebody sheared the top of it right off. And the one on the other end of the street looks like it was hit by a Mack truck loaded with India ink. You couldn't read it if your life depended on it.

IMMANUEL: This is Andvari Strasse.

ARCHER: That's not the point. The point is that whoever is in charge of keeping those signs in good repair is falling down on his job. What you people on this block ought to do is complain to the City Street Commission. Get them to send someone down here and fix up what should be fixed up.

IMMANUEL: Some things will not be fixed.

ARCHER: Everything can be fixed but you have to have the right attitude. You can't just give up about it. I'll tell you something else that's mighty sad about this street. There isn't a house on the entire block with a number on it. Next time you're out take a look.

Wait a minute. I take that back. There was one house with a number on it and some kid with a dachshund was digging out the number plate with a screwdriver.

IMMANUEL: This is seventy-four.

ARCHER: [*Starts searching his pockets.*] Wait a minute. I got the number my brother gave me. [*Searches a few seconds more and then finds it. Looks at it to confirm the wrong address.*] This is what he wrote. [*Hands it to* IMMANUEL. IMMANUEL *more or less pulls it out of his hands and stares at it.*]

IMMANUEL: Seventy-two. [*Stiffly hands* ARCHER *the fishy slip of paper.* ARCHER *with some trepidation takes it. He looks around for a place to dispose of it.*]

ARCHER: You have a garbage pail or something? [IM-MANUEL *lets the question hang in the air just a second or so more than is necessary, to create a feeling of imposition. Then he holds out his hand.* ARCHER *puts the paper in his hand.* IMMANUEL *goes to the hall door.* IMMANUEL *limps on his left foot. He opens the door and throws the paper out in the hall. He turns and comes back limping on his right foot.* ARCHER *doesn't seem to notice that the limp has switched feet. All* IMMANUEL's *walking will be done this way.*] If it wasn't for an old lady walking a Pomeranian I'd still be marching up and down the street. How Harry can write down seventy-two when he lives at seventy-four I'll never know. Wait, I take that back. [*He gives an irritating little laugh.*] The summer he flunked his pre-flight physical he decided to come into the family business and help the accountant. You know what he did? He confused the figures in the purchase and sales ledgers and debited where he should have credited and credited where he should have debited. He just could not get it right.

IMMANUEL: You have yesterday's address.

ARCHER: What?

IMMANUEL: Today we are seventy-four because the building that was seventy-four when we were seventy-two fell down. If the building next door falls down we advance to seventy-six. If we fall down, they advance to seventy-eight. Last month we were sixty-eight. [IMMANUEL *becomes particularly vicious toward the fish.*] Only sixty-eight. Soon we will be the highest number on the street! [*Said with the gusto usually reserved for such statements as "Today Europe; Tomorrow the World."*]

ARCHER: [*Holding his stomach*] Oh, damn. Stomach's been sour as hell since I got off the train. If the public health people did their job inspecting the fruit that's peddled around . . . Look, excuse me a second, will you. [*Puts magazine on table, takes off his overcoat and suit jacket, and heads for the small toilet. Once inside, he tries to shut the door. The door keeps swinging open.*] What's wrong with this door?

IMMANUEL: It keeps opening.

ARCHER: Yeah, I know it keeps opening. What you need is a lock so you can get some privacy. You don't wanna have to sit here with your foot hooked under it.

IMMANUEL: It can't be fixed.

ARCHER: Of course it can be fixed. All you need's a latch. Anybody can put a latch on. [ARCHER *comes out and begins dressing again as he makes his speech. He is extremely fastidious.*] What I don't understand is why Harry left the art school in Florence four months ago without notifying the family. People in close-knit families don't do things like that. The girls, Harry's sisters, were sending food packages to Florence and somebody down there all the months Harry's been wandering around Munich was signing his name and eating his food. I don't expect American postal standards from the Italians, I remember the Italians from the war when they were stealing your eyeteeth, but there are some standards that have to be maintained. Improper handling of the mail is a federal offense, it just is that. If a Lion friend of

mine . . . that's a business fraternity . . . didn't have
a son stationed in Munich who accidentally ran into
Harry in a museum we'd still be sending food packages to the thief in Florence. When Harry found out
the school was no good—and that's the general
trouble with Europe, it's overrated—he should have
written me and I woulda started hunting him up a
good school in America. The kid knows the family's
behind him all the way, right to the goalpost. The
better the mind you got the longer it takes to find
yourself. A lot of people like Harry don't find themselves until they're in their thirties. Then, all of a
sudden, they turn out okay. Harry'll make it okay.
But you just don't run out of Florence, drop down in
the middle of nowhere and vanish. You just don't do
that when you belong to a family. The Bible'll tell
you that . . . no man is an island all by himself. All
Harry needs is a good art school in America. A fresh
start again. There's nothing wrong with Ohio State.
Some damn fine Americans came out of Ohio State.

IMMANUEL: [*Gestures with an air of surprise toward
the toilet.*] You are finished?

ARCHER: I'll wait till I get to the restaurant.

IMMANUEL: It is not good to wait.

ARCHER: I'm all right. Did Harry say when he'd be
back?

IMMANUEL: To suffer is not good.

ARCHER: I'm all right! Let's just drop it. You said he
was at the museum before. Do you know when it
closes? [IMMANUEL *starts mumbling in German to
the fish. He wildly scrapes the scales.*] What?

IMMANUEL: [*Mumbles.*] It is not good to wait. [*Fever-
ishly*] Soon. Soon. He's at the museum. All have
different closing times. One closes one hour, another
closes another hour, another closes later, another
closes . . .

ARCHER: What's the matter here? I just . . . [IMMANUEL
continues as if ARCHER *had said nothing.*]

IMMANUEL: . . . another hour. Some of them close at three, some at four, two of them at five, one stays open to nine. [*And then, emphatically, as if it really matters*] To nine!

ARCHER: What the point here is, is that I made reservations for Harry and me to eat at the Hermitage at five. [*Looks at his watch.*] And that's what it almost is now. I don't want to have to eat that train food and neither does Harry. Look, do you have a phone? I'd better move up the reservations.

IMMANUEL: This fish is for Harry and me. There isn't enough for others.

ARCHER: [*Still looking for the phone*] You're missing the point. Harry and I are going out to eat. What you wanna do is get this room shaped up. I can't seem to find the phone.

IMMANUEL: We always eat in. It isn't fair changing the eating arrangements without notice. It's a small fish. [*Holds the fish up. The fish is quite large.*]

ARCHER: Where's the phone?

IMMANUEL: [*Looks around as if searching for a phone. ARCHER impatiently waits. IMMANUEL reaches behind him into a cupboard, presumably reaching for the phone. He pulls out a salt shaker and furiously shakes it over the fish.*] There is no phone.

ARCHER: Oh, this is something to write home about.

IMMANUEL: Harry made me take it out. He doesn't want me calling my friends. He's got it in for them.

ARCHER: [*Stares at him for a second. Seems about to say something, but doesn't.*] Okay, you just clean the fish. [*Goes over to the comfortable chair.*]

IMMANUEL: That's Harry's chair. Nobody sits in Harry's chair.

ARCHER: I'm sure Harry won't mind. I've come four thousand miles to escort him home, so he won't mind if I rest in his chair. [*Sits down and is greeted by a rising cloud of talcum powder.*] What the hell! [*He stands up and begins brushing off the back of his*

trousers.] There's powder all over my pants! Jesus
Christ. What is this? Some kind of joke?

IMMANUEL: Harry doesn't want Juju and Michael sitting in his chair.

ARCHER: [*Hits the cushion and a cloud of talcum powder rises.*] My God.

IMMANUEL: Juju and Michael always want to sit in
Harry's chair.

ARCHER: [*Now trying to pound the powder out of his
pants*] Boy, this is great, just great. Harry did this?
Oh, this isn't going to come out.

IMMANUEL: I have fluid that will cleanse a stain. [*Starts
searching in the cupboard.*]

ARCHER: Hurry up. Jesus H. Christ! I don't understand this. How do you go about putting powder in
chairs? What kind of a thing is that? [IMMANUEL
*comes limping out, pouring the cleaning fluid in a
sponge. He starts wiping the back of the pants with
it.*] Christ, it's on the jacket too. [*Takes off his jacket.*]
Is it coming off? What kind of cleaning fluid is that?

IMMANUEL: It will cleanse a stain. Take off your pants.

ARCHER: Can't you get it?

IMMANUEL: You must take off your pants. [*There is a
pause.* ARCHER *is dubious about taking his pants off.
He gives* IMMANUEL *the jacket.*]

ARCHER: Get some of that fluid on the jacket. [IM-
MANUEL *rubs the cleaning fluid on the jacket while*
ARCHER *begins taking his pants off.* IMMANUEL *brings
the pants over to the ironing board and rubs furiously, with* ARCHER *hovering over him.*] Some of
those newer cleaning fluids work like magic.

IMMANUEL: [*Supposedly annoyed because* ARCHER *is
hovering over him*] Please. [*And then loudly and
angrily*] Please! [ARCHER *goes back and sits on the
little cane chair.* IMMANUEL *rubs and rubs.*]

ARCHER: Watch the nap. You can't rub it too hard.
What kind of cleaning fluid is that?

IMMANUEL: Please! [*He hangs the suit up on the line.*

*The pants should be hung so that the audience can
see that the stain is not going to come out.*] Now they
must dry. [*From across the street the bells of the convent start tolling the hour. They toll five times.*] The
sacred bells from the convent of Our Sisters of Heal-
ing, Grace and Forgiveness.

ARCHER: Fine.

IMMANUEL: They ring every fifteen minutes.

ARCHER: Fine.

IMMANUEL: [*Goes over to a dresser and pulls out a
selection of beads and crucifixes. He brings them
over.*] You are interested in things of religion? Perhaps a purchase? Here it is possible to make a fantastic purchase. [*Displays them.*] Beads? Crucifixes?

ARCHER: No. I don't think . . . [IMMANUEL *begins waving them in front of his face.*] Must you wave them
in front of my face?

IMMANUEL: This is a fantastic purchase for you. Harry
doesn't know I have things of religion. [*Still waving
them.*]

ARCHER: I'll bet he doesn't. How much are they? Get
them out of my face.

IMMANUEL: All prices.

ARCHER: [*Picking up a string of beads*] How much are
these?

IMMANUEL: Fifty cents American money.

ARCHER: [*Pointing to another set of identical beads*]
And these?

IMMANUEL: Nine dollars American money.

ARCHER: [*Takes them both in his hands and studies
them.*] I can't see any difference.

IMMANUEL: There is a difference. [ARCHER *looks at
them more closely.*] Can't you see the difference?
[IMMANUEL *begins squinting at them as well.*]

ARCHER: They look the same to me.

IMMANUEL: [*Grabs them out of his hand and squints
at them by himself.*] There is a difference. A difference. [*He starts to put them away in the dresser.*]

ARCHER: Never mind. I'll take the fifty-cent beads. [*But* IMMANUEL *puts them back in the dresser as if he didn't hear* ARCHER *speak.*]

IMMANUEL: I have some holy water.

ARCHER: Don't bother. I'll take the beads.

IMMANUEL: Harry only wishes he possessed holy water. [*He goes over to the refrigerator and pulls out a milk bottle full of water and carefully pours some of it into a little stoppered flask. He returns with the flask.*] Fresh because you are Harry's brother. You perhaps noticed that the holy water was kept in an ordinary milk bottle. That is done to confound thieves. Do not be deluded by appearances. [*Holds out bottle.*] Smell it. [ARCHER *is hesitant.*] Just smell it. Smell it! [ARCHER *smells it.*] What does it smell like? Egypt? Babylon? Syria?

ARCHER: It smells like water. I can't smell anything.

IMMANUEL: [*Grabs it out of his hands and smells it himself.*] There is a difference. A difference. [*Limps off with it to the refrigerator, where he carefully begins pouring it back into the milk bottle. He faces* ARCHER.] You are the only one who does not smell the difference! [*Before* ARCHER *has a chance to reply he turns back to the refrigerator and finishes pouring the liquid back.*] There is a difference. The sisters of the convent assured me. There were assurances made.

ARCHER: What do you do, buy your stuff at the convent?

IMMANUEL: [*Slams refrigerator door and turns around.*] Relics? I had some bones, knee and thigh and finger bones in good condition . . . but there were dogs . . . aaagh! [*Falls down on his knees and starts searching under the bed.*] Harry doesn't know I have bone relics. He would envy me.

ARCHER: Look . . . Harry wouldn't know a bone relic from a church door. I don't know what he's been telling you but . . .

IMMANUEL: [*With* IMMANUEL *under the bed,* ARCHER

has a chance to pick his nose in private.] What I possess here is special. Special! You are familiar with the beautiful Christian virgin, St. Juliana? Eh? Eh?

ARCHER: No.

IMMANUEL: Beautiful virgin, beautiful thighs. Aagh. Her father gave her to a pagan for his bride, but she would not marry a pagan. She must renounce Christ. They threatened her with torture. She tried to flee but it was no use . . . her beautiful thighs were not fast enough . . . beautiful thighs. Aagh. They hung her upside down and beat her. Scourged by whips, the blood ran up the soft flesh of her thighs. Aagh. They said to keep the holy nail clippings in the dark, and that if I put them in the sun they would grow. There was much blood. The more she refused her cruel father's wishes, the more they caressed her thighs with whips. Into a vat of boiling lead. Then the chopping. There were nail clippings taken from her fingers and toes. Thighs. Aagh. White thighs. Yes. Clippings taken. [IMMANUEL *pokes his head suddenly out from under the bed.* ARCHER *is caught with his finger in his nose.* IMMANUEL *looks at him for a second.* ARCHER's *hand drops.*] Nail clippings? [*He comes forward. Somehow the limp in his leg has turned into a walk that is overtly feminine and suggestive.*] Nail clippings? [*Thrusts an ashtray filled with nail clippings under* ARCHER's *nose.*] You are interested in the nail clippings of saints? [*Here we must believe that there is a sort of hypnosis going on, effected both by* IMMANUEL's *sexual movements and also by a kind of eye contact.*]

ARCHER: No. [*And then slower, as if apologetic*] Not at all. Really.

IMMANUEL: Harry would envy you. Relics like these are unobtainable elsewhere. If you do not purchase here . . . Do you wish to touch them?

ARCHER: No. Not . . . I don't wish to touch them.

IMMANUEL: Touch them. Do not torment yourself. I can see you long to touch them.

ARCHER: I don't long to touch them. I wouldn't touch those filthy . . .

IMMANUEL: You wish to touch them only you are ashamed. You imagine there will be laughter, that you will seem foolish. I will not laugh at your heart's desire. Here you may do as you please.

ARCHER: [*Feebly*] I'm not ashamed.

IMMANUEL: Don't be ashamed.

ARCHER: I don't . . .

IMMANUEL: [*Suddenly and authoritatively*] Touch them! [ARCHER *almost instinctively reaches out and sticks his hand in the ashtray.*] You feel better now. Here there is nothing to be ashamed of. [*And then, almost casually, as* IMMANUEL *turns from him*] You ought to use a mouthwash. No matter. No matter. [*This jolts* ARCHER *out of whatever state he was in.*]

ARCHER: What did you say?

IMMANUEL: [*Puts the ashtray on the nightstand, picks up a black glove, and starts putting it on.*] Do you mind if I wear my medical glove?

ARCHER: What did you say about the mouthwash?

IMMANUEL: There are some who mind the medical glove. Do you mind?

ARCHER: No.

IMMANUEL: I have a skin condition. Perhaps you noticed?

ARCHER: No.

IMMANUEL: That is kind of you. When I was born there were certain handicaps . . . but it is boring for Americans to listen to recitals of infirmities. You would like to see Harry's American art while you are waiting? So. [*Escort's* ARCHER *by the arm over to the paintings.* ARCHER *doesn't enjoy being touched.*] To have bad breath is not the worst calamity. You have never had eczema, of course.

ARCHER: No.

IMMANUEL: Impetigo? Seborrheic dermatitis? Acne vulgaris? Ringworm?

ARCHER: Look, I don't want to be rude. . . . I've always been well. [*Looks at* HARRY'*s paintings.*] Harry was doing more representational things in Ohio. Portraits. Landscapes. He did one of sailboats in a harbor that the whole family liked. [*Holds one out from him. The painting is a garish blotch of discordant color.*] What's this one represent?

IMMANUEL: Hunchbacks eating strawberries. They are looking at the thighs of a young girl. She is sweet, clean. As a child, my skin became greasy and I noticed small holes appearing in the skin. I washed and washed with soaps and salts but there was dirt I could not wash out.

ARCHER: Wait a minute. [*He puts the canvas down and steps back a few feet.*]

IMMANUEL: Do you see their half-shut dreamy eyes contemplating what must not even be thought? The slow movements of the child's naked shoulders inviting their languid blue eyes.

ARCHER: I can't make it out. I don't see any child.

IMMANUEL: You see? You see? The thighs. . . . I was meticulous in cleanliness, but the disease lay dormant for months and years. Foul-odored sweat that perfume could not conceal, nor baths of potassium permanganate dispel. I rubbed the clefts of my toes, but plugs of dirt were already forming in the skin. . . . She will break their hearts. Their hearts will not be mended. She is without pity.

ARCHER: [*Still staring at the painting*] I can't make this out. Where is the child?

IMMANUEL: [*Violently pointing*] There is the child!

ARCHER: [*Pointing doubtfully*] And those are the hunchbacks?

IMMANUEL: Yes. Yes. They are suffering. They long for what they may not have. She taunts them. She teases them. She leads them on. She is without mercy.

ARCHER: I can't . . . Which is the girl again?

IMMANUEL: [*This time he runs over to the painting and shoves his finger against it.*] This! This! Look how wicked she is with her innocence. She thinks because she is innocent she can break their hearts. She thinks they are foul toads; that there is no limit to the warts that may be trust upon them. There is a limit to the number of warts! It is not enough for her that their backs are bent under the sun and under her yoke. That . . . [*Points again.*] is all she thinks she must do . . . smile . . . but she does not smile . . . she is lewd . . . she leers. You like this?

ARCHER: When Harry gets back to Ohio, he'll get in the swing again. What's under the towel?

IMMANUEL: I do not understand. Swing? This is wonderful art, for any house. Matches all colors.

ARCHER: This . . . [*Goes over and picks up his magazine, the* Saturday Evening Post. *Shows it to* IMMANUEL.] . . . this is art. Norman Rockwell. Ever hear of Norman Rockwell? If Harry'd get on the stick he could paint rings around him.

IMMANUEL: What are they doing?

ARCHER: Whatta ya mean, what are they doing? They're eating a turkey. It's Thanksgiving.

IMMANUEL: [*Pointing*] What's that?

ARCHER: That's the turkey. You better get yourself a pair of glasses. Skip it. What's under the towel? [IMMANUEL *pulls the cloth off the* Stone-blind Kid, *a small Victorian cupidlike statue without eyes.*] That's more like it. That's good. This has got it. I've seen lots of homes with these cupids. What's the matter with its eyes?

IMMANUEL: It's blind.

ARCHER: It's unfinished, that's all. You don't make blind statues. He hasn't even put the fig leaf over the . . . the organ.

IMMANUEL: It's finished. You wish to buy? You have

plaster deer on your lawn? Stone water fountains? This could be ideally placed near a stone water fountain. Harry says American lawns have blue mirrored balls. This could be placed near such a ball.

ARCHER: If Harry wants to give it to me, he'll give it. I don't buy from Harry.

IMMANUEL: You buy from me! It is mine. I buy all Harry's work. Notice the upraised supplicating arms. Useful to hold magazines in bathrooms. *Saturday Evening Post, Ladies' Home Journal, Reader's Digest.* You read in bathrooms?

ARCHER: That's none of your . . . No. I don't read in bathrooms. [*He has been scratching his nose.*]

IMMANUEL: Harry reads in the bathroom. [*He begins scratching the glove.*] When the skin is hypersensitive the slightest little irritant that would be entirely harmless upon healthy skin erupts and must be scratched and once scratched the itch grows and grows in an inflammatory temptation that cannot be resisted. A demon. [*Suddenly he switches from scratching the glove to scratching his nose.* ARCHER *immediately drops his hand to his side.*] No matter. No matter. [IMMANUEL *goes over to the bed, removes* ARCHER's *topcoat, places it across the back of the upholstered chair, and then sits down on the bed.* ARCHER, *slightly taken aback by* HARRY's *art work, walks backward a few feet still looking at it. He finally sits in the small cane chair. He is obviously thinking.*] You do not mind if I sit?

ARCHER: What?

IMMANUEL: You do not mind if I sit?

ARCHER: [*Waves his arm.*] Why should I mind if you sit?

IMMANUEL: At present I am contemplating a book attacking Hegel's dialectic. [*He removes a slipper from his foot.*] Will you hand me the scissors? [*The scissors rest on a small table in between the cane*

chair and HARRY's *chair. Motions to the scissors.*
ARCHER *brings them over.*]

ARCHER: He used to paint the damnedest harbor scenes.
[*Hands scissors to* IMMANUEL.]

IMMANUEL: Good of you. You are familiar with Hegel's
dialectic?

ARCHER: What?

IMMANUEL: Do you regard the absolute as pure being,
as nothing, or as the union of being and not being?

ARCHER: I don't regard it as anything. I'm not much
for philosophy. I'm just a businessman.

IMMANUEL: Most *businessmen* are not aware that Hegel
studied under Thomas Aquinas. That's where Hegel's
error comes from. There is no unmoved mover. There
is only the moved moving.

ARCHER: I told you I wasn't much for philosophy.

IMMANUEL: No matter. No matter. Consider the case
of an arrow in flight. In terms of existence what is it
that exists, the arrow or the flight?

ARCHER: I'm just not getting through to you.

IMMANUEL: Or consider the question of self. What is
the self that it should be hounded and not left to die?
To be left to die, a dark corner to scratch all the
itches. To scratch.

ARCHER: How long have you and Harry been living
together?

IMMANUEL: What is time? Illusion. What is illusion?
What we will. The perfume, please. [ARCHER *reaches
out to the same table and gets the perfume. He brings
it over.* IMMANUEL *dabs his feet with the perfume.*]
Would you like me to wash your feet in perfume?

ARCHER: For God's sake! I'm all right. Are you sure
Harry's at the museum?

IMMANUEL: Yes. Every afternoon he goes to the museum, but he will be here any moment now. Harry
and I find the perfume relaxing to the legs.

ARCHER: I thought you didn't know when he was coming back.

IMMANUEL: I assure you, any moment. Will you hand me my cigarettes?

ARCHER: Where are . . . [*They are on the same table everything else was on. He silently brings them over.*] If you put that table over here you'd be organized. [*Meaning the table* ARCHER's *been fetching from.*] The both of you could use a little of that. [IMMANUEL *lights his cigarette and inhales deeply. He puts the cigarette down and, sticking the leg fully out of the bathrobe, proceeds to rub the perfume on.*] You both sleep in this bed?

IMMANUEL: Yes. It is our bed. Do you wish to relax till Harry gets here?

ARCHER: I'm comfortable here.

IMMANUEL: Do not feel embarrassed. I can see you're tired and wish to relax. Your spine must be paining you on that little chair. Come. Lie down, here. [*Patting the bed.*]

ARCHER: I'm fine.

IMMANUEL: No matter. No matter. [*He reaches into the night table drawer and pulls out a woman's nylon stocking. He begins massaging his leg and putting the stocking on.* ARCHER *is revulsed, tries to look away.*] The cold dilates the blood vessels in my leg. Special precautions must be taken. You can see the leg is weak. Hair cannot seem to grow on it. Therefore I must keep it warm. Perhaps you are familiar with legs like mine? Doctors have been unable to help. I go to bed early in the evening when the blood is most active. Then I sleep. The leg is warm. The thigh is hot. I am delirious with happiness. While I sleep, the snow falls layer upon layer, the chill advances through the window, under the door. It comes under the bed and touches my leg. I ignore it, but the pain grows. I will not have anything to do with it. Out. Out. But the pain stabs at the heel, at the arch. It cannot be ignored. It lowers the temperature in my calf, it chills the thigh. My leg is now encased in ice. The pain is exquisite. The ligaments are torn at, they stretch, they twist, they tighten into the bones, I am in torture. I cannot bear to be touched. I throw the bedclothes from me. I move from this side to that side, but it is worse. The pain heightens; it grows more exquisite, fits of terror overtake my thigh. There is no respite from the pain. No movement that will free the leg. I twist; I turn; my leg is encased in icy pain; there is no fleeing, no remedy, I die . . . but the night passes, the sun comes, I throw my leg in the sun, the yellow heat flames upon the calf, the thigh . . .

ARCHER: Well, I'm going to wait at the restaurant. [*Gets up and goes over to the clothesline to feel the stain on his pants.*] It still isn't dry! What did you put on it?

IMMANUEL: It will be cleansed. Do not keep touching it, and handling it, and fondling it.

ARCHER: Then why is it still wet? I don't understand that. Any cleaning fluid should be dry by now.

IMMANUEL: You do not mind if I stretch out further?

ARCHER: Why should I mind? Why should . . . [*He holds his stomach, and winces.*] Goddamn it.

IMMANUEL: You wish to use my toilet?

ARCHER: I'm all right.

IMMANUEL: It is there for your use.

ARCHER: [*Recovers.*] The pants should be dry in another minute or two, then I'm leaving. You can tell Harry to meet me at the Hermitage!

IMMANUEL: No matter. No matter. [*He begins cavorting under the covers. He turns and twists, in a rather sexual manner.*] My spine is damaged. Perhaps you noticed? That is why I must twist about.

ARCHER: I didn't notice.

IMMANUEL: Ah, kind of you to say so.

ARCHER: I didn't notice!

IMMANUEL: You did not notice the stoop?

ARCHER: No. I told you I don't notice things like that.

IMMANUEL: With most people it is the first thing they notice, but I have become philosophical about it. Once in the park I was set upon by children. Several stones were thrown. I chased the children but they ran and my leg is twisted. [*Dangles leg out of the bed and then coquettishly withdraws it.*]

ARCHER: It looks all right.

IMMANUEL: No matter. No matter. It is of no importance. I accept. It is for that reason I must stretch the length of my spine against the mattress. You understand? It is all right?

ARCHER: Please! Do as you like!

IMMANUEL: [*Crawling farther under the covers.*] I will just pull the coverlet up to my neck, no higher. I find that unless my neck is warm my shoulders ache. [*Managing to thrust a shoulder out and then withdrawing it.* ARCHER, *uncomfortable on the cane chair, has moved over to the side of* HARRY'S *chair. He sits on the arm.* IMMANUEL *begins patting the bed.*] Come, you are tired. Sit beside me on the bed and we will talk.

ARCHER: I'll be leaving in a minute.

IMMANUEL: Why weary your back? Why torment your spine . . . if only for a minute . . . You must be tired. There is no need for formality. Come, stretch yourself beside me. It is too cold not to be together. Come. Come.

ARCHER: I don't understand why it takes those pants so long to dry. Can I see Harry coming from this window?

IMMANUEL: No matter. Yes. You can see all the way down the street from that window. [ARCHER *walks over to the window.*] Do not touch the curtains! Please!

ARCHER: I only wanted to pull . . .

IMMANUEL: The window faces a convent. The curtains are never pulled.

ARCHER: I just wanted to look out in the street.

IMMANUEL: It is a matter of religious principle, the Catholic mysteries.

ARCHER: I can't see what religion has to do . . .

IMMANUEL: I have made a Catholic vow. You mustn't tell Harry I'm a Catholic.

ARCHER: I'm not going to say anything.

IMMANUEL: Harry doesn't know anything about the beads. I tell him they are for children. I pretend the holy water is ice water. I don't want him to know. You won't say anything?

ARCHER: I'm not going to say anything.

IMMANUEL: I pretend the nail clippings are from my feet. He thinks I'm an orthodox Jew. I was forced to buy a yarmulke and go to synagogue on Fridays because Harry wanted to see, but then on Sunday I took in an early-morning mass.

ARCHER: Look, I don't care about your religion. That's the American way. If you wanna sit on a flagpole bowing to Mecca that's your business.

IMMANUEL: I confessed on Sunday. The priest said it would be all right if I confessed on Sundays. Do you think that makes it all right—if I do evil and then confess on Sunday?

ARCHER: If the priest said it was all right, it's all right.

IMMANUEL: Yes. Of course. But if the priest made a mistake, then I'm doomed. It's a matter of grave importance. [ARCHER *has wandered close to the bed.*] Come, give me your hand. [*Seizes* ARCHER's *hand.*] Come, come. [*Pulls* ARCHER *down on the bed beside him. As he mentions each part of his body he puts* ARCHER's *hand on the part.* ARCHER *is increasingly repelled.*] Feel my hands. Like ice. That may be a sign. A foreshadowing. I don't want to wait till the eleventh hour. If the priest made a mistake, I'm doomed. [*His hopes pick up.*] But my throat is warm. Feel my throat. It's warm. Do my shoulders seem hot or cold to you? The left is warmer than the right, is that not so? That is a good sign. [*Hopes fade.*] But here, here, the heart is cold. Feel my back. The hump is hot. Feel my hump.

ARCHER: [*Manages to pull his hand free.*] Get hold of yourself. What's wrong with you?

IMMANUEL: It is a matter of grave importance.

ARCHER: Priests are infallible. If he told you it's all right, it's all right.

IMMANUEL: Only the Pope is infallible. That's what tortures me. Priests can make mistakes. Hell is full of priestly mistakes. The soul in hell melts like a wax candle, the blood dries to red powder, the eyes burst and flow like jelly down the cheek. [IMMANUEL *is all upset.* ARCHER *puts his arms around* IMMANUEL *and comforts him. Rocks* IMMANUEL *like a baby.*]

ARCHER: It's all right. All right. [*Suddenly* IMMANUEL *recovers, lies back, and smiles at* ARCHER.]

IMMANUEL: I feel better now. That is why I'm writing this book attacking Thomas Aquinas.

ARCHER: [*Gets up and pulls his pants off the clothesline. He begins dressing.*] Listen, you were just writing on Segel or somebody.

IMMANUEL: You're mistaken. You do not see things as they are. I am revising. I cannot continue with Segel. My father wants me to continue with Segel but I cannot.

ARCHER: [*Has the pants on, but he sees they are too wet.*] Jesus. It's getting through to my underwear. [*He goes over to the stove and keeps his back to it.*] What kind of cleaning fluid doesn't dry? Jesus Christ.

IMMANUEL: Perhaps you saw him selling balloons at the corner?

ARCHER: [*Not paying any attention*] If these pants are ruined . . .

IMMANUEL: [*Shouting*] Perhaps you saw my father selling balloons!

ARCHER: No. All right? All right? [*From below somebody has been disturbed by the yelling and knocks up.* IMMANUEL *reaches out and grabs a thick wooden cane. He pounds the cane on the floor until the pounding below ceases. And then, as if there had been no interruption:*]

IMMANUEL: He keeps a vicious red monkey to attract the children.

ARCHER: I didn't see him.

IMMANUEL: He's at the corner every day.

ARCHER: I didn't see him. . . . All right?

IMMANUEL: Once a week he lets a single balloon loose. The string slips through his fingers. The balloon rises over the roofs and then lunges for the moon.

ARCHER: [*Looking at his pants*] Jesus.

IMMANUEL: You didn't . . .

ARCHER: No!

IMMANUEL: He wears a red jacket. Will you look?

ARCHER: What?

IMMANUEL: Will you look and see if he's there? He wears a red jacket.

ARCHER: I thought you didn't want me to look out the window!

IMMANUEL: Yes, you may look. If you look just to the right. The convent is to the left.

ARCHER: I tell you he isn't there. I would have seen him when . . .

IMMANUEL: Will you look? Please! [ARCHER *goes over to the window.*] Just move the curtain back a little. You will not look at the convent?

ARCHER: I'm not going to look at the convent. Why should I want to look at the convent?

IMMANUEL: Sometimes he takes a little child in back of the convent. You have only to move the curtain back a hairsbreadth to see him.

ARCHER: All right. All right.

IMMANUEL: Only a hairsbreadth. Slowly, slowly. There are mysteries. Do not move it too much. He goes in back of the altar of the convent where the nuns never come. He thinks he will be safe there. [*Sharply*] Do not look to the left.

ARCHER: I'm not looking to the left.

IMMANUEL: Please do not look to the left.

ARCHER: There's nobody there.

IMMANUEL: He is wearing a red jacket. He always wears a red jacket. He's always there.

ARCHER: Well, maybe he left. All right?

IMMANUEL: You're looking to the left.

ARCHER: I'm looking to the right. All they got out there is two nuns waiting for a trolley.

IMMANUEL: Are they moonfaced? Sometimes it is a matter of disguise.

ARCHER: Just two nuns! . . . Which way does Harry come?

IMMANUEL: From the left. Don't look to the left. Please. Please.

ARCHER: [*Slamming the curtain closed*] Listen, you . . .

IMMANUEL: Do you mind if I slip a bit further under the covers? Only when I lie flat does my spine rest.

ARCHER: Do as you please. You tell Harry that train leaves at eleven and I expect him to be down there packed and ready to leave. I expect . . .

IMMANUEL: I can converse quite well under the covers. I shall direct you from under the covers.

ARCHER: I don't need directions. He's not there. You tell Harry it's track four, track . . .

IMMANUEL: First, do you see the bakery?

ARCHER: [*Slowly returns to the window and draws back the curtain.*] All right. All right.

IMMANUEL: Next to the bakery is a mailbox. You see the mailbox?

ARCHER: I'm not sure. The street is dark.

IMMANUEL: He always wears . . .

ARCHER: I know. I know. A red coat.

IMMANUEL: Always a red coat.

ARCHER: I see the mailbox. After the mailbox is a lamppost. The light is out. Where is he? By the lamppost? Is he by the lamppost?

(*There is no answer from* IMMANUEL. *When* ARCHER
turns around, IMMANUEL *seems to be asleep. There
is a gentle snore or two.* ARCHER *looks down on the
bed for a second or two, then angrily takes his jacket
off the line. As he puts it on preparatory to leaving,
he is seized with stomach pains. Once more he walks
into the bathroom and cautiously closes the door.*
IMMANUEL *immediately throws the covers off and
leaps from the bed. He begins vigorously chopping
and hacking at the fish.*)

IMMANUEL: Sometimes it does not work quite properly.
Sometimes the pipes clog and will not flow. Sometimes there is noise and flakes of rust fall. Sometimes
the water backs up and thrusts itself through the
pores of the weary metal. Sometimes the metal groans
and the apparatus shakes. Sometimes the water is
stagnant and smells.

ARCHER: It's all right.

IMMANUEL: Do you wish to read?

ARCHER: No.

IMMANUEL: I shall slip your magazine under the door.

ARCHER: Just leave me alone. I'll be out in a second.

IMMANUEL: There is no rush. Do not rush yourself.

ARCHER: I don't want to talk while I'm in the bathroom. All right? [*A few seconds go by.*] Where's the
toilet paper?

IMMANUEL: There is always a roll in the bathroom.

ARCHER: There's no toilet paper in here.

IMMANUEL: [*Approaching the toilet*] I will check.

ARCHER: Keep out of here.

IMMANUEL: You must allow the door to open. I will
check.

ARCHER: There's no paper in here. I'm not blind. I can
see what's here.

IMMANUEL: I will check the cupboard. [*Goes over to
the cupboard and looks inside.*] We have no toilet
paper.

ARCHER: Jesus Christ.

IMMANUEL: We have soft table napkins.

ARCHER: All right.

IMMANUEL: [*Reaches into the cupboard and pulls out a single napkin. Stands in front of the bathroom door.*] I have it.

ARCHER: [*Opens the door a fraction of an inch.* IMMANUEL *stares in.*] Give me some more of them.

IMMANUEL: That was Harry's responsibility to buy! There is no more! I only buy the food. I am not to blame.

ARCHER: Do you have any Kleenex?

IMMANUEL: There is no Kleenex. [*He picks up* ARCHER'S *copy of the* Saturday Evening Post *and, ripping off the cover, silently passes it under the door.* ARCHER *silently takes it. Some moments pass.* ARCHER *pulls the flush chain. Nothing happens. He violently pulls it a number of times.*]

ARCHER: It's not flushing.

IMMANUEL: Sometimes there is trouble. I shall come in and help.

ARCHER: Stay out. I'll take care of its myself. [*He climbs on the toilet seat and looks into the water box.*] The rod on the float ball is twisted. [*He tries to straighten it by hand.*] Damn.

IMMANUEL: [*Shouts.*] It can't be straightened.

ARCHER: [*Still at it*] Damn it.

IMMANUEL: Aaagh! Some things are worn crooked.

ARCHER: [*With deep anger*] Anything can be straightened! You could straighten out the whole world if you wanted to. Get me a pair of pliers. The whole world if you had the right attitude. If Columbus didn't think the world was flat he wouldn't have even bothered sailing. They'd still be thinking the earth was going around the sun. You know something is wrong, you get off your butt and you fix it up. You move out. You get on the stick. You put your shoulders to the wheel. You throw up in a plane, you clean it up and keep going. You just don't stand around whining about it. That's how you fix things up. That's how everything gets straightened. [IMMANUEL *starts limping toward the cupboard.*] Come on. Come on. [*He returns with the pliers and hands them to* ARCHER.]

IMMANUEL: Not everything can be straightened.

ARCHER: Everything can be straightened. Everything. I'll straighten this. I'll straighten this son of a bitch. Get me some water. [*While* IMMANUEL *fills up a bucket,* ARCHER *works furiously on the float ball.*] We'll see if it can't be fixed; oh yeah, we'll see . . . All right. . . . Come on with that water. [IMMANUEL *hands him the bucket.* ARCHER *pours the bucket full of water into the water box.*] All right, we'll see what can and what can't be fixed. [*He steps off the toilet seat and pulls the chain. There is a loud flushing sound.*] Oh, God. It's not stopping. It's coming up. It's coming up. Oh, God! [ARCHER *comes running out. His feet are soaking wet. The water flows under the door.*]

IMMANUEL: It's Harry's toilet! His! His!

CURTAIN

SCENE III

To divide what is thine from what is mine

PLACE: HARRY *and* IMMANUEL'*s room.*

TIME: *Ten-thirty that night.*

ON RISE: IMMANUEL *is huddled under the covers in* *bed. There is the sound of the downstairs door slam-* *ming. Offstage, we hear* HARRY *shouting.*

HARRY: [*Offstage*] Hey, Archie, Archie! [*Pause, then* *he starts singing and laughing.*]
   From this valley they say you are going
   I shall miss your bright eyes and sweet smile
   For they say you are taking the sunshine
   That brightens our pathway awhile.
HERMAN: [*Offstage, in German*] Be still, you American bum. American go home! We don't want trash over here.
HARRY: [*Offstage*] Sieg heil! Sieg heil!
HERMAN: [*Offstage, in German*] I'm going to call the police.
HARRY: [*Offstage, with German accent*] Achtung, ach-tung, make ready the gas chamber. Lower the chil-dren into the soap vats, knock out the gold teeth.
HERMAN: [*Offstage in English*] I'm going to call the police.
HERMAN'S WIFE: [*Offstage, in German*] Don't aggra-vate yourself, Herman. Come inside.
HARRY: [*On stage*] Call the Gestapo too, you potbellied cretin Nazi bastard. The only reason they didn't get

50

you clowns at Nuremberg was international big business. I'm the one guy who remembers Pearl Harbor. I'm the one guy who doesn't forget. Sieg heil! Sieg heil! Right in the fuehrer's face. You want something to remember? I'll give you something to remember. Here it comes. Get set. Here it comes. [HARRY *runs over to the phonograph and turns it on. It starts with a blare. The song is "The Fuehrer's Face," a satire on the Germans.* HARRY *goosesteps around the room. Song, on record.*]

Ven der Fuchrer says, "Ve iss der Master Race,"
Ve heil, ve heil, right in der Fuehrer's face.
Not to love der Fuehrer iss a great disgrace,
So ve heil, ve heil, right in der Fuehrer's face.
Iss ve not der supermen, superduper supermen?
Ya ve iss der supermen, superduper supermen.
Ve bring der Verld to order.
Heil Hitler's vord is order . . .

[*A severe banging begins from* HERMAN'S *apartment downstairs.* HARRY *grabs the same stick* IMMANUEL *had used and returns the banging with vicious glee. Runs to the door. Shouts in hall.*] I remember Pearl Harbor. Achtung, achtung, make ready the medical experiment.

HERMAN: [*Offstage, in English*] Chicago gangster!

HERMAN'S WIFE: [*Offstage, in German*] Come inside, Herman. He is a madman.

HARRY: [*Long Bronx cheer.*] Right in the Fuehrer's face. [HERMAN'S *door slams shut.* HARRY *shuts his door and leans against it for a moment as if catching his breath. He is breathing hard. He calms down, switches off record in such a way that record just comes to a slow stop. He leans against the door for a few more seconds taking in the situation. A slow smile appears, and then in a "hide and go seek" voice*] Hey, Archie, Archie, Archie, where is you? [HARRY, *pretending to be a combat soldier sneaking up on the enemy, backs along the wall toward the toilet. He kicks open the toilet door and machine-guns the area. The game done, he turns to look at the huddled mass of* IMMANUEL *under the bed covers.*] Hey, roach, where's my brother? It's ten-thirty. Half hour to train time. Bong! Bong! Hey, cockroach. Come on, little cockroach. [*Goes over to the bed.*] Cockroach? Cockroach? Black Ugly Man is home. Do you know what makes this night different from all other nights? Do you know why on this night we have to get our chin whiskers standing taller than ever tall they stood? It's going back to Ohio night. All the little lights at *American Farm and Garden* . . . Pow . . . Pow . . . Pow. My brother waiteth at the station. All things waiteth on the hour and for me. So let's get those antennae standing tall, roach-cock.

(HARRY *with one sweep pulls the covers halfway off* IMMANUEL. IMMANUEL *is in a fetal position, his back to* HARRY.)

IMMANUEL: [*Grabbing back the covers*] What are you doing? [*Throws them back over his head.* HARRY *starts to pull at the covers.* IMMANUEL *resists.*] What are you doing? What are you doing?

HARRY: [*Imitating him*] What am I doing? What am I doing?

IMMANUEL: Don't imitate me, Harry. Don't do that.

HARRY: Come on outa there, spider. The web is ripped. The strands playing on the breeze. The hunter is home from the hill, the sailor from the ocean, and the time has come to part, to sunder, to pluck up, to divide what is thine from what is mine.

IMMANUEL: Leave me alone, Harry. If you're going, go.

HARRY: Aw, he was sulking under the covers!

IMMANUEL: I was sleeping, Harry. I was just sleeping.

HARRY: He was sulking because Black Ugly Man was unhibernating himself.

IMMANUEL: I was sleeping.

HARRY: You lying eight-legged son of a bitch. You never sleep. You haven't shut your eyes since DDT. Get the hell out of my bed. [*Continues pulling at the covers.*]

IMMANUEL: A third of the bed in mine, Harry. You'll be late. Your brother wouldn't like that. Leave me alone. The train leaves at eleven. You'll be late.

HARRY: You'd like that. Tell me you'd like that.

IMMANUEL: Don't get the covers all mussed up, Harry.

HARRY: Tell me how much you'd like Black Ugly Man to stay, roach. Let me hear it.

IMMANUEL: You know I can't sleep when the covers get all mussed up.

HARRY: Tell me.

IMMANUEL: The sheet's getting all tangled, Harry.

HARRY: Tell me before I pull seven of your legs off.

IMMANUEL: I'm sleeping, Harry. I'm sleeping.

HARRY: [*Stops tugging at the bedding.*] Swear you were sleeping.

IMMANUEL: I don't want to swear, Harry.

HARRY: I want you to swear. Swear!

IMMANUEL: I swear.

HARRY: Swear on something you hold near and dear.

IMMANUEL: I swear on my mother's life.

HARRY: Swear on something sweet and innocent.

IMMANUEL: On the blood of virgins, Harry. My mother is sweet and innocent. On her sainted life.

HARRY: [*While talking he is surreptitiously working to pull down the clothesline strung across the room.*] You're lying. You're an habitual liar. You lie about everything. The spring, the fall, the winter, flowers, teakettles, bathtub rings.

IMMANUEL: Not on my mother's life. I wouldn't swear on my mother's life and lie, Harry. Not on my . . .

HARRY: You never had a mother.

IMMANUEL: I had a mother, Harry. Her hair should fall out if I'm lying.

HARRY: How about the milk? You lied about that.

IMMANUEL: A mother's life is sacred. Let her tongue hang out if I'm lying.

HARRY: You ordered plain and you told me homogenized.

IMMANUEL: Some things are sacred, Harry. It was homogenized.

HARRY: It was plain and you drank off all the butterfat and all the cream with the vitamin A and D and you left the scummy water part for me.

IMMANUEL: In the sacred bowels of Jesus it was a mistake, Harry. I forgot to shake the bottle.

HARRY: You use me all the time. [*Starts imitating him.*] Harry, my feet are cold. Harry, scratch my balls. Harry, my ass itches. Harry, buy another fish. And all the time you were skimming off the cream. Every last lousy day. [*Suddenly* HARRY, *having secured the rope, pulls* IMMANUEL *widthwise across the bed and begins rolling the mattress up.*]

IMMANUEL: What are you doing? My spine. Don't damage the blood vessels into the spine!

HARRY: The thing was you thought you had me. The web here; the plotting board there. You thought this stinking room was it for me. It. Every last lousy day. But I'm bigger than this room! You know I'm bigger than this room.

IMMANUEL: I ordered homogenized. I swear on the Holy Ghost. The Holy Ghost, Harry.

HARRY: [*Begins tying* IMMANUEL *in.*] A thousand times bigger than this room. That's why I'm going back to Ohio. There isn't enough air in this room to last me five minutes. If you took all the air in Europe and put it this room, it wouldn't be enough.

IMMANUEL: Don't do this to me, Harry. I'm not an animal. Don't tie me up like an animal.

HARRY: [*Finishes tying the rope around the mattress.*] You are an animal! Don't fool yourself, that's all. I got a blue guitar, you know. I see things as they are.

You better see things the way they are. Tell me you don't want me to go back to Ohio. [*Harry jumps up and down on the mattress.*]

IMMANUEL: My spine.

HARRY: Tell me you'd rather have this than Black Ugly Man going back.

IMMANUEL: My spine.

HARRY: Tell me!

IMMANUEL: Don't go back, Harry. You're my best comrade, Harry. Till the end of time.

HARRY: [*Imitating him*] Don't go back, Harry. [*Stops the imitation.*] Well, it's all up. [*Leaves IMMANUEL all trussed up and goes over to the closet. He pulls out a valise and starts throwing odds and ends in it.*]

IMMANUEL: What are you going to do in America, Harry? Are you going to be a big success in America? Are you going to fight World War II and win Congressional Medals, Harry? Are you going to open up a used-car business and make mountains of money? What are you going back to, Harry?

HARRY: It's summer all the time in Ohio. Even when it snows it's summer. In the winter you can hunt unicorns in Ohio. Whole fields of them.

IMMANUEL: There are no unicorns in Ohio, Harry. You can't even paint. Why do you think they wouldn't keep you as a student in Florence? Why do you think you only sell your stuff to me? I'm the only one. Isn't it strange? The only one. It seems strange to me. Do you want to go to another art school in America? Lots of damn fine Americans went to Ohio State. Then you can go to another one and another one and another one. You'll never run out of schools. They never let you run out of schools in America. You can't add. You can't fly. The only thing you know how to do is vomit in Air Force planes.

HARRY: [*Searching around for something*] Where's my gym shorts? Where's my tennis balls? Where are the Florida coconut patties from my sisters? I'll kill you if you ate them. [*Finds them.*] Where's my oxblood shoes? [*Begins searching with intensity.*] What did you do with my oxblood shoes?

IMMANUEL: People die in Ohio, Harry. Black things, worms, beetles, flies, die in Ohio. Things die. Don't forget the lederhosen, Harry.

HARRY: I don't want the lederhosen. I want my oxblood shoes. Nothing dies in Ohio.

IMMANUEL: It isn't Christmas in Ohio. It isn't poetry.

HARRY: Nothing dies in Ohio. Where's my oxblood shoes?

IMMANUEL: I didn't touch them. They're in the closet.

HARRY: I don't see them. You're lying to me.

IMMANUEL: They're in the closet where you put them.

HARRY: Why can't I see them then? Why can't I find them if they're in the closet? I'm not going to be cheated out of my shoes.

IMMANUEL: They're in the closet, Harry. What's the matter with you?

HARRY: Why can't I find them then. I can't find them. They're not here.

IMMANUEL: They are, Harry.

HARRY: [*Starts jumping up and down on the mattress.*] They're not here. I won't go without them.

IMMANUEL: My spine. My bones.

HARRY: Don't give me that spine shit. What did you do with what's mine?

IMMANUEL: Remember when I bought the lederhosen for you, Harry? The sparrows had come back to Munich and they were standing in the snow puddles like thin sticks. You said everybody was wearing lederhosen and you wanted a pair and I took the check my father sent me and I spent it all for you.

HARRY: You didn't touch my stuff all day today?

IMMANUEL: I don't want to play the games, Harry.

HARRY: You didn't touch my stuff all day today?

IMMANUEL: [*After a pause. Suddenly with loud sin-*

cerity] I swear on the Virgin's womb. The fruit of the womb. On the holy fingers of the Magi, Harry.

HARRY: You didn't touch my two thirds of the dresser? You didn't stick your hands in my two thirds of the dresser and put on my stuff and show my stuff off to your friends?

IMMANUEL: My mother's breasts should rot if I touched anything of yours.

HARRY: I can tell if you touched my drawers. You know that? Should I tell you how I always know when you're fondling my stuff? Should I tell you? [*Turns the mattress around so that* IMMANUEL *faces the dresser.* HARRY *goes over to the dresser.*] You think I put paper matches in the corner and the matches fall to the floor when the drawer's opened. So all you had to do was replace the matches and I wouldn't know. Well, it wasn't the matches. The matches are a decoy. That's how you get fooled. A decoy. It was the talcum powder. All along the edges I put talcum powder and when anything is touched the talcum powder falls to the floor. Puddles of talcum. You thought it was the paper matches, didn't you? [*Pulls the drawer. Talcum falls.*]

IMMANUEL: I never touched your dresser!

HARRY: So you opened the drawer, slowly, slowly, and then carefully put back the match. But you overlooked one detail. One small detail.

IMMANUEL: I can't feel my legs, Harry. My rib cage is bending.

HARRY: The secret's in the talcum powder. I put the talcum powder in the shoes and when you wore them there were footprints. In the crotch of the pants, too. Last week the corduroy pants. [*Runs to closet, pulls out the corduroy pants and shoves them in front of* IMMANUEL.] You see that? [*Turns them upside down and the talcum falls out.*] You don't do a damn thing I don't know about. [*Crawls up on top of the mattress and, reaching over into the night table, grabs handfuls of talcum and begins throwing them inside the mattress.*]

IMMANUEL: Don't treat me like this. I can't breathe.

HARRY: You can breathe.

IMMANUEL: I can't breathe.

HARRY: [*Jumping up and down on mattress.*] You can breathe. You throw the covers over your head. You breathe that, don't you? You breathe stale air, old air, used air. The air people forget about: in closets, in corners, old tires. Last week's air. Last year's air. When did you change the air in this room? Did you change it last week when I told you to?

IMMANUEL: I did. By Christ's holy bladder I did.

HARRY: The hell you did.

IMMANUEL: [*Excited by being able to prove the air was changed.*] We had bluefish a week ago. There's no bluefish smell in the room. Smell, smell.

HARRY: When we were in Rome . . . [*Imitates IMMANUEL's voice.*] "Harry, let's stay down in the catacombs just another hour. Let me suck up the air around the crypts just another minute."

IMMANUEL: I'm telling the truth by the warm milk in Mary's bosom. Just smell. One smell.

HARRY: All right, I'm going to do that. I'm going to do that. [*Stops and smells.*] It's that same goddamn fish smell.

IMMANUEL: It's not, Harry. This is codfish. I bought a codfish. The first Friday of every month it's a sardine fish, then a pickerel fish, then a bluefish, then a codfish.

HARRY: [*Reaches over and picks up the black glove that is lying on the night table.*] You wore the rubber glove?

IMMANUEL: You know what we'll do. We'll go skiing at Garmisch. You always wanted to do that, Harry. Just us. Juju and Michael won't know. We can spend all winter huddling and cuddling and drinking rum.

We'll buy ski outfits as soon as my check comes. You always wanted a white ski outfit.

HARRY: But you wore the glove for Archer?

IMMANUEL: He was confused. I spoke of illnesses and touched him. I touched his arm and the flesh below shrank. I spoke of skin conditions and infirmities. I hinted at certain handicaps, at foul odors that emanate from the mouth, at smells that rise between the toes.

HARRY: And then the suggestions of greasy skin and scales on the thighs? You didn't forget about that and the soaps and salts?

IMMANUEL: I thrust my leg through the robe. He was confused. He rose slightly in the chair, fell back, gazed away.

HARRY: He does that. When I used to ask him for things or try to tell him things he would look up to the ceiling.

IMMANUEL: I mentioned the blood vessels. Infirmities. The lack of hair.

HARRY: Archer is covered with hair. The whole family is hairy.

IMMANUEL: I suggested vague disorders that could not be cleansed.

HARRY: They bathe twice a day. God, they hate dirt.

IMMANUEL: Vague illnesses involving worms and acnes.

HARRY: And the ones with Latin names? You didn't forget the ones with Latin names?

IMMANUEL: I remembered them all. He was weakening. I twisted my leg and perfumed it. I spoke of colds and snows and exquisite suffering. Encasements in ice and the tortures of tearing ligaments. I called him to my side.

HARRY: That was when he resisted.

IMMANUEL: I slid his hand upon my shoulder. "But my throat is warm. Feel my throat. Do my shoulders seem hot or cold? The left is warmer than the right.

My heart is cold. Feel my back. The hump is hot. Feel my hump."

HARRY: You did the hump? That's when you found out about his iron will. Right? Right? That was the moment when you had to stop. That iron will.

IMMANUEL: But it was too late, Harry. He felt less, that he was reduced. I could see it in his eyes.

HARRY: Had you done the beads?

IMMANUEL: The crucifix, too, and the holy water and then the nail relics. I made him touch the nails.

HARRY: But he wasn't overcome. He has perfect control. He never loses control!

IMMANUEL: He moved to the window, but it wasn't the same man. He was reduced, confused, less than he was. "You will not look at the convent." "No." "You must not look at the convent." "I won't look at the convent." "Don't look at the convent." I had my rubber glove on, my twisted spine, my hump and my limp. He didn't want to sit on the bed, but he sat. He didn't want to stroke me, but he did. The powder had risen about him; it clung to his coat; he couldn't shake himself free; the church bells rang and he was less and less and then he couldn't find the balloon man, but he kept looking, and I directed him. I was in command. "Can you see the bakery? Can you see the mailbox?" He was growing weaker, a bull weakened by a dozen pics. I didn't relent. I moved further below the covers. I was conquering, his will was collapsing. I ran him through, Harry. I ran the bull through. I could feel the bleeding in my mouth, I . . .

HARRY: Oh, goddamn you! God *damn* you! [*He begins pulling the mattress off the bed with* IMMANUEL *inside.* HARRY *is in a real panic.*]

IMMANUEL: You are pleased! You are. I did it for you.

HARRY: You did it for yourself.

IMMANUEL: You wanted it. You wanted me to do it.

You couldn't do it. [*He screams out like a madman while* HARRY *drags him across the floor.*]

HARRY: I didn't want it.

IMMANUEL: You wanted it.

HARRY: Never! I never wanted it. Never. Not once. Not one time. Not to my brother.

IMMANUEL: Always. Everything you did, you wanted it. I did it for you. You knew he was coming. You got out. You left him for me.

HERMAN: [*At that moment* HERMAN *shouts up the stairway, offstage, and his* WIFE *starts banging on the ceiling.*] You crazy maniacs. I'm going to have you locked up in an insane asylum. Do you hear! Stop that noise!

HARRY: [*Jumping up and down on the floor.* HERMAN'S WIFE *answers by banging up.* HARRY *runs over to the door and opens it*] Where were you when they were turning people into soap? When they were making lampshades? What were you doing then? What about the noise then? Why didn't you hear the noise then when they needed you? Who needs you now?

HERMAN: [*Offstage*] I'm going to call the police.

HARRY: Call the police. [*Looks around the apartment for something to throw.*] I'll give you something to call the police for. Let them throw me in a concentration camp. I'm not afraid of your lousy concentration camps. [*Grabs a flowerpot. Runs out into the hall.*]

HERMAN: [*Offstage*] You madman.

HARRY: You son of a bitch. [*Throws the flowerpot. It evidently strikes* HERMAN, *who is coming up the stairs. We hear him fall down the stairs.*]

HERMAN'S WIFE: [*Offstage in German*] My God. My God. You've killed him!

HARRY: You open your mouth. I got one for you, lampshade-maker. Heil Hitler. [*Runs back, grabs another flowerpot.*]

IMMANUEL: [*Screaming out*] Harry! Harry! [HARRY *runs*

to stairwell. Throws flowerpot. This one misses. We hear it break.]

HERMAN'S WIFE: [*Runs down the stairs, screaming in German.*] He's killed my husband. Help! Police!

HARRY: You think it's enough if you keep the railroad stations clean? It's not enough. You gotta keep clean in the heart. In the heart. You Nazi bitch. Call the storm troopers. Nazi bitch! You don't fool me. [*Runs over to the window. Flings it open. Shouts out.*] You Nazi bitch! [*Starts wandering around the room.*] You crazy. You crazy. You crazy.

IMMANUEL: Harry, you must run from here. She's going to call the police. You don't know our police, Harry.

HARRY: What do I care about your lousy police. Where are my ox-bull shoes? My ox-bull shoes!

IMMANUEL: They'll take you away. Get out of here. Go back to the Dolly Bar. I'll meet you. What do we care about the rest of the world?

HARRY: What are you talking about? I'm meeting my brother at the Bahnhof at eleven. I want a drink of water.

IMMANUEL: There isn't time. [*He struggles to free himself but he cannot.* HARRY *goes over to the refrigerator and pours out some of the "holy" water. He drinks it. Watches almost with detachment* IMMANUEL's *struggles with the mattress.*]

HARRY: [*Tapping the empty glass against his teeth*] You'll never get out. Once you're in, you're in. It's mathematics. It's figured on computers. Columns add up. Add up one side, add up another side. So much for this side. So much for that side.

IMMANUEL: Get out of here, Harry. Please. Please.

HARRY: [*Refills the glass and walks over.*] There's always been something I've wanted to see. You know what that is?

IMMANUEL: There isn't time.

HARRY: [*Sits down beside* IMMANUEL.] I've always

wanted to know if a clown is a clown always—if you are a clown or not a clown.

IMMANUEL: I'm not a clown, Harry. [HARRY *sticks his hand in the mattress and begins pulling* IMMANUEL'*s head out.*] Leave me alone, Harry.

HARRY: I'm gonna pull your head out.

IMMANUEL: You're hurting me. I'm hurt, Harry. [HARRY *finally succeeds in pulling* IMMANUEL'*s head out. He pushes the glass filled with water in front of* IMMANUEL'*s mouth.*]

HARRY: You gotta get the glass in your teeth. I want you to pick up the glass and drink the water.

IMMANUEL: I can't get my arms out.

HARRY: You gotta drink it without your arms.

IMMANUEL: I can't.

HARRY: This is confidential. Entre nous, you know what I mean?

IMMANUEL: There isn't time.

HARRY: Don't worry about time. You have nothing to do with time. This is about the circus that came to Columbus when I was in the Cub Scouts.

IMMANUEL: I don't want to hear about circuses, Harry. I want to go skiing at Garmisch.

HARRY: Archer said that the clowns were clowns even when they weren't wearing clown suits. How about that? Isn't that an amazing thing to hear? What do you think about it? Isn't it amazing?

IMMANUEL: It's stupid, Harry.

HARRY: But it implies things. You see that? You see how it implies things? Once you're in, you're in. What do you think?

IMMANUEL: I don't know.

HARRY: Neither did I, then. But after the circus, Archer took me downstairs below the arena to see Moko. Moko was a failure clown. The kind that everything goes wrong for. He just wants to get out of the arena. But they won't let him. That's essential. They won't let him go. He tries to climb the wall, but he keeps falling back, so they try to shoot him out of a cannon, but the cannon won't fire. It blows up in his face. He runs to the phony doors they keep shoving in front of him, but the doors won't open. They drag him over to a spinning ball, but he can't stay on. He runs up to the other clowns for help, but they throw water on him. He can't win. The other clowns steal his shoes; they beat him up. They lie to him. They kick him in the behind. And all this time he's saying, "God, let me escape; God, let me escape."

IMMANUEL: This has nothing to do with me, Harry. I don't want to listen.

HARRY: I'm shouting, "Let him go. What do you want from him?" But my sisters and Archer are laughing.

IMMANUEL: Let me out, Harry. Please. Please.

HARRY: So Archer takes me under the arena and there's Moko sitting in front of his dressing table. An old, old man bent over. Archer doesn't knock. He doesn't even knock! Most of the paint is off. Long silver lines of tears running down Moko's face. God! I remember that. How weird. He looks up into the mirror and stares at us and then he turns around with the saddest expression I ever saw. I wanted to cry, but Archer starts laughing and laughing. And Moko got sadder and sadder. Archer couldn't stop laughing. He kept trying to turn away and Moko wouldn't let him. Archer ran all over the arena and Moko kept chasing him around and around making him look, sticking his face in front of him. When I cried, Archer laughed, it was always that way, but now Archer had to hold his ribs. The clown wanted to kill him.

IMMANUEL: I want to get out of here, Harry. I don't want to be tied up.

HARRY: It's not a matter of what you want! It's a matter of what you get. Drink!

IMMANUEL: I'm not a clown.

HARRY: Try. You never know till you try.

IMMANUEL: I don't want to try. I'm not a clown. I'm

a human being, Harry. [IMMANUEL *looks up at him, pleadingly.* HARRY *stares mutely at him.* IMMANUEL *takes the glass in his teeth and, painfully raising his head, drinks. The glass falls out of his mouth and the water spills to the floor.* HARRY *wearily gets up.*]

HARRY: You see how you dropped it? You couldn't do it. You're a clown after all. That's the way it is with clowns. They think they can make it till every cannon in the world blows up in their face, till every ball slips out under their feet. You start out life thinking you can do it. Nobody has got you down for pantaloons and colored hair because you're just starting out. You haven't vomited in the plane yet. You think, boy, I'm going to sail! Boy, I'm going to get out of that cannon with a flying roar! Boy, I'm going to get in that sky and really move! Your brother is sailing in the blue, your sisters are sailing in the blue, the whole God-clean world is sailing in the blue, and you're fading out. You're dimming. You've got a green head. You got purple eyes. Whoever is in, you're out. You're growing radishes in swamps, you're doing it all wrong, nothing's coming up. Maybe they won't notice you're dimming. You never make it. In or out. In or out. Right from the beginning. [*Sound of a police car.* HARRY *picks up the statue of the stone-blind kid and puts it near his valise.*] Out on the ocean by tomorrow. The wind blowing clean. Skimming. Cutting the water like a knife. America. America.

IMMANUEL: Oh, Harry.

HARRY: You keep quiet. I wanna see those shoes produced. That's what I want from you. [*Sound of people running up the stairs.*]

HERMAN'S WIFE: [*Offstage, in German*] This way. This way. He dropped a flowerpot on my husband's head. He is a madman.

HARRY: [*Closes his valise and touches the statue.*] I'm gonna give him eyes to see with. Big granite eyes.

POLICEMAN: [*Offstage, in German*] This is the police. Open up.

HARRY: Anne Frank doesn't live here. You wanna find Anne Frank? She's dead. Gone. [HARRY *runs over to the record player and starts a new record. It is "The Emperor's Waltz."*]

POLICEMAN: [*Offstage, in German*] Open up.

HARRY: She's gone away. Heil Hitler. This is the Fuehrer speaking. Tomorrow we will put on the clown mustaches and make with the goosestepping.

POLICEMAN: [*Offstage, in English this time*] If you do not open up, I will force the door.

HARRY: Go ahead. I'm an American. I'm sure the American ambassador will be interested in the revival of Nazi fascism. [*The door is forced.*]

HERMAN'S WIFE: [*Standing back a bit. In German*] That's him.

HARRY: I wish to prefer charges against this woman.

HERMAN'S WIFE: You madman. You want to kill. That's what you want.

HARRY: [*In German*] She is a war criminal.

POLICEMAN: [*In English*] We will talk this over at the police station, sir.

HARRY: Talk it over here. I've an eleven o'clock appointment. [*The* POLICEMAN *grabs* HARRY. HARRY *resists and is forced down the stairwell. He screams out.*] Hey, wait a minute. Wait a minute, you fascist. Can't you wait just a minute? Just that minute. I'm an American. Just that minute. I'm an American. I am an American. [*As soon as they have left the room,* IMMANUEL *begins violently struggling to free himself. He rolls about the floor with maniacal determination and desperation. The bells of the convent are tolling. Far down the stairwell* HARRY *calls out.*] Archer! Archer! [IMMANUEL *answers in a voice full of rage.*]

IMMANUEL: Me, Harry. What about me? Me! [*The music on the record player, "The Emperor's Waltz," has grown very loud. It fills the entire room with the glorious sounds of another era. The spotlight focused on* IMMANUEL'*s enraged face suddenly blacks out, leaving the stage in darkness and a cacophony of suddenly stopped sound.*]

CURTAIN

The Journey of the Fifth Horse

A Play in Two Acts

Based, in part, on the story
"Diary of a Superfluous Man"
by Ivan Turgenev

For Wynn and Bobbie Handman

The first performance of *The Journey of the Fifth Horse* was given on April 13, 1966, at the American Place Theatre in New York City. It was directed by Larry Arrick. The scenery and costumes were by Kert Lundell; the lighting by Roger Morgan.

THE ORIGINAL CAST
(In Order of Appearance)

TERENTIEVNA, housekeeper to Nikolai
   Alexeevich Chulkaturin .... *Mary Hayden*
ZODITCH, first reader in the Grubov
   Publishing Company .... *Dustin Hoffman*
SERGEY, grandchild of Terentievna ... *Christopher Strater*
*RUBIN, apprentice reader in the Grubov
   Publishing Company .... *William H. Bassett*
*MISS GRUBOV, owner of the Grubov
   Publishing Company .... *Susan Anspach*
*PANDALEVSKI, supervising printer in
   the Grubov Publishing Company .... *Lee Wallace*
KATERINA PROLOMNAYA, a landlady ... *Catherine Gaffigan*
NIKOLAI ALEXEEVICH CHULKATURIN,
   a landowner .... *Michael Tolan*
DR. KORVIN, a physician .... *Mark Hammer*
LEVINOV, a lawyer .... *Harry Miller*
*FEATHERS, a cleaning girl .... *Susan Lipton*
KIRILLA MATVEICH OZHOGIN, a landowner .... *Allan Rich*
*ELIZAVETA KIRILLOVNA, his daughter ... *Susan Anspach*
*BIZMIONKOV, family friend of the
   Ozhogins .... *Lee Wallace*
ANNA, wife of Kirilla .... *Martha Greenhouse*
GREGORY, a neighbor to Zoditch .... *Jack Aaron*
*VOLOBRINA, a servant girl .... *Susan Lipton*

*CAPTAIN IVAN PETROVICH NARVINSKY,
a cavalry officer .... *William H. Bassett*
TANIA, an unmarried girl .... *Jane Buchanan*
LIEUTENANT ZIMIN, a cavalry officer .... *Jim Doerr*
OFFICERS .... *Brian Turkington, Ron Seka*
  *The following roles are doubled:
    RUBIN and CAPTAIN IVAN PETROVICH NARVINSKY
    MISS GRUBOV and ELIZAVETA KIRILLOVNA
    PANDALEVSKI and BIZMIONKOV
    FEATHERS and VOLOBRINA

ACT I

Scene 1:
  The Grubov Publishing House
Scene 2:
  Zoditch's apartment

ACT II

The entire action takes place in Zoditch's apartment house.

TIME: *The late nineteenth century*
PLACE: *St. Petersburg, Russia*

ACT I

Scene 1

PLACE: *An office space in the Grubov Publishing House occupied by* ZODITCH *and* RUBIN.

TIME: *Late afternoon.*

SCENE: *There are two desks:* RUBIN's *on the left side of the room;* ZODITCH's *on the right side.*

ON RISE: *The stage is completely dark. We hear a voice.*

VOICE: In Samarkand I saw a monkey yellow-splotched and dying in a cage, and as I made to hasten by, he grasped my sleeve as if there might be something more to the matter.

(*Lights up.* RUBIN, *a young man of about twenty-five years of age, sits behind his desk tweezing and clipping his mustache. His desk is bare, in rather sharp contrast to the fairly well-cluttered desk of* ZODITCH. ZODITCH *stands on a little ladder near the back wall of the room, engaged in hanging a border of black crepe around a large portrait of* MR. GRUBOV, *the founder of the firm.* ZODITCH *is about ten years older than* RUBIN. *He is thin, wiry, quick, and nervous in his movements. When he puts his glasses on you can hardly see his eyes. He is of somewhat less than average height, and losing his hair. In front of* ZODITCH's *desk sit two visitors:* TERENTIEVNA, *a peasant woman in her early sixties, and her grandson,* SERGEY,

72

about seventeen years old—a simple-minded boy who is stylishly dressed in clothes that are obviously too small for him. His arms dangle out of his sleeves. The clothes seem ready to burst.)

TERENTIEVNA: [*To* ZODITCH] Did you say something, mister?

ZODITCH: No.

TERENTIEVNA: Oh, I thought you said something. I thought you was saying you wanted to read the writing, mister.

ZODITCH: I said nothing, madam. I am hanging the crepe now.

TERENTIEVNA: Because if you want I can let you read the writing now, mister.

ZODITCH: [*Exasperated*] I cannot read your master's manuscript now, madam. I am hanging the crepe now. You have come at a bad time. There has been a death in the firm; our employer, Mr. Grubov, has passed away.

TERENTIEVNA: Oh, has he?

ZODITCH: Yes.

TERENTIEVNA: That's a sorrow.

ZODITCH: Yes.

TERENTIEVNA: And a sorrow it was when my master died, him being so sadly reduced in fortune.

(ZODITCH *stares at her for a moment and then resigns himself to the fact that she will not be silenced.*)

SERGEY: He didn't have a kopeck what you could call his. And them what he owed money to was fierce.

TERENTIEVNA: There was always the moneylenders banging at the door of the house, but I never let none of them get at the master. I kept the doors locked in their faces I did, and I told them what they could do with their bills receivable. As God is my judge, mister, they woulda pulled the sheets off the bed he was dying on, if I'da let 'em, so vicious they was about getting their monies. What makes people get that way over money, do you suppose, mister?

RUBIN: [*He speaks before* ZODITCH *has a chance to answer. He gestures at the painting of* MR. GRUBOV.] Well, what do you think, Mr. Zoditch, have they buried him yet? [ZODITCH, *without answering, starts down the ladder.*]

TERENTIEVNA: The master's house was what they called the Chulkaturin family house. [ZODITCH *looks at her.*] Chulkaturin, mister. It's a name what nobody gets right, and him, poor soul, being the last of 'em what bore the name, who's to care now what the rights and wrongs of sounding it be?

RUBIN: Now that Mr. Grubov is tucked away, we can expect some changes, wouldn't you say, Mr. Zoditch? [ZODITCH *still doesn't answer.*] I'd imagine Mr. Pandalevski would be the man to watch. [ZODITCH *sits down and begins adjusting himself. He removes the garters from his arms, pushes down his sleeves, runs his hand through his hair.*]

TERENTIEVNA: And a hard thing it is to say "family house" when all that were near and dear to poor Mr. Chulkaturin, his mama and papa, was already gone and buried.

SERGEY: They was dead, wasn't they? Tell 'em about the rats.

TERENTIEVNA: During the winter I took service with the gentleman, I found the house overrun.

SERGEY: Rats big as horses' heads.

TERENTIEVNA: Not only rats, mister. Moles and other creature things what come burrowing in through the cellar to get in from the snow. He wouldn't let me drive them out, though I could have easy enough without him knowing because by that time he was near finished with this world, but I didn't have the heart to go against his wishes, him being perishing like he was and the doctor telling us to leave him be about the little things.

ZODITCH: Madam, I am not interested in rats, moles, and medical reports.

SERGEY: And the lousy stream? What about that?

RUBIN: Of course the fact that Mr. Pandalevski accompanied Miss Grubov to the cemetery may not mean anything definite, unless it's a step in the right direction. A young girl has to rely on someone when her father's dead, don't you think? [ZODITCH *starts angrily over to* RUBIN's *desk. He slams down a stack of manuscripts on it.*]

ZODITCH: Work. Tweeze on your own time.

TERENTIEVNA: The boy is meaning a stream what belonged to the properties. When the master died the water went particularly bad.

SERGEY: It stank, that's what it did. And the garden had nothing to eat from it.

TERENTIEVNA: It was a flower garden, you see, mister.

SERGEY: Well, ya can't eat flowers, so what's the sense in that?

TERENTIEVNA: The flowers was particular treasured by him. You see, mister, he was a gentleman, which was why he didn't need to plant vegetables. And then after he died the spring came around again and everything was coming up, and that's a sorrow, him dead and everything coming up colorful.

RUBIN: Only who would have thought it would turn out to be Mr. Pandalevski she relied on. My money was on you, but he's a comer, he is. Well, it's all a ladder, Mr. Zoditch. It's up or it's down. We can't be keeping our feet on the same rung.

ZODITCH: Be still. I warn you. I'm the first reader.

TERENTIEVNA: The good Lord has His ways, I know, and none of us can choose the comings and goings of things, but I prayed for him that he would last through the spring so the flowers would give him pleasure.

SERGEY: So why didja pour the soap water on 'em?

ZODITCH: Madam, I have already told you, you have come at a bad time. There has been a death in the firm.

TERENTIEVNA: [*Begins coughing. A very bad cough. She pulls out her handkerchief and spits into it.*] That clears it up, it does. So that's how it is with us, mister. All Mr. Chulkaturin left us in exchange for the cruel months of our services, is what I got here. [*She takes a small parcel from her bag.*] And it's for getting it made into a book with you bookmongers, which is what the gentleman himself was most insistent on so we could get paid something for our kindnesses to him, that me and the boy came to Petersburg. He didn't pay us a bit of wages so it's a fair thing we're doing now trying to make a little money off his writings, wouldn't you say, mister?

ZODITCH: Yes. Yes. [*Annoyed, he takes the offered parcel.*]

TERENTIEVNA: Not that I begrude working for the sick. Doing a Christian duty to another fellow creature is doing no more than what Christ expects of us. [ZODITCH *starts to unwrap the parcel. Suddenly there is the sound of a bell—the kind of bell that hangs over a door. Then the door slams shut.*]

RUBIN: They're back. [*There is a flurry of motion.* RUBIN *shoves his manicuring equipment into the desk and hurriedly begins reading and taking notes at the same time.* ZODITCH *puts on his coat. In come* MISS GRUBOV *and* MR. PANDALEVSKI. *They are dressed in black. As they pass by* ZODITCH, *he scurries out from behind his desk.*]

ZODITCH: Miss Grubov. [PANDALEVSKI *and* MISS GRUBOV *stop.* ZODITCH *searches his pockets for an envelope and then remembers it is on his desk. He takes the envelope and hands it to* MISS GRUBOV.] A note of condolence.

MISS GRUBOV: Thank you, Mr. Zoditch. [*She starts to leave, but* ZODITCH *tries to get in a few more words while he has the opportunity.* PANDALEVSKI *frowns.*]

ZODITCH: [*He speaks falteringly.*] I just wanted to say that I thought your father was wonderful, Miss Grubov, wonderful, a man to be admired, respected. It was an honor to be employed by him these past twelve years. We all miss him: a loss, a great loss . . .

MISS GRUBOV: Thank you. [*Starts to go again. Again* ZODITCH *dribbles out a few words.*]

ZODITCH: I hope it was not too cold for you, Miss Grubov. I thought of you in the carriage and I said they will forget the extra blankets. I . . . [*Starts backing away.*] Excuse me. Excuse me.

MISS GRUBOV: It was fine in the carriage, Mr. Zoditch, thank you. [*She walks offstage.*]

PANDALEVSKI: Bring up the tea to Miss Grubov. [*He starts to exit after* MISS GRUBOV *and then turns.*] And a cup for me.

RUBIN: [*Although* PANDALEVSKI's *words were spoken mostly to* ZODITCH, RUBIN *answers.*] Yes, Mr. Pandalevski. Right away. [*He starts out from behind his desk.*]

ZODITCH: Where are you going? It is my privilege to bring up the tea. [RUBIN *just smiles and exits.* ZODITCH *runs after him.*] Where do you think you're going? [*We hear him running down the steps after* RUBIN.] It is my privilege. [*As soon as* ZODITCH *leaves,* TERENTIEVNA *spits into the wastepaper basket. She opens her purse and, withdrawing a small flask, takes a quick snort.* SERGEY *begins hitting his boots.*]

SERGEY: [*To boots*] Damn you. Damn you. [*To* TERENTIEVNA] I don't like it here, Grandma. I don't like him. I don't like anybody. [*Grabs his boots and starts wringing them with his hands.*] Arrrh, Arrrh, Arrrh. They're haunted. They're killing my feet. His ghost is in them. What's the sense in having boots to kill you? I don't want them. I told you to let him have his boots right from the beginning. [*Strikes boots again.*] Arrrh. Arrrh. I don't feel well. Let's go to another bookmaker's place. You remember I wanted

him to have his boots? You remember that? I don't
like it here.

TERENTIEVNA: Be still!

SERGEY: Listen, I want a regular suit. While we're in
Petersburg I want you to buy me a regular suit.

TERENTIEVNA: You have a regular suit.

SERGEY: This is not a regular suit. It hates me. It's his
suit. His suit is not a regular suit. It doesn't fit me. The
pants are too tight. Look how they make me walk.
[*Gets up and walks as uncomfortably as possible. He
keeps grabbing at the pants.*] You see? Look. You see
how I'm walking? They're tearing my legs to pieces.
I can't put anything in the pockets. [*Flings himself
back in the chair.*] The jacket is crushing my chest. It
cuts me under the arms. It twists my shoulders. Look
at the collar. Do you see how tight it is? I can't breathe.
Arrrh, Arrrh. Listen, you know what I think? [*Leans
forward confidentially.*] This was the suit Mr. Chulkaturin was meant to be buried in. Not the lousy one.
This was the one he wanted. That's why it doesn't fit.
It was supposed to go with him to the grave. I told you
to let him take this suit. Let him take the good suit
was what I said.

TERENTIEVNA: Be still!

SERGEY: I can't be still. It itches me. It chokes me. It
tears my legs. It rubs my neck. It doesn't let me alone.
Arrrh. Arrrh. [*Beats at the boots and tears them off.*]
Leave my feet alone, damn you. Damn you! [*Switches
topic.*] And when are we going to see the wild animals? I want to see the wild animals of Petersburg.
You promised me. [*Again switching topic*] And
maybe they won't buy his writings and then we won't
make any money and then we've come all this way for
what? For what? [*Rubbing his feet*] Arrrh. Arrrh. And
then what? What about my yellow sled? What about
that? Where's the money for that? [ZODITCH *and*
RUBIN *enter fighting over possession of a tea tray containing a teapot, two cups, and a stack of biscuits.*]

ZODITCH: It is my responsibility to bring the tea. Will you let go of it?

RUBIN: Mr. Pandalevski was talking to me.

ZODITCH: He was not, Mr. Rubin. He was talking to me. I have always brought the tea to Mr. Grubov and now I will bring it to Miss Grubov.

RUBIN: Will you let go? I am to bring the tea. He was talking to me.

ZODITCH: I am not going to let go. You let go. He was talking to me. Don't be silly, Mr. Rubin.

RUBIN: I am not going to let go. I'm not being silly.

ZODITCH: Let go. You are being very silly.

RUBIN: No. It is you who are being very silly.

ZODITCH: You.

RUBIN: You.

ZODITCH: You. [*There is a real skirmish.* RUBIN *pulls the tray free with a final jerk.*]

RUBIN: You! [*He walks offstage.* ZODITCH *begins wandering about the stage.*]

TERENTIEVNA: [*Thinks this is a good time to continue her monologue.*] The master was a very refined type such as yourself, Mr. Zoditch, and he had a good handwriting, too, which comes from being so sensitive to things. You could tell he was delicate just from looking at his hands. [ZODITCH *is at this moment in his pacing wringing his hands, and making almost animal noises in his frustration. He sits down on* RUBIN's *chair.*]

ZODITCH: Madhouse. Madhouse. Up the ladder, is it? [*He picks up a small bundle of* RUBIN's *pencils and breaks them.*]

TERENTIEVNA: Yes, mister, a madhouse it is for sure, which is something of what the master said when he was trying to save the family properties which his father had gambled away. That was what they all said at the burial.

ZODITCH: [*Highly distracted, jumps up.*] Who said? Why do you go on and on? What are you talking about?

TERENTIEVNA: It was "they" what said it, mister. Those at the church what knew the family. They was coming and going in the law courts all the time, the mother and father was, and after the mother and father passed on, the poor gentleman continued fighting to save what was his. If you ask me, it was the courts what drove him back and forth like a poor pigeon across the country. It was them what broke his heart. That was what done it, mister. The law stealing his property. Even down to the summer house which the law stole away from him for taxes. Didn't he get in a rage when he learnt that. [RUBIN *reenters carrying the empty tea tray. He crosses over to his desk and, sitting on the edge of it, stares at* ZODITCH. ZODITCH *stares back at him furiously.* TERENTIEVNA *continues, trying to regain his attention.*] You should have heard him, mister. "I won't have it. They won't get away with it," he says and such like, but they did get away with it. [*And then in a different tone of voice, as if what she now has to say has particular significance to* ZODITCH] Which is what they always do, ain't it, mister? The worst getting away with it all. [ZODITCH *looks back at her as they exchange a quiet stare.* TERENTIEVNA *then continues as before.*] Oh, he was as much a fighter for things what was his as ever Death took away. He was never one to give up on things on account of him being a delicate soul. He was a brave sort and nobody can grudge him that. God love him for it.

ZODITCH: So? So? You are finished? Eh? [*Angrily unwraps the parcel containing the manuscript and glances at it.*] This is a diary. [*Pushes the manuscript back to* TERENTIEVNA. *Keeps looking at* RUBIN, *off and on.*] We do not publish diaries. You have talked all this time for nothing.

TERENTIEVNA: Oh no, mister. It ain't a diary. It's papers.

ZODITCH: It's a diary. [*Madly opens up to one of the pages and shoves it under her nose.*] You see? March 20? A day of the month. That's a diary.

TERENTIEVNA: No, mister. I can't read dates. Me and the boy can't read. [*At this moment* MR. PANDALEVSKI *stands unseen at stage right, a cup of tea in his hand. Only* RUBIN *sees him.* RUBIN *gets instantly to work.*]

ZODITCH: Well, I read dates, and it's a diary, madam. I assure you. And I assure you that we do not read diaries, nor have we ever in the entire history of Grubov Publications published one. So if you will excuse me . . . [*When* ZODITCH *looks over toward* RUBIN *and sees* RUBIN *working, he imagines it is because he has asserted himself with* TERENTIEVNA, *and put* RUBIN *in his place. It fills him with renewed determination to be assertive. He keeps looking at* RUBIN.]

TERENTIEVNA: You see, mister, it was just as a favor to the poor gentleman what wrote it because he wanted to see us paid for our goods and services that we come at all. He was a fine talker and word writer.

ZODITCH: Oh, he was, was he?

SERGEY: [*To* TERENTIEVNA] You're going to take me to see the wild animals of Petersburg!

ZODITCH: [*With mounting anger*] A good writer, was he? [*Whips open the pages of the diary.*] Well, he had a bad handwriting. How does that suit you? He wrote with the hand of a pigmy. Tiny, tiny letters, too backward, too feminine. And where is the punctuation? Do you see the punctuation? What has he done with that? Perhaps it is a very long sentence and all the punctuation is at the end? [*Turns the pages.*] Ah, here is a comma. I have found a comma! But where are the periods, the colons, the semicolons, the question marks? Where?

TERENTIEVNA: It's just writing, mister.

ZODITCH: Perhaps he has placed all his punctuation on the last page. [*Turns to the last page.*] No. I do not see them. In the middle, perhaps they are stored in the middle. [*Turns to the middle.*] No. They are not in the middle. So I will shake the pages and see if they fall out. [*Shakes the pages.* SERGEY *stares at the diary*

81

*and the floor as if he expects the punctuation to fall
out.*]

TERENTIEVNA: It's just writing, mister.

ZODITCH: There is no *just* writing! There is only proper
and improper writing. Your Mr. Chulkaturin doesn't
cross his *t*'s, he ignores his *t*'s, he makes his *t*'s look
like *l*'s, and the *l*'s like *b*'s, and the *b*'s like *h*'s, and
the *h*'s like nothing at all. And why doesn't he dot his
i's? Why doesn't he loop his *e*'s? I'll tell you why.
Because he doesn't know anything; because he doesn't
know how to write. We have here a babbling of con-
sonants, a scribbling scribble, a disease that knows
no punctuation, no sentencing, no paragraphing, a
singular disease . . . [*At this point he sees* MR. PANDA-
LEVSKI, *but he cannot stop. He would like to stop, but
he goes on and on.*] that rambles, that goes no place,
that floats on streams of bombast, a leaking hulk of
language in a sea of rhetoric, a babbling monument of
incoherency . . . [*He rises in his chair until he stands.*]
a vacuum, a wasteland, a desert, a void, a . . . [*He
stops. There is a moment of absolute silence, as*
PANDALEVSKI *comes forward.*]

PANDALEVSKI: Read it! Take it home with you, Mr.
Zoditch. Read it! [*Lights out.*]

CURTAIN

Scene 2

PLACE: ZODITCH's *apartment.*

TIME: *Early evening. Same day.*

SCENE: *The apartment is poorly furnished. It contains a
coal stove, a desk, a bed, sundry other things.*

ON RISE: *The apartment is unoccupied. Outside the
apartment, offstage right, we hear the shrill sounds of*

many small dogs barking. We next see ZODITCH *hastening up the staircase. When he reaches the door to his room he stops and turns around.*

ZODITCH: [*Speaks out loud, although the words are directed towards himself.*] Bark your lungs out, you bitches. You thinks I'm afraid of your dogs, Katerina Prolomnaya. I'll take a stick to them. I'll beat their brains out. And where is the hall light, Katerina Prolomnaya? You are quick enough to ask for the rent. [*The barking ceases.* ZODITCH *enters his room and, standing near the door, shouts into the hall.*] There will be no rent without a hall light! [*Shuts door quickly. Barking immediately begins again. Offstage sound of a woman's voice,* KATERINA PROLOMNAYA, *the landlady.*]

KATERINA: [*Offstage*] Who opened his mouth? Show yourself! You miserable pack of cowards. I'll set my dogs on ya, if I hear another word. You hear me? It'll be a cold day in hell before Katerina Prolomnaya takes garbage from the pack of you. [*From somewhere in the darkened hall comes a feeble* VOICE.]

VOICE: No rent without a hall light! [*This call is picked up by another* VOICE, *and then another, until there is a chorus of* VOICES *chanting one after the other.*]

VOICES: No rent without a hall light! No rent without a hall light!

KATERINA: No rent? A hall light? I'll throw the lot of you useless pieces of baggage out on the street where you belong. I'm coming up. [*Dogs bark louder. To* TENANTS] We'll see who it is that keeps his door open now. [KATERINA *ascends the stairs. Sound of doors shutting.*] So you're shutting your doors, you crawling pack of cowards. [*Stops right outside* ZODITCH'*s door. He is plainly frightened.*] Well, which one of you will stick his head out now and ask me for it? Which one? [*Pause.*] Which one? [*She bursts into a laugh that echoes and reechoes through the halls of the house.*

ZODITCH, *terribly frightened, keeps his back against the door. Sounds of the dogs sniffing around, scratching at his door.*] Come along Porshy, Potshy, Pinchy. [*Sound of the pack of them descending the stairs. Sound of her door shutting, and then silence.* ZODITCH *goes over to his stove and looks inside. He takes some paper and puts it in. He goes over to a small bucket— the bucket has only a few pieces of coal in it. He spills the entire amount into the stove and, striking a match, lights it. He stands in front of it for a moment, rubbing his hands. Then he picks up a pot of gruel which has been sitting on the stove and takes it over to the desk. He reaches into his pocket and pulls out the* CHULKATURIN *manuscript. He eats while he talks.*]

ZODITCH: Take it home with you. Read it! I will not take it home with me! I will not read it! Aagh. [*Slowly pronounces* CHULKATURIN's *name.*] Chulkaturin. Mr. Chulkaturin. You impossible name. You gentleman. So much the worse for you if you believe worms make distinctions underground. There are no distinctions underground. No better classes of worm. No gentleman's worm. No worm with an uncommon body, an uncommon mouth. You won't find them to your liking. I can assure you. [*Takes a whiskey bottle out of his coat and a glass out of the desk. Wipes the glass with his handkerchief. Pours in a tiny drop and spends a few seconds savoring it and smacking his lips over it.*] Rest assured. Worms don't get down to boot level. You won't get their tongue on your boot. They don't know about the summer houses you had, your Mediterranean villas, your ladies. Damn your ladies. Damn your fruits and peppermint creams. Damn their parasols, their lawn parties, your fresh meat and ice creams, your sailboats, your insolences. Aagh. [*Pours out another tiny drop, and drinks it down the same way.*] Here you come to me. Down to me, and you satisfy me or I'll ship you into oblivion. I'll take your bones and mangle them, I'll break your head, I'll break your back. I'll . . . [*In his anger he bends the spoon in his mouth. All subsequent action, real or imagined, will be played out within the room. The following is imagined.*]

PANDALEVSKI: [*His voice comes from somewhere in the dark.*] Why don't you shut your mouth, you sack of hot air! [*Lights up on* PANDALEVSKI.]

ZODITCH: You scum. You garbage. You dregs. You horse's tail. Do not think injustice goes unpunished. Do not think this is the office. Here there is freedom. Here you watch what you say to me. A trip to the cemetery does not make a love affair. Keep your hands off my water jug.

PANDALEVSKI: [*Pours the water from the jug into a basin.*] On the trip to the cemetery it was boringly obvious which direction the affection of Miss Grubov lay. Spreading the blanket to cover our legs from the chill, I found that by a subtle snaky motion of her torso she connived it so that one two three our thighs and hips were dancing flank to flank to the rolling of the wheels. Hand me the soap.

ZODITCH: Who do you think you're ordering about? I am the head of the reader's section, the first reader, you carbuncle, you wart, you pimple. I do not take orders from you. I will dance on your grave before I'm through.

PANDALEVSKI: Hardly had this dance begun when by a writhing of her arm, a heaving breathing of her bosom, as if the desire in her must burst, she seized my fingers one by one and locked them in the compass of her hand. Get me the soap!

ZODITCH: I'm warning you, Pandalevski. Watch what you say. Do not push me too far. Be careful. I will not put up with these lies.

PANDALEVSKI: Seizing thus my hand, she covered it with kisses and sent it, as it were, on a foreign exploration to private lands best left undiscovered outside the marriage bed. I pretended fright, surprise, but her

importunities and protestations were of such severe
necessity I at last gave way and exposed her bosom.
Get me the soap!

ZODITCH: You liar! You defamer! What right do you
have to say such things?

PANDALEVSKI: The soap!

ZODITCH: The soap is it? [*Reaches over and grabs the
soap bar.*] Here is the soap. [*He brings the bar of soap
down on top of* PANDALEVSKI's *hat and proceeds to
hammer* PANDALEVSKI *into the ground.*] I'll drive you
into the ground. I'll beat your brains out. We'll see
who's whose superior. We'll see about trips to the
cemetery, you carcass, you liar, you buzzard, you ink
pot. [ZODITCH *drags* PANDALEVSKI *to the door and out.*
PANDALEVSKI *holds on to his hat.*] Down the stairs
with you! [*Curiously enough there is no barking from
the dogs.* ZODITCH *returns and stands by the door.*]
Monstrous liar. Vilifier. What right to say such things?
[*The voice of* PANDALEVSKI *is heard from the direction
of the washbasin. He is lathering his hands with soap.*]

PANDALEVSKI: What right to say such things? Once having seduced Miss Grubov, once having aroused in her
the fevered breath of passion, which I found most sour
to the smell, I suppose I have all rights to say what
pleases me. Hand me the towel. [ZODITCH *doesn't
move.*] It was then that I thrust your name into the
conversation where it fell like a small stone dropped
from some low height into the sea. "And what of
Zoditch," I said, and when there was no sign of recognition on the lady's lips, I pressed forward with en-
couragements to her remembrance: "The rude fellow,
the crude fellow, the open-the-door and 'if you please,'
fellow, the tea fellow, the biscuit fellow, the a b c
and loop your e's fellow." But there was no remembrance. You are, nevertheless, welcome to the wedding along with the bookkeeper and the printer's
apprentice. Hand me the towel.

ZODITCH: There will be no wedding!

PANDALEVSKI: Oh, yes, a very large wedding. Hand me the towel!

ZODITCH: There will be no wedding. She is untouched.

PANDALEVSKI: I have washed my fingers, have I not? Do I wash my fingers for no reason? Hand me the towel!

ZODITCH: I'll give you the towel. [*Takes the towel and suddenly wraps it around* PANDALEVSKI's *throat. There is a struggle this time.*] Sleep with the devil in hell tonight. Enough of your insults. Your lies. Enough. Enough. [PANDALEVSKI *slumps to the floor.* ZODITCH *nudges him a few times to make sure he is dead.*] It is finished. Idiot! [*He drags* PANDALEVSKI *out, returns. He sits at his desk once again. He spoons in his gruel.*] Was it too cold, Miss Grubov? I thought of you in the carriage and I said they will forget the extra blankets and Miss Grubov will be cold. It's a long drive to any cemetery and the horses move so slowly. [*Following is imagined.*]

MISS GRUBOV: [*From the dark. Her voice flat, almost as if hypnotized.*] Yes, it was cold. [*As she speaks, the light goes up revealing her seated on* ZODITCH's *bed.*]

ZODITCH: [*Still eating*] That is too bad. In the winter when Death comes to Petersburg, he takes the large and the small: I have heard forty to fifty cats, their eyes like jelly ice, their whiskers stiff as banjo wire, die each night. I have heard a like number of cur bitches with teats so locked with rime they could not suck their puppies die each night. I have heard birds innumerable die each night seeking warmth in chimney smoke—and I thought of you huddled in the carriage, your father before you, his great black coat wrapped about him and his eyes shut to eternity come, and I said she will listen to the horses kicking up the ice and she will know in her heart she is alone. [*He stands up and wipes his mouth with the back of his hand. Goes through his obsequies: rubs shoes against pants, wets fingers and runs them up and down trouser crease, cleans wax out of ears, slicks down hair.*]

MISS GRUBOV: I sat in the chapel with my father, and the cold sunlight shone over the length of his body and I was alone.

ZODITCH: [*Stands by her side and begins unbuttoning her jacket.*] There was loneliness.

MISS GRUBOV: I was alone. Lonely.

ZODITCH: What were you thinking of?

MISS GRUBOV: I thought of nothing. I saw nothing.

ZODITCH: [*Begins ravishing her.*] Without me, nothing. Nothing. [*She responds and they embrace on the bed.*] I am to be promoted.

MISS GRUBOV: Yes, I will promote you.

ZODITCH: I will fire Pandalevski. I will set my desk in the main office. I will be served tea and I will have what is mine to have. I will buy a sailboat. I will buy a house. I will buy a carriage to go to the operas.

MISS GRUBOV: Yes. Yes. You shall have all.

ZODITCH: I love you.

MISS GRUBOV: Marry me. Marry.

ZODITCH: Yes. Yes. Yes. Yes. Yes. [*They embrace for a few seconds. Suddenly* RUBIN *appears. He watches them for a second or two and then, bending down, picks* ZODITCH *up by the seat of the pants and the scruff of his neck and tosses him to the floor.*] You! You! You! You! [RUBIN *is already in the bed on top of* MISS GRUBOV. ZODITCH *tries to grapple with* RUBIN *but* RUBIN *shoves him to the floor with his foot.* ZODITCH *remains on the floor.* MISS GRUBOV *speaks as she engages in lovemaking with* RUBIN. *They roll from side to side in the bed. They laugh.*]

RUBIN: It's all a ladder, Mr. Zoditch. We can't be keeping our feet on the same rung, can we?

MISS GRUBOV: There are matters that have come to my attention, Mr. Zoditch.

ZODITCH: [*Scurrying over to the bed.*] What matters?

MISS GRUBOV: Complaints that may lead to your dismissal.

ZODITCH: This is impossible. Your father promised to

advance me. I have told everybody I am to be advanced.

MISS GRUBOV: My father is dead. Death causes change.

ZODITCH: There can be no change in this. I have served with loyalty for twelve years.

MISS GRUBOV: Those who have watched you say you seek a strange advancement.

ZODITCH: They are madmen. You must not believe their lies.

MISS GRUBOV: Do they lie?

ZODITCH: They lie. Dear Miss Grubov, believe me. I think of you only as a person above me. I do not dream. I'm not a man driven by dreams. You don't know them. How they connive. How they watch me to discover evil. They distort me. They twist me into shapes I am not. It is they who harbor these evils. Yes. It is they. I can give you their names.

MISS GRUBOV: Can you?

ZODITCH: Yes. Yes. It is the man in the bookkeeping section, and the printer's apprentice. You see? I know them. I spit on them. They do not respect your virginity. They make jokes. It is they who seek strange advancement. [MISS GRUBOV *and* RUBIN *laugh and throw the covers over themselves.*] Do not treat me this way, Miss Grubov. I am a man of feeling. I am not a nothing. I am a man of respect, of sentiments. [*They just continue to make love.*] Stop it. You have no right to do this. Stop it. Stop it. What do you think I am? You think I am a toad? I am a man to be respected. Everybody in this house comes to me because I am a man of influence. This is my bed! [*Once again he is pushed away from the bed by the feet of* RUBIN *and* MISS GRUBOV. *He falls to the floor and yells from the floor.*] You think there were not affairs I had? What do you know of that? There were women who loved me. When I was not even twenty there was a woman who wanted to marry me, who said I was handsome. She thought I was a soldier. [*The muted sounds under the covers have become increasingly animalistic.* ZODITCH *speaks in a calmer tone as he returns to his desk.*] I could have been an officer, but there was no one to speak for me. [*Lights out on bed.* ZODITCH *slumps down at his desk and opens* CHULKATURIN's *diary.*] I would have been a captain by now. [*As* ZODITCH *silently reads, the lights come up on* CHULKATURIN *standing near the bed.*]

CHULKATURIN: I, Nikolai Alexeevich Chulkaturin, in my twenty-ninth year, certain in the hope of the resurrection and the life to come, begin this my diary at Lambswater, March the twentieth, eighteen-seventy.

ZODITCH: [*Still thinking of his own problems, calls out.*] I had no one to speak for me!

CHULKATURIN: The doctor, the same doctor that brought me into this world, came this morning with his black bag of useless medicines to tell me that I must now prepare myself to be shortly ushered out of it. At the end of all his medical subterfuges and hem-hawing terminologies he told me only what I already knew— I am to die. So be it. My life has been as brief as it has been meaningless, and death's a goodness for all we know. [*Lights up on* DR. KORVIN *standing near the bed.*]

DOCTOR: I will leave this here for you, Nikolai. [*Places a bottle on the night table.*] If you are troubled by pain you are to take a teaspoonful. In any event have a teaspoonful before you retire. It will assure you a good night's sleep. It's opium. If you dream, do not pay any attention to it.

CHULKATURIN: [*Speaking as if to himself*] This morning I dreamt I was in a great cage in some marketplace I had never seen before. The sun burned down upon me and I could not escape. I kept sticking my hand through the bars of the cage, grasping at those who passed by, but they would not stop and I had lost all power to speak. I could not breathe. I felt myself suffocating, and no person stopped. [*He turns to look at the* DOCTOR *as if expecting an explanation.*]

DOCTOR: I will have that Terentievna of yours open the window a crack before you retire this evening. [SERGEY, *without knocking, opens the door a trifle and sticks his head in.* CHULKATURIN *lies down on the bed.*] Oh, there you are. It's about time. What took you so long?

SERGEY: I was chasing the cats away.

DOCTOR: Away from what? [SERGEY *just shrugs his shoulders.*] Well, come in, come in. There are some sheets in the closet I want you to take down to your grandmother to wash.

SERGEY: [*Pointing to the closet*] In here?

DOCTOR: Yes. Be quick about it. [SERGEY *opens the closet and looks at all the clothes before he bends down to pick up the sheets. He suddenly backs away, letting out a cry.*] What's the matter with you?

SERGEY: There's blood on 'em.

DOCTOR: Never mind what's on them. Just take them down to your grandmother. [SERGEY *picks up the sheets with great distaste and leaves.*] Stupid lout. If your father were alive he'd pick them both up by the neck and toss them out.

ZODITCH: [*Interrupting with a comment. Action freezes.*] I'll pick you up by the neck and toss you out!

DOCTOR: [*Action resumes.*] Do you know what she was doing when I came in this morning? Sleeping! Big as you please, sprawled out in bed with a bottle of vodka clutched to her chest and her legs dangling to the floor. She's allowed the downstairs to become a rat's den.

CHULKATURIN: Terentievna's old and she drinks, but she is here when I need her. The boy is somewhat backward. Every day he sticks his head into the room to see that I have not made off with the closet. He fancies my clothes.

DOCTOR: And the old woman? What does she fancy?

CHULKATURIN: The house.

DOCTOR: Look here, Nikolai, this is none of my affair, but if you do not watch what you are doing they will rob the teeth out of your head before they are done. Do not underestimate the cunning of poor people. You do not know them.

CHULKATURIN: [*Seriously*] I have never known anybody, Dr. Korvin. [*Changing mood*] But do not worry, nothing is settled yet. We negotiate day by day. Besides, to whom else should these clothes and this house belong? By the time I am gone she will have earned this roof over her head.

DOCTOR: And the summer house? What has become of that?

CHULKATURIN: Sold at auction. A cloth merchant from Novgorod. A man who had to have a summer house.

DOCTOR: This is all quite distressing to hear, Nikolai. Surely some other alternative presented itself to you.

CHULKATURIN: No, Doctor. Let the summer house be gone. What it meant to my father, it never meant to me and for it the Chulkaturins, father and son, are at last quits with the human race. I have paid off the last of my father's obligations, and if no man will be the richer for the Chulkaturins having lived, well, no man can say he is the poorer either. Do not look so concerned, Dr. Korvin. Obligations must be met.

DOCTOR: Your friends will not permit this, Nikolai. To sell your property this way is demeaning. You are no merchant's son.

CHULKATURIN: I have no friends, Doctor.

DOCTOR: You have had friends, Nikolai. At the university I'm sure you made many friends. [*There is no answer from* CHULKATURIN, *so the* DOCTOR *makes his own.*] Every man has friends. [*The* DOCTOR *busies himself putting back his medicines and collecting together his odds and ends. He pays no attention to* CHULKATURIN.]

CHULKATURIN: Upon meeting my friends on the street of the university: "Why, it's Chulkaturin," they say, and when I approach, the circle of friends parts as if a slightly leprous thing had been thrust into their midst. And the eyes which had been set upon my eyes begin dropping from my face to my chest to my knees to the bottom of my feet, and everybody stands absolutely struck-still desperately trying to remember what it was they were saying before I arrived. Once I am ten feet past, the circle once again shrinks, the eyes once more rise, and conversation moves like fish hustling down the Don. Oh, Christ, that the circles of this world might shrink and find me standing locked inside! [*Unaware of what* CHULKATURIN *has said, the* DOCTOR *turns to him.*]

DOCTOR: Try not to have too many visitors, Nikolai. . . . You must get your rest.

CHULKATURIN: Doctor? I'll see that you are paid as soon as I can. [*The* DOCTOR *exits as* TERENTIEVNA *comes in, broom in hand.*]

TERENTIEVNA: He's a bit of nose, ain't he? He was staring into everything downstairs when he first come. Even poked into my room and me with a bottle of furniture polish in my hand at the time and the dress about the knees from bending over.

CHULKATURIN: I'm sure he meant nothing by it, Terentievna. He used to visit this house often when my parents were alive.

TERENTIEVNA: I'm not a housekeeper to have her work looked after by them what ain't of the family. I do my job.

CHULKATURIN: Yes, I'm sure you do.

TERENTIEVNA: I do my dusting and my window washing and my floor cleaning and my cooking and them what ain't of the family has other business to mind. [CHUL-KATURIN *reaches over to take his writing pad and pencil out of the night table.*] Let them stick their noses to their own face.

CHULKATURIN: Terentievna, there is something you can do for me.

TERENTIEVNA: And what would that be?

CHULKATURIN: I'm going to do some writing and when I am finished I want you to promise me that you will take it downstairs to the kitchen stove and burn it.

TERENTIEVNA: Burn it, sir?

CHULKATURIN: Yes. You are not to show it to anybody, or get anybody's advice about what to do with it. You will take it straight to the stove, you understand?

TERENTIEVNA: Is it letters, sir?

CHULKATURIN: No. Just writing that I wish to do for myself. Just a whim, it will be of no value or concern to anyone, so it is to be destroyed.

TERENTIEVNA: Yes, sir.

CHULKATURIN: You will do this without fail, Terentievna?

TERENTIEVNA: That I will. Is it bad news the doctor was bringing about the cough, then?

CHULKATURIN: Yes.

TERENTIEVNA: The cough's not to go away?

CHULKATURIN: No, Terentievna, it will not go away.

TERENTIEVNA: I'm sorry for that, sir, truly I am.

CHULKATURIN: I know you are, Terentievna.

TERENTIEVNA: It's the good what always go before us and the bad what come dragging after. It's a bad world, sir, that's what it is, and none of us can look for justice in it. [*Pause, and then slyly*] Is it soon you'll be leaving us, sir?

CHULKATURIN: I don't know, Terentievna. [*She nods her head up and down as if thinking something over.*] Is there something else?

TERENTIEVNA: No, sir, only . . . well, it's the boots and the clothes in the closet. I was wondering if you'd be wearing them again.

CHULKATURIN: [*Softly*] No.

TERENTIEVNA: Sir?

CHULKATURIN: You can have them, Terentievna.

TERENTIEVNA: You see, it's for the boy. He doesn't have

much in the way of shoes fit for the snow and all, and him without a winter coat. . . .

CHULKATURIN: Yes. You are right. There is no need to wait.

TERENTIEVNA: [*Goes to the closet and pulls out the boots and winter coat.*] We'll be obliged to you for this kindness, sir. You're a gentleman what understands.

CHULKATURIN: Those were my father's boots, Terentievna.

TERENTIEVNA: Yes, sir, and fine leather they are, too. Would the overcoat be your father's, too?

CHULKATURIN: No.

TERENTIEVNA: It's hardly worn at all, is it? It's the changing of the styles what do it for gentlemen more than the wearing of them out, I suppose. There are some what get a new coat every year just for the new look of it, they say. Will we be needing the services of a lawyer, sir?

CHULKATURIN: For what?

TERENTIEVNA: The house, sir. Can we make our agreements by the speaking of them, or do we have to have them writ down by the lawyers?

CHULKATURIN: They must be written down.

TERENTIEVNA: Oh, must they? Everything is a fuss, ain't it?

CHULKATURIN: You can tell Sergey to fetch Lawyer Levinov tomorrow. I will have him draw up the transfer papers.

TERENTIEVNA: Yes, sir. And don't you trouble yourself about anything. I don't mind at all about the sheets. I'm going to do the wash right now.

CHULKATURIN: You won't pour the wash water in the stream, will you, Terentievna? I don't want the carp and grudgeon killed by the soap.

TERENTIEVNA: Don't you worry about that, sir. Don't you worry. I'll find another place. [*Exits. Lights dim to indicate a passage of time.*]

CHULKATURIN: March twenty-second. Lawyer Levinov

came yesterday and as I signed the papers giving the house over to Terentievna upon my death, I felt that by that simple signature I had somehow set myself irrevocably free: as a piece of ice that has been bound all winter flows at last down to the sea, so I too have become unbound. To flow where? God knows. [*Lights up on* LEVINOV.]

LEVINOV: I find myself hard put to even describe the coach ride over. The driver, a lunatic of a fellow, was absolutely insensitive to anything other than meeting his schedule. Although the four horses we had were good and we were flying along, this madman insisted on adding a fifth horse. This poor horse was completely out of place, completely superfluous. [*Points to a spot on the page.*] Sign there, too, Mr. Chulkaturin. [*He continues with his story.*] And how was this unnecessary horse fastened to the carriage? Absolutely all wrong. By means of a short thick rope that constantly cut into his flank so that his flesh was at all times positively lacerated. How he expected the beast to run naturally when its entire body was arched in pain I don't know. And what was this lunatic's reaction when I informed him that we would do better without this superfluous horse? [*Points to another spot.*] And here as well, Mr. Chulkaturin. [*Continues with the story.*] He began lashing the horse, a dozen additional strokes across its back and swollen belly, and screaming out to the wind, "What the hell. It's been tied on, and if not to run, then what the hell for?" [CHULKATURIN *and* LAWYER *stare at each other. Lights out on* LEVINOV. ZODITCH *flips a page.*]

CHULKATURIN: March twenty-third. Sunday. The church bells have been ringing all morning, heavy, slow, melodious, and so they will ring when I am no longer here to listen. I cannot bear to hear them. I have had Terentievna shut the window tight, but still the sound washes into the empty room, filling every corner. In darkness I see the meadow where once I played, the branches of my plum tree bending with fruit, the small stream where I caught carp. Oh, my Christ, if I cannot say goodbye to the summers that warmed me, the winters I put my fur hat on to! If I cannot say goodbye, what shall I do? Who will have pity for us all? [ZODITCH *runs over to the bed.* CHULKATURIN *stares frozenly ahead.*]

ZODITCH: Pity? Why do you waste my time with pity? There is no pity. Up the ladder. Down the ladder. Make up your mind to it. Do not live in the delusion you will put tears in my eyes. In me you do not deal with an amateur of suffering. [*Mimics* CHULKATURIN.] "The church bells have been ringing all morning." Let them ring! Every bell rings; every dog cries; every sheep bleats tears. The public is not interested in suffering. In me you deal with the public, Chulkaturin. Who is to buy the lungs and brains of you, that is what I am to decide. That is why I am a first reader. That . . . [*Finally becomes aware of a slight but persistent knocking on his door. Lights out on* CHULKATURIN. ZODITCH *goes over to his door.*] Who is it?

FEATHERS: It's me, sir, the house girl, Feathers.

ZODITCH: [*Opens the door.*] What do you want?

FEATHERS: [*A young girl, filthy from coal dust and in rags. She smiles constantly, nervously.*] Katerina Prolomnaya sent me with a bucket of coal.

ZODITCH: [*Imitates her.*] Katerina Prolomnaya sent me with a bucket of coal. [*Lets her in. Harshly*] Well, don't stand there smiling all night. I've important work that must be done. We can't all afford to live like princesses.

FEATHERS: Shall I put the coal in the stove for you, Mr. Zoditch?

ZODITCH: [*With a wave of his hand indicates she is to do so.*] Yes. Why have you brought the coal to all the others and only now to me? Why am I the last? I won't forget that, Miss Feathers.

FEATHERS: Oh, no, sir. You're not the last. The mistress

says the others aren't to have any coal at all tonight, only you, sir. She says let 'em freeze and the city would be better off without them.

ZODITCH: Do not give me stories. Coal doesn't grow on plum trees, madam! I do not live in fairy tales. [FEATHERS *busies herself putting the coal in the stove.*] She expects something for this, eh? Eh? What does she expect? Nobody does anything without expectations. If she expects to be paid now, I cannot pay now. To be advanced in the publishing business is not to be made a prince. I didn't ask for any extra coal.

FEATHERS: The mistress said nothing about asking for money, sir.

ZODITCH: Nothing? What nothing? You watch what you're doing there. You're putting in too much at once. You're not dealing with a spendthrift, Miss Feathers.

FEATHERS: And I was to bring you this kerosene, sir. [*She hands him the kerosene. He just stares at it.*]

ZODITCH: Why? [*Hesitantly takes it and, opening the jar, sticks his nose to it to make sure it's what she says it is.*] She expects to make up on the coal by overcharging me on the oil. That's it, isn't it? Well, I will not pay a kopeck for the oil. I will not pay for the coal. I asked for nothing and from nothing comes nothing. I do not need these extravagances.

FEATHERS: The mistress said nothing about money for the kerosene, sir.

ZODITCH: Tell Katerina Prolomnaya I cannot afford extravagances . . . I live close to the bone. Do something about that smile! [*Ushers* FEATHERS *out and locks the door. Once again he smells the kerosene.*] Is she so rich that she can give something for nothing? Rich? From what, rich? Her husband died owing the moneylenders. Everybody knows he died owing the moneylenders. [*Stands in front of the mirror and stares at himself. He runs his hands through his hair and preens a little.*] But if he didn't die owing the moneylenders. If . . . Bah! [*Turns from the mirror. Picks up the diary and begins reading. Immediately there is a stabbing cry of pain that comes from* CHULKATURIN *in bed. Lights come up dimly.* CHULKATURIN's *arm extends itself, opening and closing as if seeking to grasp onto* ZODITCH. *The* DOCTOR *steps out of the shadows.*]

DOCTOR: So, Nikolai, so. What has happened is a certain flow of blood from the lung. You understand? Now we must engage in the removal of a like quantity of blood. You will feel better after you are bled. It is to be expected that spittle from the lungs, since the hemorrhage, will be somewhat pasty, like clay, even like clay. A slight disruption of the digestive organs, the increased frequency of intestinal discharge in turn brings about an additional grabbing and uncontracting, as it were, of the bowels, which in turn produces the diarrhea. Do not distress yourself with keeping your sheets clean. That is nothing to distress yourself about. A trifle of blood, a trifle of excrement. You understand? So. So. [*Lights out on* DOCTOR *and* CHULKATURIN.]

ZODITCH: [*Nervously*] Who's to say what handsome is? Katerina Prolomnaya's first husband was short. What was Napoleon if not short, or Caesar? *Veni, vidi, vici.* It is a medical fact that the short man, by having his heart placed closer to his brain, enjoys a richer supply of blood, ergo, a proportionate enlargement of the cranial area so that he becomes quicker in wit, more active in deed, greater in accomplishment. To marry Katerina Prolomnaya would be a diminishment. . . . [*He begins biting at his nail, and then laughing and then biting and then laughing. Glances at manuscript. Lights up on* DOCTOR *as he pours a beaker of* CHULKATURIN's *blood into* ZODITCH's *washbasin. Lights out on* DOCTOR. *Lights up on* CHULKATURIN *in bed. He is writing.*]

CHULKATURIN: Think, dear Christ, have you made me

anything more than Lawyer Levinov's fifth horse? If I had never lived it would have made no difference to anyone. My entire existence has been superfluous. That is the central fact of my being: the central word that sums up my total meaning. Think, dear Christ, is that not so? Have you not made me a fifth horse fastened uselessly to the coach of life? To whose benefit do I run? For whose benefit am I beaten? O my Christ, where is my posthouse? [*Action freezes.* CHULKATURIN *looks straight ahead.*]

ZODITCH: So it is a husband she is after. She sends Miss Chimney Sweep with the kerosene to keep me from getting an eyestrain. Five feet four inches can hardly be considered short in any event. She doesn't wish me to be eyestrained because she is concerned. The coal alone might be construed as meaning no more than a mere landlord-tenant relationship. So if she just sent the coal she might expect no more than a thank you, but more than a thank you is floating around here. The time I left my gloves on the hall table and she called out to me on the street: "Oh, Mr. Zoditch, your gloves." And the payment of the rent, did she not say, "Ah, Mr. Zoditch, your rent." What was the "Ah" about? "Ah, Mr. Zoditch." Ahs and ohs have meanings. They don't just blow around the air! One does not say "ah" . . . "oh" just for the pleasure of opening a mouth. [*Begins biting his fingernails again and looking at himself in the mirror.*] Surely she loved me even while her husband was alive! [*Does a stupid little jig. Begins to read.*]

CHULKATURIN: April the second, Wednesday. It rains now. A cold soundless rain that falls into the snow and vanishes. I struggle to separate the days one from the other. It is useless. I think of you, Liza, my rainbow, my bird, caught now forever fixed in the timeless grace of your seventeen years, and I know as truly as I must have known all these years that in you and in you alone exists all I shall ever know of useless happiness, and useless agony. Now I begin. Now at the end of my life I prove, dear God, that had I never lived it would have made no difference to anyone. [*Takes a slight pause before continuing.*] Some years ago, I was obliged to spend some months in a small town lying in one of the more remote districts—a town overrun by mud and goats. Fortunately, the parents of Illya Ozhogin, an acquaintance I had known for a single term at the university, lived there, and before I found myself desperate with boredom I resolved to pay a call. I sent a boy from the inn I was lodged at, to announce my arrival to the Ozhogins.

(*Lights out on* CHULKATURIN. *Scene with the* OZHOGINS *becomes animated. Light remains on* ZODITCH. KIRILLA MATVEICH OZHOGIN *sits with his hands folded on his belly.* ANNA, *his wife, is sewing.* BIZMIONKOV, *the family friend, plays a game of solitaire.* LIZA *toys with a caged bullfinch.* ZODITCH *identifies the characters in* CHULKATURIN's *story with people familiar to him in his own life. Thus:* KIRILLA MATVEICH *is* MR. GRUBOV, *the man in the portrait at the publishing house;* BIZMIONKOV *is* PANDALEVSKI; LIZA *is* MISS GRUBOV.)

KIRILLA: [*Pulling a watch from his vest and looking at it.*] If he's going to call, why doesn't he call? And why isn't the dinner ready yet? It's already after twelve. How much longer must we wait to eat? Liza, go into the kitchen and find out what they're doing there. [LIZA, *busy playing with the bullfinch, doesn't hear.*] Elizaveta!

LIZA: Yes, Papa?

KIRILLA: Go into the kitchen and find out what the delay is. [*She can scarcely tear herself away from the bird. She exits, staring at the bird all the way.*] That girl is turning deaf, positively. And crazy, as well. All day with that bird. [*Imitates* LIZA *with the bird*.] Eech. Eeech, eech. Ooooch. Ooooch. Eech, eech.

BIZMIONKOV: [*Calmly continuing with his game*] It is the same with all young girls, Kirilla Matveich. There is nothing to be concerned about.

KIRILLA: We will see if you sing the same tune, my friend, when you marry and have a daughter who arranges flowers all day and tickles bullfinches. Maybe you should marry my Liza and then we will see what you say. [ANNA *offers one of her little social laughs. Pulling out his watch again*] Is he coming for lunch, or what?

BIZMIONKOV: [*Calmly*] When you send a messenger at lunchtime, you are coming for lunch.

ANNA: I'll have them set another place. [*Leaves excitedly*.]

KIRILLA: Don't get rich, Bizmionkov. Take my advice. Stay poor. When you live in poverty, you live in happiness. Your meals are served on time.

BIZMIONKOV: Money is a curse. [LIZA *returns*.]

KIRILLA: Liza, dear, go back into the kitchen and get a little snack to hold Mr. Bizmionkov over to lunch.

BIZMIONKOV: I can wait for lunch, there is no need to go to extra effort.

KIRILLA: There is no need starving yourself, my friend. Why be a martyr? If we have to wait for Mr. Chulka . . . Chulkaturin, we have to wait, but there is no need to starve. We are not at the gates of starvation here. Just bring some fish, Liza . . . [*She keeps starting out, but his additional requests keep calling her back*.] . . . with lemon . . . bread . . . some olives . . . five or six . . . better bring the same for me . . . some kvass to drink . . . you want some kvass, Bizmionkov? [BIZMIONKOV *nods*. LIZA *has started toying with the bullfinch again*.] Some kvass for Mr. Bizmionkov, too. Eh? What, are you playing with that bird again? Leave the bird alone. [LIZA *exits back to the kitchen*. KIRILLA *looks after her to make sure she is gone*.] Listen, Bizmionkov, I have something I want to talk to you about. [KIRILLA *tries to start, but isn't quite sure how to frame his remarks.*]

BIZMIONKOV: Well?

KIRILLA: It's about Liza. [*Still hesitates.*] When you're a father you notice things.

BIZMIONKOV: Yes?

KIRILLA: Don't rush me.

BIZMIONKOV: Who is rushing you?

KIRILLA: As I was saying, you notice things when you're a father.

BIZMIONKOV: What things?

KIRILLA: What do you mean, "What things?" Things! What I want to know is what kind of a bird is that?

BIZMIONKOV: [*Going up to the bird.*] A bullfinch. What else would it be? You thought it was an owl?

KIRILLA: I know it's a bullfinch, but what kind of a bullfinch?

BIZMIONKOV: A Russian bullfinch.

KIRILLA: A female? Is it a female?

BIZMIONKOV: What difference does it make what sex it is? Isn't it singing all right?

KIRILLA: Will you look under the feathers and stop asking a thousand questions.

BIZMIONKOV: It won't raise its tail.

KIRILLA: Wait a minute. [*He opens the cage and starts to stick his hand in just as his wife comes in.*]

ANNA: What are you doing?

KIRILLA: [*Quickly pulling out his hand*] Nothing. I was merely placing my hand in the bird's cage.

BIZMIONKOV: Kirilla Matveich wants to know if the bird is a male or a . . .

KIRILLA: Sha. [*To* WIFE] Nothing. It is nothing.

ANNA: Isn't it singing well?

KIRILLA: It is singing well. I just felt like feeling its feathers, that's all. Have you set another place for our son's friend?

ANNA: Yes.

KIRILLA: Well, let's not stand in front of the bird's cage

all day. [*Return to seats.* KIRILLA *makes a big production about sitting down.* ANNA *eyes him suspiciously.*] Ah! My favorite chair. [*Nobody says anything. To* WIFE] Are you going to be sitting there for a while, Anna?

ANNA: Is there some reason I should not sit here?

KIRILLA: No reason. Of course there's no reason.

ANNA: Then I will be sitting here for a while.

KIRILLA: There is nothing further that needs your attention in the kitchen?

ANNA: What else should need my attention in the kitchen?

KIRILLA: I don't know, Anna. I was only asking. [*Pause.*] Things do not go well all the time in the kitchen, that is all. [ANNA *gets up.*] Where are you going?

ANNA: Back to the kitchen.

KIRILLA: If things are going well there is no need to go back to the kitchen. [ANNA *starts to return to her chair.*] But if you feel it needs your attention . . . [ANNA *leaves the room, almost tearfully.* KIRILLA *hastens over to the cage and, opening the little door, sticks his hand in.* ANNA *returns unexpectedly.* KIRILLA's *hand gets momentarily caught in the cage.*]

ANNA: If the meal is not right, it is not my fault. I do my best. [*Almost in anguish*] What do you want from that little bird?

KIRILLA: [*Exasperated*] Nothing. We are going into the garden. Come, my friend, come, come. Why must you exasperate me so, Anna? [*Takes* BIZMIONKOV's *arm and escorts him out of the room.* ANNA, *still distraught, exits—passing her daughter, who has just entered with a tray.* LIZA *puts the tray down and stands looking about her for a second. Then, for no apparent reason, she whirls about the room, ending up in front of the birdcage. She dances about the cage and begins whistling to the bird. There is a knock at the door, which brings* LIZA *out of her little trance. She looks about her for a second and then, seeing that there is*

no one to answer, she goes to the door. CHULKATURIN
*comes in. He is rather overdressed, almost foppish,
somehow ill at ease. He tends to make little mistakes
in manners due to his anxiety.*]

CHULKATURIN: Excuse me, I am Nikolai Alexeevich
Chulkaturin.

LIZA: I am Elizaveta Kirillovna, Illya's sister. [*They just
stand looking at each other.*]

CHULKATURIN: Is there anything wrong? I sent a messenger to say I was to follow.

LIZA: Oh, no, there is nothing wrong. Illya used to talk
so much about his university friends . . . we are expecting another of Illya's friends to call later this
summer, you must know him . . . Captain Ivan Petrovich Narvinsky.

CHULKATURIN: No, I don't think so.

LIZA: Illya used to talk about him all the time. He's the
terribly handsome one that I was absolutely forbidden
to meet. The one who went into the army.

CHULKATURIN: No, I'm afraid I don't recall . . .

LIZA: Shall I try to place you? I know all of Illya's
friends.

CHULKATURIN: Well, I don't think that outside of being
roommates we were very . . .

LIZA: [*Clapping her hands*] You were the roommate who
never came in from parties earlier than four in the
morning. The boy who never attended a single lecture
for two years.

CHULKATURIN: No. I think that was the roommate your
brother had during his senior year. We were roommates during the second year, the first half of the second year. Then Illya moved out.

LIZA: Oh. [*Pause.*] Then you must be the one Illya had
that terrible fight with over some dreadful woman. He
wrote Papa all about it in a letter.

CHULKATURIN: No. Illya and I never had a quarrel.
That was Peter Richter from Prussia.

LIZA: If you give me time I will remember just exactly

your place in my brother's life, because Illya wrote me without fail a letter every week from Petersburg and I'm sure I know everything he did. [*Pause.*] You were the one who gambled at the races. [*A line of pain momentarily crosses* CHULKATURIN'S *face but the girl does not see it.*]

CHULKATURIN: That was Ivan Vorontzoff. I never went to the races.

LIZA: You did not own a white stallion? [CHULKATURIN *shakes his head.*] You know what I think? It will come to me suddenly. Oh!

CHULKATURIN: What is the matter?

LIZA: I hope you have not come all this way just to see Illya, because he is not here. He left to go abroad for the Czar; he is in the diplomatic service now, you know, since last April, but I'm sure he wrote you about that. [CHULKATURIN *shakes his head.*] No? He must have forgotten. Poor Illya, it was a very busy time for him so you must excuse him. He left for Austria a month after his wedding to Frieda Semeonova who is a blood relative of Prince Adrian. I'm sorry you were unable to come for the wedding. So many of Illya's friends and yours from the university came, but you must have been busy. [*It is obvious from the look on* CHULKATURIN'S *face that he realizes what a small part he must have played in* ILLYA'S *life, and that* ILLYA *did not even consider him enough of a friend to extend a wedding invitation to him. He is saved from any further embarrassment by* LIZA'S *running over to her bullfinch.*] Isn't it darling? Illya gave it to me when he left. I have been teaching it to sing. [*To the bird*] Sing a song for the gentleman, Popka. [*She whistles to the bird, then turns to* CHULKATURIN.] He really sings his heart out when he wants to. Come. [*Motions for* CHULKATURIN *to come over to the cage. He stands close to* LIZA *as she talks.*] See, he is not afraid of you at all. That's a good sign. It is a well-known fact that birds and animals can instinctively look into the hearts of people and know if they are good or bad. Did you know that?

CHULKATURIN: No.

LIZA: Oh, they can. If you trust the judgment of your pets they will always tell you who your real friends are. See how he is not afraid of you.

CHULKATURIN: Then we shall become friends.

LIZA: [*To bird*] Brave little bird. That's a brave little bird. [*To* CHULKATURIN] I would find it impossible to love someone that an animal feared, wouldn't you?

CHULKATURIN: I don't know.

LIZA: Will you whistle for Popka? See if he will sing for you.

CHULKATURIN: Oh, I don't think I could.

LIZA: Please. [CHULKATURIN, *after a moment's hesitation, begins to whistle.*]

ZODITCH: Already he must prove he is an ass. Already the fool.

CHULKATURIN: [*Turns and faces the audience.*] Is it possible that one day you could open the door to some stranger's house and fall in love? [ZODITCH *lets out a cry of disgust.*] Yes, it is possible. That was the exact moment I fell in love. I say that without reservation. The moment the door swung open into that household was the exact moment I came to love and to shut out all the impossible loneliness and misfortune of all the years before: my father's failures, my mother's long-suffering virtues, my less than human isolation from mankind. I had now for the first time placed myself in contact with one whose steps would not flee from me, one whose eyes would behold my face and not turn away. It didn't matter that now I stood in front of a bird's cage and forced myself to whistle. Not even forced myself. I whistled joyfully.

ZODITCH: You ass!

CHULKATURIN: The tune, whose melody I can no longer remember, rose from my heart. A nameless tune from

the so-long-shut closet of my heart broke forth and
I brushed against the sleeve of her dress and she did
not move and the bird broke forth answering me and
I thought as I stood there, God, oh, God, don't let me
be shut up anymore. [*Lights out on* CHULKATURIN
scene.]

ZODITCH. What are you talking about? What do you
think you're talking about? [*Pours himself a drink.
Sound of someone shuffling about in the hall. The
shuffling goes back and forth as* ZODITCH *drinks.*
ZODITCH *goes to the door and listens. In a whispered
voice, as he opens the door a crack.*] Who is that?

GREGORY: It's me, Zoditch, Gregory from downstairs.

ZODITCH: [*Practically hissing in annoyance*] What the
devil are you doing marching up and back? Have you
lost your wits?

GREGORY: I must talk to you.

ZODITCH: [*Suspiciously*] About what?

GREGORY: Let me come in. I don't want to stand in the
hallway. [*After some hesitation* ZODITCH *lets him in.*]
Something must be done to increase the amount of
coal provided the tenants. We will all freeze to death
unless steps are taken with Katerina Prolomnaya. The
woman is mad to think a family can survive a winter
night on half a bucketful of bad coal. Do you know
the dogs are freezing to death out on the street? Have
you heard even as much as one of them howl tonight?
By morning there won't be a live dog left in Petersburg. Already the water basin in my kitchen has pieces
of ice in it the size of your fist.

ZODITCH: Why do you bother me with your family problems? Go see Katerina Prolomnaya. I have no time to
get involved in this.

GREGORY: That is what must be done. Katerina Prolomnaya must be visited.

ZODITCH: Then go. Go!

GREGORY: That is what my family has instructed me to

do. My wife will not put up with it another night. And my children . . . the eyes they turn to me . . . it would break the heart of a monster. . . . Even Katerina Prolomnaya would see the necessity of more coal if she could hear my children crying in their beds. We must not be ignored because we are poor. She must not be allowed to prey on our misery.

ZODITCH: Then why do you stand here? Be off. Speak to her. This is a family problem.

GREGORY: She must be spoken to. It's not right to be cruel when people are suffering. But I don't know what to say to that woman. Every time I have to speak to her the words tumble together in my mouth. I am no good with words . . . that is why I was in the hall . . . I kept saying if I start down the stairs I will find the right words to make my position clear by the time I reach her door, but then I think what if I knock on her door and she opens it and I do not have the words yet, what then? Eh? What then?

ZODITCH: [*Anguished*] What do you want of me? Leave me alone.

GREGORY: And I think what if those rotten brown dogs of hers come for me even while the words are glue in my mouth? How many have those dirty beasts sunk their teeth into already?

ZODITCH: I cannot help this. I want only to be left alone. I am a busy man.

GREGORY: Zoditch, come with me.

ZODITCH: What are you saying?

GREGORY: You are a man of words. Everybody knows that. Everybody respects you for that. Just the other day my wife was commenting on your fine methods of address and speech deportment. "How fine Mr. Zoditch speaks. How quickly. How precisely. . . . He is a master of the Russian language." You are much in respect because of it. If you went with me the other tenants would follow. I know they would. Come.

Come. We will face her together. You will say all the right things. You will say what only you know how to say. One, two, three, it will be done.

ZODITCH: Leave go of my arm. This is not for me. I tell you leave go! [*Jerks his arm free.*]

GREGORY: What are you doing to me? We are neighbors. We live side by side.

ZODITCH: Side by side? What is that, side by side? When my mother died, who came to me with fruit? When I lay in my bed sick with fever for three days, who knocked on my door? Who said to me, "Zoditch, my friend, we have come. Zoditch, are you alive? Here is soup to warm you, a cool towel for your head. Zoditch, we have come." Nobody. Nobody came.

GREGORY: But nobody knew. Nobody was informed.

ZODITCH: [*Pulling open the door*] Nobody cared! [GREGORY *seems about to say something, then changes his mind. He exits.* ZODITCH *closes the door after him.*] Nobody. [ZODITCH *leans against the door intently listening as* GREGORY *descends the stairs. We hear the shrill barking of a number of small lap dogs.* KATERINA PROLOMNAYA'S *door opens and the barking becomes louder and more shrill. Through the barking we hear* GREGORY.]

GREGORY: Katerina Prolomnaya, I have come . . . [*The rest is blotted out by the barking. After a moment*] We won't survive the night. Already the frost is through the window. Surely there is enough compassion in you to . . . [*There is the sound, the mad sound, of* KATERINA PROLOMNAYA'S *laughter. The barking has increased.* GREGORY *runs up the stairs shouting.*] Get them away from me. Get away. You get away. In the name of Christ, if we don't get some more coal . . . Oh, God . . . get away . . . aaagh . . . aaagh. Help me. Zoditch, help me. Help me. Get away, you bastards. Get away. [*Pounds on* ZODITCH'S *door.*] Zoditch! Zoditch, help me. Oh, God. [*The scene ends in a wild crescendo of pounding, barking, yelling, and laughter, as* ZODITCH *presses his back to the door.*]

ZODITCH: Leave me alone. Leave me alone. This is a family problem! [*He slides down the door and collapses to the floor.*]

CURTAIN

ACT II

PLACE: ZODITCH's *apartment*.

TIME: *A few moments later.*

ON RISE: *All sounds have stopped.* GREGORY *is gone.*

ZODITCH: [*Suddenly shouts out, nervously, excitedly, clearly in an anguish of some kind.*] Let the house freeze, Gregory! What else are winters for if not to put frost on dogs! [*Shovels in the remainder of the coal. Stands in front of the stove, his arms wrapped about him.*] I am not to freeze. She would be a fool not to take my attainments into consideration. Is it nothing to be a first reader in a famous publishing house? Is it nothing to have read Seneca, Cicero? O tempora! O mores! Senatus haec intellegit, consul videt; hic tamen vivit. Vivit? Where is the wonder then that Katerina Prolomnaya should reach for me? Is it every widow who can snatch twice at the gold ring? [*Goes over to the table and picks up the diary for a second and then puts it down.*] Katerina Prolomnaya, do not underestimate my value! I am no ring for your finger without considerations. You are not the voice of springtime. Bear in mind assets. Ah. This marriage is a diminishment for me without your assets. I do not mind the diminishment if there are assets. [*Pulls out a piece of paper and makes notations.*] Rents. Movables: tables, chairs, sofas, beds, et cetera. Drapes, linens, clothings, furs, equipments, carriages. Personal

112

assets: the pleasures of the bed . . . marred, gray streaks in the hair, brow wrinkles, crow's-feet, throat wrinkles, worn-down teeth, yellow and fallen-out teeth, breasts good, too-full waist, a mouth forever at the food box, a brain stuffed with candies. [*Shaking the paper in his hand*] It is well to bear in mind, Katerina, that we do not live by bread alone. In me you will not find a husband who is fondly foolish, one of those husbands who thinks to satisfy a woman's whims is to satisfy all. In me you will have a husband gentle but firm, a husband capable of great understanding and compassion, but a husband capable of being the master of his house, a husband whose hand, though not often set down, set down becomes immovable. [ZODITCH *smashes his hand on the table. And then, satisfied with his speech, picks up the diary. Lights up on* CHULKATURIN.]

CHULKATURIN: O sweet summer. Sweet lost summer of days that are no more. Summer of bright birds. Summer of flowers. Summer of strawberries and golden mornings. Summer of musical harmonies in the sky. Summer when my heart stood in tune with every living thing. Summer when I was not myself. Summer when I was in love. [*Lights out on* CHULKATURIN. *Lights up on a public garden.*]

KIRILLA: [*Offstage*] Why don't they watch where they plant their damn vines? Must a man break his skull or strangle to death in order to keep on the path?

BIZMIONKOV: [*Offstage*] This way, my friend. Be careful. Do not trample down the flowerbeds.

KIRILLA: [*Offstage*] Is that you, Bizmionkov? Blast their flowerbeds. What idiot planted flowerbeds in a public garden? [*He comes out on stage.*] Here, this way. It's clearer over here. [*He plunks down exhausted on the bench.* BIZMIONKOV, *book in hand, calmly appears.*] Where's Anna?

BIZMIONKOV: She was with you. You were hand in hand when we left the fountain.

KIRILLA: No. She was with you.

BIZMIONKOV: [*Turns a page.*] I'm sure she was with you.

KIRILLA: Don't be foolish. [*Calls out.*] Anna! Anna! [*To* BIZMIONKOV] And where is my daughter? [*Shouts.*] Liza! [*To* BIZMIONKOV] This park was designed by a madman whose sole desire is to lose half of Russia in a vine tangle! And where is Chulkaturin? The poor fellow can't find his way from one end of the street to the other.

ANNA: [*Halloing from somewhere offstage*] Yoo hoo. Yoo hoo.

KIRILLA: Anna! Anna! Is that you?

ANNA: [*Offstage*] Yoo hoo. Yoo hoo.

KIRILLA: Over here, woman. Yoo hoo. Yoo hoo.

ANNA: [*Offstage*] I can't.

KIRILLA: What do you mean you can't?

ANNA: [*Offstage*] I'm in the middle of a flowerbed.

BIZMIONKOV: Watch how you step, Anna. Don't crush the flowers.

KIRILLA: [*To* BIZMIONKOV] The devil take the flowers. [*To* ANNA] Come forward. Watch the vines; damn the flowers! [*Sound of* ANNA *crashing through the brush.*]

ANNA: [*Offstage*] I'm coming. I'm coming. Yoo hoo. Yoo hoo.

KIRILLA: I can assure you, my friend, this park will be looked into. Monstrosities do not just create themselves. There are madmen at work here. [ANNA *breaks into the clearing. Her large white hat is crushed.*] You see? You see? Look what those madmen have done to my wife.

BIZMIONKOV: It is only a matter of staying on the path, my dear friend. It is all geometrically laid out. One has only to follow the path.

KIRILLA: Bah! Here, Anna, sit on the bench. [*To* BIZMIONKOV] We will see what is geometrically laid out and what is not. Do they imagine we are bees? My poor Anna.

ANNA: [*Practically in tears*] Oh, my hat.

BIZMIONKOV: They do not imagine we are bees.

KIRILLA: They think because we are an outlying province they can send their madmen out here to create monstrosities, but that is a mistake, I can assure you. The businessmen of this town will not put up with it.

ANNA: Oh, my hat.

KIRILLA: [*In a quick aside to his* WIFE] Enough with the hat, Anna. [*To* BIZMIONKOV] I have a son in the diplomatic service. All I have to do is write a letter and there will be repercussions. It isn't every family that has a son involved in the intricate workings of government, or is expecting a visit from a captain of cavalry.

BIZMIONKOV: The diplomatic service and the park department are totally separate.

KIRILLA: Ah, you think so. But you are mistaken. They are hand in glove.

ANNA: My hat, look at what has happened to my hat.

KIRILLA: Enough with the hat! [*To* BIZMIONKOV] It is only to a political novice such as yourself, Bizmionkov, that things appear unrelated. In government the toe is connected to the foot and the foot to the arm and so forth.

BIZMIONKOV: The Department of Parks is connected to the Department of Fish. It is not connected to the diplomatic service.

KIRILLA: [*Calls, after giving* BIZMIONKOV *an angry stare.*] Liza! [*To* BIZMIONKOV] That is only what they want you to think, Bizmionkov. Listen to me. I am aware of what is and what is not.

ANNA: And where is Elizaveta? You were holding her hand when we left the fountain.

KIRILLA: I was not holding her hand when we left the fountain. Do not exasperate me, Anna. [*Shouts.*] Liza! [*To* BIZMIONKOV] There are things I could tell you about the working of the government that would completely shock you. You would say to me, "Kirilla Matveich, that is impossible. Kirilla Matveich, you are mad, such things cannot be."

ANNA: She is lost.

KIRILLA: She is not lost. She is with Chulkaturin.

KIRILLA and ANNA: [*Suddenly aware that to be with* CHULKATURIN *is to be lost, both call out.*] Liza! Liza! [*They exit.* BIZMIONKOV *follows, reading his book. Sound of* LIZA'S *laughter is heard.* LIZA *bursts out into the open and whirls herself around.* CHULKATURIN *appears and watches her as she is lost in her reveries. She spirals to the ground. For a long moment she remains on the floor of the forest as* CHULKATURIN *stares at her.*]

ZODITCH: Go to the Petersburg ballet! Don't dance on my time! This is not the ballet!

CHULKATURIN: I could not move. I could not breathe. There were wildflowers in her hand. Her cheek pressed to the floor of the forest as if feeling the unheard music of grass and earth. I clung to the edge of the clearing afraid to approach, afraid to be seen, afraid of a moment into which I had transgressed. Though love had brought me, I came only as a stranger. [LIZA, *resting on her extended arm, slowly opens her eyes and stares at* CHULKATURIN. *The moment is poignant and* CHULKATURIN *breaks the mood abruptly by striding forward in cheerful embarrassment. A bit too loud*] Well, you see you have fallen. That's what you get for running so fast. Come. Let me help you up. [*Extends his hand to her. She looks at him for a moment and then turns away. He drops his hand.*]

LIZA: I'm all right. Please, just a moment.

CHULKATURIN: [*Stands by her, uneasily feeling that something should be said but not knowing, or rather not daring, to say what is in his heart. Instead, he makes conversation.*] I suppose they will be wondering what happened to us. I cannot imagine how we came to be separated from your parents. [*Pause in which there is no answer.*] Well, we've certainly taken our exercise for the day. If the summer continues at such a pace we shall all be in fine health. I haven't run this far since my father raced me in the meadows of Lambswater. [*Pause. Change of tone. Serious*] You grow older you run less.

LIZA: [*Suddenly turning to him*] You think it was childish of me to run?

CHULKATURIN: No. No, I didn't mean to imply that.

LIZA: Well, it was. Perhaps it will be a long time before I run again. [*Her mood changes from seriousness to fresh exuberance.*] Come. Sit down beside me. [*Extending her hand to him as he had before to her.*]

CHULKATURIN: We ought to sit on the bench. Your dress is going to be covered with grass stains.

LIZA: [*She drops her hand as he, before, had dropped his. She becomes thoughtful for a second, and then that passes and she smiles again, playfully.*] If you make me sit on the bench, I shall fold my hands in my lap and not allow you to become what you should become.

CHULKATURIN: And what is that?

LIZA: What do you think that is?

CHULKATURIN: I don't know.

LIZA: Guess.

CHULKATURIN: I can't.

LIZA: Then you shan't become it. [*She plays with the wildflowers.*]

CHULKATURIN: Tell me.

LIZA: What would you like to become?

CHULKATURIN: I don't know.

LIZA: Poor Nikolai Alexeevich Chulkaturin doesn't know what he would like to become. Shall I be kind and tell you, then? [*Pause, and she breaks into a smile.*] King of the May! The king of all the hearts of young ladies. Here and now I shall give you your new identity. But you must kneel properly and lower your head. Come. On your knees, or else I shall be forced to find another to be King of the May and you shall have lost your identity for good. Don't dally. Shall you be crowned or not? [*There is a moment in which they look at each other directly in the eyes, and then* CHULKATURIN *goes on his knees and lowers his head. She begins putting the wildflowers in his hair*.] What fine silky hair you have, Nikolai Alexeevich. Have there been many young ladies who have loved you for your fine brown hair?

CHULKATURIN: There has been no one.

LIZA: Perhaps you have forgotten them. The woods are full of the sighs of young girls. I think there must be many girls you have loved and forgotten.

CHULKATURIN: Do not think that there have been others.

LIZA: You must hold still. If you raise your head the flowers will fall.

CHULKATURIN: There has been no one who has loved me. Do not think that of me.

LIZA: I think men must be very cruel creatures to play with the heart of a girl and then not even remember her name. Men are like that according to my brother. [*She laughs.*]

CHULKATURIN: Why do you laugh?

LIZA: Illya says that the hearts of young girls are strewn about the world like grains of sand upon the shore and that there are not as many stars in the night sky as unremembered girls. Do you think that is true?

CHULKATURIN: I think that is poetic.

LIZA: And is that the same as true? What is your answer to that, Nikolai Alexeevich who has fine silky hair?

CHULKATURIN: You are making fun of me.

LIZA: [*Stops as if suddenly wearied.*] Yes. [*She stands up and turns to face the sun.*]

CHULKATURIN: Have I offended you?

LIZA: [*Wearily*] No.

CHULKATURIN: Then what is the matter? Why are you staring into the sun?

LIZA: Must I have reasons for everything? Is it not enough reason to stare at the sun because it is up there, because it is flaming across the sky, because we may never see the light again, because, because, because, because. [*The mood becomes a trifle lighter as if she attempts to recover.*] Have I found enough "becauses" to satisfy you? [*He is hurt. She reaches out to him, sincerely.*] Poor Nikolai, it is I who have offended you. Am I completely intolerable to be with?

CHULKATURIN: [*As he stands up, the flowers fall off his head.*] No. You cannot offend me. How could you ever think that you . . .

LIZA: See how soon every flower must fall. [*Brushing her hand through his hair to dislodge the other flowers.*] Every flower. [*To* CHULKATURIN] Don't be angry with me, ever, Nikolai. [*She takes his hands in hers and kisses them.* CHULKATURIN *bends down to kiss her, but she almost flippantly turns away.*] Papa thinks young girls should be placed in hibernation along with Siberian mastodons until we become eighteen years old, then we are to be melted from the ice and returned to our homes in time for marriage. Isn't that terribly clever of papa? [*She begins to cry.*]

CHULKATURIN: [*In surprise and confusion*] Liza, why are you crying?

LIZA: [*Tears running*] Isn't that terribly clever? I suppose I should take my dear bullfinch to sing to me in the ice and . . .

CHULKATURIN: What is wrong? Please don't cry. Please, Liza, Liza. Please! [*She turns her back to* CHULKATURIN *and, bowing her head, runs off.* CHULKATURIN *picks up the fallen flowers.*] Are the tears of women ever insignificant? And the tears of young girls, the young girls of our youth that so haunt us in after years, are they so much salt water lost from us forever? Did she not then, standing there in the final light of the sun, love me? Think, think, if I could not claim every tear, might not there have been a single tear that was for me, a fragment of a tear, a thousandth part of all that running flood loosed for me?

For me alone? Could those tears have fallen without me?

ZODITCH: They fall. They fall. Having no mind of their own, women have tears. It is not necessary to philosophize these things.

CHULKATURIN: I danced that night. I opened every window to the summer air, struck every candle, from every corner of the room dispelled every shadow. I took the wine from the landlord's table and brought it to my room. I took the books from the shelves and threw them in the closet. I locked the closet. The tears of a young girl, no . . . the tears of a young woman are bashful trembling tears. Shall I quote to you important works of important philosophers that will tell you that, precisely just that? There is no other way for girls to come to love but through tears. Shall I tell you about my future plans? In my happiness, my love, I made future plans. The world was to become involved with me, and I, through Liza, like some rose flung to the shores of the universe was to become involved with the world. There was the plan involving a wedding that the little provincial town would never forget. The entire town was to be invited, down to the last shoemaker.

ZODITCH: You cannot make weddings out of tears! There is nothing written down here to make weddings from! What are you making weddings from? [*Furiously begins rereading the previous pages. He turns the pages backward and forward while* CHULKATURIN *goes on in his happiness.*]

CHULKATURIN: Why should not the lowest shoemaker share in my happiness? I wanted everybody that I had ever brushed against to be happy. Let all those whose hearts were sick, be healed. Let those who were pained in silence, be pained no more. I saw the house of the Ozhogins preparing for the feast. Tables decked out: linen cloths, silverware, breads, steaming urns of soup, caviar, chicken boiled, chicken roasted, assortments of dainties, teas black and green, chocolates and mints, fruits, oranges, lots of oranges.

ZODITCH: [*Calling out while hunting for anything written that might have provoked* CHULKATURIN'*s outburst.*] Insane madman! You are making a wedding out of nothing!

CHULKATURIN: Old man Ozhogin stuffed into his leather chair, delightful, wondrous old man Ozhogin, patting his stuffed belly, checking the time with a gold watch drawn from his vest, blowing fantastic vast clouds of smoke from a miraculous black cigar; my father's watch, I had given Father Ozhogin my father's watch, and Mother Ozhogin crying tears on her voluminous breasts, she was my mother now. . . . [ZODITCH *lets out a cry of disgust.*] I had a family . . . Ozhogin . . . how rich that simple name sounded. . . . Ozhogin . . . has there ever been a more lovely name? A more beautiful sound upon the air? And Liza, my Liza before me in her wedding dress, her long unbound hair fallen to her shoulders, her eyes lit with happiness. The happiness that would be mine forever. [*Lights out on* CHULKATURIN.]

ZODITCH: No more of this! [*Starts flipping the pages for a new beginning. As he hunts, a spotlight falls on* CAPTAIN IVAN PETROVICH NARVINSKY, *a spit-and-polish officer. The kind of young man that traditionally sways a young girl's heart . . . he is* RUBIN. *The* CAPTAIN *is apparently engaged in conversation with* OTHERS. *Spotlight on* CHULKATURIN.]

CHULKATURIN: In brass, in leather, in saddle soap, the captain of cavalry called. Volobrina? [VOLOBRINA, *a servant girl to the Ozhogins, approaches . . . she is* FEATHERS.] Who is that?

VOLOBRINA: The friend of Illya's, Ivan Petrovich. A distinguished officer and rich. Come to organize recruits for the Czar.

CHULKATURIN: Illya's friend, ah. What the hell does he want here? Doesn't he know Illya isn't at home?

VOLOBRINA: What does anyone want here? Eh? [*She goes. Lights go up on the* OZHOGIN *living room. Present are the* CAPTAIN, KIRILLA, ANNA, BIZMIONKOV, *and* LIZA.]

CAPTAIN: At present my stay in this district is quite indefinite. A month, perhaps two. It is difficult to say at the outset.

ANNA: And have you found a suitable place to stay, Ivan Petrovich?

CAPTAIN: Yes, thank you. I have engaged a number of rooms at the inn for my officers and myself.

BIZMIONKOV: I'm afraid you will find the inn somewhat less than what you are accustomed to.

KIRILLA: I'm sure that will be the case. There are no decent accommodations in this entire town.

BIZMIONKOV: But then hardly anyone ever comes here, so there never seems any pressing need to have decent accommodations. [ANNA *laughs at the little joke.*]

CAPTAIN: I am a soldier, Mr. Bizmionkov, and for a soldier luxury is an unnecessary vice.

BIZMIONKOV: Yes, of course.

CAPTAIN: A soldier must take the terrain as he finds it. If he finds his feet are wet, well, then he must accept his wet feet. In my life such things are of no significance.

BIZMIONKOV: And what is of significance, Ivan Petrovich?

CAPTAIN: To serve the Czar and the motherland. To fight the enemies of Russia and to serve with courage and with faith.

LIZA: [*With a sigh*] Yes, that is right. [*Before she has a chance to be embarrassed at her outburst,* CHULKATURIN *enters the room waving a white rose.*]

CHULKATURIN: Good day. Good day. [*They* ALL *turn toward* CHULKATURIN. *The* CAPTAIN *alone stands.*] Oh, you have a guest! [*As if in complete surprise*] I hope I'm not intruding, but I was just passing by and . . . [*In his gesture, the rose flies out of his grasp and lands at* LIZA's *foot. He tries to remain nonchalant.*] Oh. [*He hastens to get it.*] I thought since I was in the vicinity I would come over. [LIZA *hands him the flower. They briefly exchange glances. He doesn't know quite what to do with the rose. It occupies much of his attention.*] I hope I'm not intruding.

KIRILLA: [*With a trace of irritation in his voice*] Not a bit.

CHULKATURIN: Are you sure?

KIRILLA: Yes. Yes. Quite all right.

CHULKATURIN: Because if you wish I could return later. I do not wish to interrupt. [*Looking about him for a friendly smile.*]

KIRILLA: [*Impatiently*] You are not interrupting! May I present Captain Ivan Petrovich Narvinsky, an officer in the Czar's cavalry. Captain, this is Nikolai Alexeevich Chulka...

CHULKATURIN: [*Used to his name being mishandled, completes it.*] Chulkaturin.

KIRILLA: Chulkaturin. A friend of Illya's from the university.

CAPTAIN: Ah! A pleasure, sir. [CHULKATURIN *has started to shake hands. However, all the* CAPTAIN *intended to do was a slight click of the heels and a bow. When he sees* CHULKATURIN *intends to shake hands, he extends his hand.* CHULKATURIN, *unfortunately, raises the hand with the rose. He switches the rose to the other hand. They finally shake.*]

CHULKATURIN: Thank you. Thank you. A pleasure for me as well. [*A kind of silence settles on the room.*] Well, please go on with whatever you were discussing. I'll just sit here. [*Starts to sit on the step leading into the living room. A step near* LIZA.]

CAPTAIN: No, please. [*Offers* CHULKATURIN *his chair.*]

CHULKATURIN: Oh no. Please. It's quite all right here. I really don't mind in the least.

KIRILLA: What? Is that our last chair? I have a thousand

chairs in this house. Wait. [*Starts to head out of the living room.*]

CHULKATURIN: Please. There is no need to bother. I'm perfectly . . .

KIRILLA: There is a need. Nobody has to sit on floors in my living room. [*Glares at* CHULKATURIN *and marches out. Silence descends. Finally . . .*]

CAPTAIN: So you knew Illya from the university, Mr. Chulkaturin.

CHULKATURIN: Yes, from the university.

CAPTAIN: Ah! [*Followed by a pause. A noticeable lapse in the conversation.*]

CHULKATURIN: [*Starts the conversation again.*] Is that where you knew Illya from?

CAPTAIN: Yes.

CHULKATURIN: Ah! [*Another noticeable pause.*]

CAPTAIN: Perhaps we've met before?

CHULKATURIN: I don't think so.

CAPTAIN: Ah. [*Pause.*] Were you one of the gentlemen Illya brought to my father's summer home?

CHULKATURIN: No.

CAPTAIN: It was a hunting trip?

CHULKATURIN: I don't hunt.

CAPTAIN: Oh. [*Pause.*]

ANNA: The captain is here to recruit soldiers for the Czar's cavalry.

CHULKATURIN: So?

CAPTAIN: Yes. [*Pause.*]

BIZMIONKOV: [*Opening his watch.*] Almost noon. [*Snaps his watch shut. Sound of chair scraping in the hall. Some grunting on the part of* KIRILLA.]

CHULKATURIN: Let me help, Mr. Ozhogin. I'll give you a hand. [*Goes offstage. We hear them speak.*]

KIRILLA: [*Offstage*] No. It's all right.

CHULKATURIN: [*Offstage*] I'll take the leg.

KIRILLA: [*Offstage*] I have it by myself. Watch your flower. You're pushing the flower in my eye. Watch it! Watch it! [*Sound of the chair falling over.*]

ANNA: [*Rising*] What's happened?

CHULKATURIN: [*Pokes his head in. The flower is bent.*] We've got it now.

KIRILLA: [*Appears holding the chair by himself.* CHULKATURIN *uselessly hovers about him.*] I can manage by myself.

ANNA: Are you all right?

KIRILLA: [*Sets the chair down.*] Fine. Just fine. [*To* CHULKATURIN] Sit! [CHULKATURIN *sits.* KIRILLA *returns to his seat. He blinks his eye.*]

LIZA: Is your eye all right, Papa?

KIRILLA: Yes. Yes. Go on with your conversation. [*Pause. Silence.* BIZMIONKOV *coughs. More silence.*]

CHULKATURIN: Would you like to take a turn around the garden, Mrs. Ozhogin? Liza?

ANNA: Perhaps after a bit, thank you. [LIZA *just shakes her head.* BIZMIONKOV *coughs again.*]

CHULKATURIN: Allow me to get you some water.

BIZMIONKOV: No need. . . . Just a tickle.

CHULKATURIN: Quite all right. I'll be back in a moment. [*Gets up and heads for kitchen. Conversation immediately picks up.*]

KIRILLA: You were saying, my dear captain?

LIZA: Ivan Petrovich was telling us about the cruel conditions under which soldiers must live, Papa. [*Lights dim on scene in living room. The rest of their conversation is played out in mime. Light focuses gradually down on the* CAPTAIN, *who continues speaking, and* LIZA, *who becomes more and more absorbed.* CHULKATURIN *has returned. He stands spotlighted in the doorway, a rose in one hand, a glass of water in the other.*]

CHULKATURIN: So he talked and so she listened and so you see . . . you see what it is to exist as an interruption, a break in everybody's conversation.

ZODITCH: [*Shouting out*] Nobody is just a break in the conversation! We all have our place! From the peasant to the Czar we have our place. Every ant, every

125

roach has his place. This is God's universe. This is not a madhouse of useless, placeless rats.

CHULKATURIN: How well the conversation proceeds now that I have left. Bizmionkov no longer coughs. He no longer even finds it necessary to clear his throat. Papa Ozhogin is no longer set to the task of moving chairs; Mama Ozhogin does not have to refuse a walk in the garden. Everybody is dug in. Conversation, now that I am gone, becomes pure song. [CHULKATURIN *extends his hand holding the rose*.] For you, Liza. Did you not know the rose was for you? Do young men carry roses for nothing? [*Only* LIZA *and* CAPTAIN *are now visible in living room*.] Go on, you Othello of the Steppes, with your big wars, your killings, your medals. Go on, Liza, fall in love with his black boots, his mustache, his eyes, and gallantries. What could I bring to you to match those gifts? And you, stand in the arches of the doorway with your water glass and your rose, stand there until the sky falls down, for all the difference it makes. It should have been enough for you to sleep through life, dreaming of happiness. [*Light goes out on* LIZA *and* CAPTAIN.] O time that was and time that never more shall be, I give you back your woods, your pathways, your shadowed glades. I give you back her whose dear sweet lips once brushed my heart. I give you back the earth I knelt upon to take a crown. I give you back the happiness of days now fled from me. I give back . . . I . . . [*Sound of waltz music growing louder*.] No. No. Nothing! I give back nothing! [*A lighted chandelier is lowered from the ceiling onto the center of the stage. Bit by bit, as* CHULKATURIN *stares about him, a dance is assembled. A table of punch, fruit, cookies, is brought in by a number of the* CAPTAIN's OFFICERS. *We hear the chatter of* PEOPLE, *the music, the laughter. In the wings of the stage, left and right, we can see some of the dancers. A young woman, perhaps twenty-five years of age, enters the stage behind* CHULKATURIN. *She pauses momentarily at the punch bowl and then, eying* CHULKATURIN, *comes forward. On her head quivers a small butterfly attached to a copper spring. The girl has an awkward smile that is constantly being flashed. She is the girl left over, the girl unchosen by any man.* CHULKATURIN, *in his anguish, cries out to the world and to the vanished* LIZA.] Nothing was definite until the night of the dance. Listen, I am not the type that deludes himself. You were no more his than mine the night of the dance. No more mine . . . [*Voice trails off as if suddenly aware he is now at the dance.*] than his. Why do you play games with me?

TANIA: [*Flirting as best as she can. She occasionally strikes* CHULKATURIN *with her fan.*] I still think it's mighty strange, Mr. Chulkaturin, that you could be in our little town so many months and we never meeting. I bet you just came in for the dance.

CHULKATURIN: [*Scarcely hears her, he is so distraught.*] What?

TANIA: I said isn't it strange we never met previously. I just bet you came in for the dance. Everybody does.

CHULKATURIN: Came in where?

TANIA: Why, in town.

CHULKATURIN: No. No. I've been here for months.

TANIA: Isn't it strange we've never met before?

CHULKATURIN: Yes. Strange, very strange.

TANIA: Just everybody is here tonight. Just everybody. I think someone has done something to the punch. Everybody seems to be having such a gay time, don't you think? I just love dances. I can't seem to remember who I am when I'm dancing. Isn't that funny? I start out saying, "Tania, you must remember your own name, you silly girl, you mustn't forget your own name," but then I feel myself saying "one, two, three, one, two, three," and the room begins spinning around and around, and the music seems to slide right into my slippers. [*There is no response from* CHULKATURIN. *She waves to someone.*] So many of the gentlemen I

know seem to be absent tonight. [LIZA *and the* CAP-
TAIN *waltz by, from wing to wing of the stage, totally
ignoring* CHULKATURIN.]

CHULKATURIN: Did he say something to me? Did you
hear him say something to me when he danced by?

TANIA: The captain?

CHULKATURIN: Yes. Yes. Him.

TANIA: Why I'm sure I don't know. I don't think so, Mr.
Chulkaturin. Isn't he a handsome man in that lovely
uniform?

CHULKATURIN: He made a noise.

TANIA: Is something wrong, Mr. Chulkaturin?

CHULKATURIN: No. Why should there be something
wrong?

TANIA: I don't know.

CHULKATURIN: Then what are you talking about? Let's
dance. [CHULKATURIN *dances wildly, angrily. He
begins to shout as he dances. The* GIRL *becomes increasingly distressed. On one of the turns, he half
thrusts her from him. He continues shouting as he
dances alone.* TANIA, *frightened, watches him for a
moment and runs from the room.*] You provincials.
You eaters of onions. You sleepers with sheep. Who
invited you to the dance? Who told you to come?
Wasn't it enough you had your fatlegged wives? Your
pimple-nosed children? And you, Captain of Killing,
weren't there enough women in Petersburg to satisfy
you? Let me tell you, my friend—go polish your
boots in another neighborhood. Why didn't you stay
away from what's mine? Did I come around bother-
ing your women? Did I ever come to Petersburg and
bother your women? Did I ever take what was yours?
[*The* CAPTAIN *enters in time to hear* CHULKATURIN's
last few words and to see the girl flee. CHULKATURIN
does not see him. The CAPTAIN *pretends he has seen
nothing. He heads toward the punch bowl.*]

CAPTAIN: Ah, Mr. Chulkaturin. Where have you been

keeping yourself all evening? Are you enjoying yourself?

CHULKATURIN: Do not mock me!

CAPTAIN: What?

CHULKATURIN: It is you who deserves to be mocked, you hollow-brained imitation of a peacock.

CAPTAIN: [*Holding the glasses full of punch*] In a moment.

CHULKATURIN: I'll kick your head in if you laugh at me.

CAPTAIN: [*Smiling*] Not here. In a moment. I understand you.

CHULKATURIN: [*Whispering furiously as he departs*] Go back to Petersburg. [*The* CAPTAIN *gives the drinks to* VOLOBRINA, *who is passing by with a serving tray. He returns.*]

CAPTAIN: [*Smiling. Puts his arm around* CHULKATURIN.] I believe we have some business to discuss.

CHULKATURIN: Take your hands off me. I am not one of your serfs.

CAPTAIN: Keep your voice down. There is no need not to handle this as gentlemen. I assume I am talking to a gentleman. [*Waves at* LIZA *as she passes by arm in arm with* BIZMIONKOV.]

CHULKATURIN: Assume what you like.

CAPTAIN: I believe you have intentionally insulted me.

CHULKATURIN: Believe what you like.

CAPTAIN: Perhaps you would prefer to settle this in a duel?

CHULKATURIN: As you wish.

CAPTAIN: If you do not withdraw your remarks it shall be my wish to challenge you. It will also be my unfortunate choice to have to kill you. Let me assure you I am an excellent shot. Therefore, consider what you are forcing me into. I do not wish to kill a man who means nothing to me one way or the other.

CHULKATURIN: Nothing, is it? I withdraw nothing, you fop, you strutting suit of peacock feathers. You think because I am not a soldier I do not know the meaning of courage? You think because I do not have brass bands and medals I do not know how to behave when I am mocked?

CAPTAIN: You mock yourself, sir. But as you wish. I shall have the honor of sending my second to you tomorrow morning. Mr. Stuccoturin. [CAPTAIN *turns and walks away, smiling, greeting others*.]

CHULKATURIN: Chulkaturin! My name is Chulkaturin! [*A circle of light illuminates* BIZMIONKOV *and* CHULKATURIN. *Light on dance scene dims*.]

BIZMIONKOV: Listen to me, Chulkaturin, you cannot persist in this. Do you hear his officers? They are laughing because they think you are a fool. They know he will kill you.

CHULKATURIN: That is their prerogative. Perhaps tomorrow I shall give them less cause for laughter than they think.

BIZMIONKOV: Have you ever fired a pistol?

CHULKATURIN: No.

BIZMIONKOV: Then you are a fool. He will kill you. He will not miss.

CHULKATURIN: Perhaps.

BIZMIONKOV: Not perhaps, certainly! Do you wish to die? Is that it?

CHULKATURIN: I do not wish to die.

BIZMIONKOV: Do not be too sure of that, my young friend. Many a man has died thinking he did not wish to die.

CHULKATURIN: If you think that, you do not understand the meaning of honor.

BIZMIONKOV: This is not a question of honor.

CHULKATURIN: He has insulted me. Something was said.

BIZMIONKOV: What was said? [*Long pause in which no answer comes from* CHULKATURIN.] What? Are your sensibilities so refined you cannot even say what has been this insult to your honor? Listen to me, go away, tonight. There is nothing for you here. You cannot make a woman love you. Not if you stood on your head till kingdom come. If you can learn that by the time you are twenty-five, you have learned much.

CHULKATURIN: You do not understand.

BIZMIONKOV: Then tell me. Tell me what it is I am to understand. Because I am glad it is not for love that you are putting your back to the wall. Because I am very glad you are not dying for love, because at this very moment the captain's affair is progressing in the back of the Ozhogin garden, in a closed carriage, in the captain's bedroom, or wherever else they have found convenient.

CHULKATURIN: Why do you lie to me?

BIZMIONKOV: Go home, my friend, go home. Do not die uselessly. [BIZMIONKOV *starts to exit.*]

CHULKATURIN: [*Shouting after him, and as* CHULKATURIN *turns toward* BIZMIONKOV, *a light goes on showing the* CAPTAIN *kissing* LIZA.] It is not useless! Don't tell me what is useless! I at least am not a sponge. I do not hang onto the coattails of a family and rob them of their food because they have money! I do not pretend friendship where there is none.

ZODITCH: [*Shouts out.*] Go on! Give it to her! Press her into the wall, Rubin! [*The scene fades out.*] Why don't you write about that? That's what the public wants to read about. There's a man to handle every bitch . . . And they're all bitches. They take your heart. They . . . they . . . [*The scene lights up and we are on the dueling field. On one side of the stage stands* CHULKATURIN *and on the other side the* CAPTAIN *and some of his* OFFICERS. *One of the officers,* LIEUTENANT ZIMIN, *slightly drunk, comes over.*]

LIEUTENANT ZIMIN: Listen, Tulkaturbin or whatever the hell your name is, can you handle a military pistol?

CHULKATURIN: Yes.

LIEUTENANT ZIMIN: [*Looks at* CHULKATURIN *dubiously for a second, and then shouts out to the other officers.*] You better watch out, Ivan Petrovich. He says he's fired a pistol before. [*The other officers laugh.* ZIMIN *and the* CAPTAIN *do not. The* CAPTAIN *hushes the others. To* CHULKATURIN] All right, Tulkaturbin, I'm going to give you some advice. The captain has no desire to blow your head off. Until you insulted him he didn't even know you existed. Take my advice, apologize and the affair is ended. [*Belches.*] Pardon. Then we can all go back to the inn and go to sleep. It's too early in the day for you to die. You're a bright fellow. What lies between the hammer and the anvil soon gets knocked flat. Huh? You understand me? Why get your nose knocked out of joint by interfering in a love affair? Go down to the stage line. Every coach brings in a new woman.

OFFICER A: [*From one of the group by the* CAPTAIN] Lieutenant Zimin, are you ready?

LIEUTENANT ZIMIN: [*Looks at* CHULKATURIN, *who remains impassive.*] My friend, it is imbeciles such as yourself who ruin the summer. [*To* OFFICER A] We are ready. [*To* CHULKATURIN] There is one round in the pistol so you will have only one opportunity to fire. You understand?

CHULKATURIN: Yes.

LIEUTENANT ZIMIN: When he tells you to cock your pistol you pull this back with your thumb. [*Indicates the hammer.* ZIMIN *pulls back the hammer, and then releases it to show* CHULKATURIN *how it's done.*] You see? Don't be too much in a rush to fire. There are no prizes for firing first. [CHULKATURIN *nods.*] All right. Let's go. Take off your coat. Give it to me. [CHULKATURIN *and* ZIMIN *walk to meet the* CAPTAIN's *party in the middle of the stage.*]

OFFICER A: Take your positions.

LIEUTENANT ZIMIN: [*To* CHULKATURIN, *who doesn't quite know what to do.*] Here, turn around. [*He turns* CHULKATURIN *around so* CHULKATURIN *and the* CAPTAIN *are back to back.*]

OFFICER A: Are you both ready?

CAPTAIN: Yes.

CHULKATURIN: Yes.

OFFICER A: You will each take five paces. At the command, "Turn," you will turn and fire.

OFFICER B: [*One of the ones who has been laughing*] Has anyone found out where we're supposed to ship the poor fellow's body?

CAPTAIN: [*Turning on him*] Be still!

OFFICER A: Cock your pistols. [CHULKATURIN's *hand is shaking slightly. He has trouble cocking his pistol.* ZIMIN *cocks it for him.*] Take your paces. [ZIMIN, OFFICER A, *and the rest back away from the line of fire as the paces are counted off. The* CAPTAIN *and* CHULKATURIN *have come to a stop.*] Turn! [CHULKATURIN *turns quickly and fires. The* CAPTAIN *is grazed along the temple. He goes down for a moment.* CHULKATURIN *instinctively moves forward.*] Stand your place, sir. [CHULKATURIN *stands still. Head erect, the pistol hanging in his limp arm, he is obviously willing to die. The* CAPTAIN *returns to a standing position and after a moment's hesitation, at which time his pistol is leveled straight at* CHULKATURIN's *head, fires into the air.* CHULKATURIN *gives a long scream of anguish.*]

CHULKATURIN: Shoot me! Shoot me! Shoot! Shoot! [*Lights out. We hear the sound of scuffling.* CHULKATURIN *calls out from the dark.*] Where's he going? Take your hands off me. Leave me alone. Come back! Shoot! Shoot me! [*Lights up on* CHULKATURIN *in his bedroom. He is writhing on the floor, the* DOCTOR *and* TERENTIEVNA *trying to hold him down. It is a melee with his last amount of energy. He appears hysterical. He seems to be wanting to pull himself out of the* DOCTOR's *grasp to get at the* CAPTAIN *in the scene before.*]

DOCTOR: There's nobody. Nobody wants to shoot you.

CHULKATURIN: [*To* DOCTOR] Listen, you don't know what that little scar across his temple did to me. Nobody in town spoke to me again. They didn't let me come to their doors because I who wasn't worth the killing had tried to kill the captain. She wouldn't see me. What right did he have to fire into the air? What right did he have to scorn me so? What right to injure me twice?

DOCTOR: Help me get him to lie down, Terentievna.

CHULKATURIN: Did I deserve that treatment? What right did he have to shoot into the air? What was I supposed to do? Take his insults lying down? Don't snakes bite the foot that crushes them? Even snakes. Just because I'm superfluous, am I to be stepped on? [*They get him into the bed.*]

DOCTOR: Where was he going? Why is he dressed, Terentievna?

TERENTIEVNA: I don't know, sir. He said he was going to a dance.

DOCTOR: Take off his boots. What nonsense! [*She begins pulling off his boots.*]

CHULKATURIN: And who was right, after all? After they didn't speak to me, after all the doors shut, after I wandered the streets like a ghost for weeks, when they came around to me. So who was right, after all? "Chulkaturin," and they knew my name, "you were right. Listen, my friend, he has made her pregnant and has deserted her. He has gone back to Petersburg. He has moved out with his recruits. What is to be done? Who will marry her now?" [CHULKATURIN *looks hard at the* DOCTOR *and* TERENTIEVNA. *They both stare at him.*] Eh? Who will marry her? You know how it is with those springtime fellows? Eh? One flower in April, one flower in May. His day, his hour, was my whole summer, my whole life. [CHULKATURIN *stares off in the distance and a spotlight illuminates* KIRILLA *and* ANNA, *who seem to be addressing* CHULKATURIN.]

KIRILLA: Chulkaturin, how clever you are. You knew what that fellow was from the start. You saw through him, my friend, when the rest of us were blind. My friend, what are words? What can I say?

ANNA: She goes nowhere now. She will not leave the house. She is invited nowhere. What can I say to you? [*Lights out on* KIRILLA *and* ANNA.]

DOCTOR: [*To* TERENTIEVNA] Get me the pan. We must remove the excess blood before it is too late. [*She exits. To* CHULKATURIN] Be calm, my friend, be calm. What are you staring at?

CHULKATURIN: What if I gave myself to her now? What if I offered to marry her? You understand how it was? She was proved worthless, dishonored. It would be a sacrifice for me to go to her and propose marriage. It would be an act of pity to love what others mocked. She would fall into my arms. She would bless me. She would think I was her savior. That was a proper expectation. A reasonable man would call it a proper expectation.

DOCTOR: Yes. Yes.

CHULKATURIN: Listen, they've taken my father's boots. Find out what they've done with my father's boots.

DOCTOR: Don't worry about the boots now.

CHULKATURIN: [*Tears running down his face*] Don't let them steal the boots. Can I rely on you? Don't let them steal my property. See to it. See to it. I rely on you. [*Lights out on scene. Lights full up on* ZODITCH *at his desk, the diary open,* FEATHERS *standing by his side.*]

ZODITCH: Well? Well? Was that all?

FEATHERS: Katerina Prolomnaya says that if you wish to come down then you are free to come down, Mr. Zoditch.

ZODITCH: And what else?

FEATHERS: Nothing else, sir.

ZODITCH: But she was anxious?

FEATHERS: I don't know, sir.

ZODITCH: She seemed excited, nervous?

FEATHERS: I couldn't say, sir.

ZODITCH: You are a stupid little girl. When I am master of this house I will not tolerate stupid servants, mark my words. I will not tolerate smiling. If you do not wish to live in the chimney do not trifle with me.

FEATHERS: Are you then to be master of this house, Mr. Zoditch?

ZODITCH: [*Thinking about something and not particularly listening*] Eh?

FEATHERS: Are you to be the new master, sir?

ZODITCH: What have *you* heard?

FEATHERS: Nothing, sir.

ZODITCH: [*Grabbing the* GIRL] You heard something. Out with it. Do not play games. She mentioned my name to you?

FEATHERS: Oh yes, Mr. Zoditch. That she has.

ZODITCH: Ah. I knew it. In what connection?

FEATHERS: In connection with the weather, sir. She said this morning that you left the house without your scarf.

ZODITCH: She noticed that, did she? [FEATHERS *nods head.*] Well? Well? What else did she say?

FEATHERS: [*Hesitantly*] She said that only a fool walks in this weather without a scarf about his neck.

ZODITCH: A fool! You did not hear her correctly. Her manner? She did not perhaps rest her hand upon her cheek . . . [FEATHERS *shakes her head.*] or tilt her head, thus . . . [FEATHERS *still shakes her head.*] or utter any oohs or ahhhs? [GIRL's *face lights up and she nods her head.*]

FEATHERS: Something of that, sir. An ooooh.

ZODITCH: Ah. Ah. [*Rubs his hands together and then anxiously shoos his hands at the girl.*] Go. Go. Tell your mistress I shall be down shortly. [*The girl starts to go.*] Wait. Just say I shall be down. Do not say shortly. [*She exits. To himself*] Shortly implies haste. Here there is no haste. A wormy apple is not to be thrown out, nor to be hastened to. [*Goes over to his closet and starts looking at his clothes. Picks a gray suit.*] Gray. Neither too gaudy nor too funereal. Gray as a sea gull. [*He pulls it out and inspects it. He starts*

to brush it off. He is plainly thinking. From the dark-
ened part of the room, in his imagination, a voice.]

KATERINA: Will you have a piece of fudge, Mitya? [ZO-
DITCH *turns without surprise. He is going to act out*
his approach to the woman. This is how he imagines
it will be. As he turns, the couch area lights up and
we see KATERINA PROLOMNAYA. *She is an immense*
woman, a good four or five inches taller than ZODITCH.
She is overstuffed, overripe, and yet sensual for it all.
Her face is heavily painted, her hair is intricately in
place with hairpins. He takes the proffered fudge and
sits down on the couch. They both eat fudge while
staring intently at each other.] Do you like the fudge,
Mitya?

ZODITCH: It is only fudge, Katerina. I do not concern
myself with fudge. A man concerns himself with taxes,
estates, properties, and bank balances.

KATERINA: [*Sighing.*] I know. I know. But surely there
must be time for . . . [*Hesitantly*] other things.

ZODITCH: Other things? I do not understand what you
mean by other things. [*Points to match.*] The match.

KATERINA: Yes, Mitya. [*She lights his cigar.*] I enjoy a
man smoking a cigar.

ZODITCH: Your late husband did not smoke?

KATERINA: No.

ZODITCH: That is unfortunate. A house without tobacco
smoke is a house not lived in.

KATERINA: Yes, that is true. [*Then a bit too forward*]
Oh, Mitya, these last few months have been lonely
ones for me. Knowing that you were near and yet so
distant.

ZODITCH: [*Raises his hand.*] You must learn to keep
your lusts under control, Katerina. The ashtray,
please. [*She hands him the ashtray.*] A woman who
cannot keep her lusts under control soon finds her
lusts keep her under control. Lust is the devil's monastery on the road to hell.

KATERINA: The seas have been rough for me, Mitya.

Women by their nature are but frail vessels. They only
have their hearts to guide them.

ZODITCH: And so I have come to consider taking the
helm.

KATERINA: Oh, Mitya.

ZODITCH: To *consider*, Katerina. *Consider*. To consider
is not to undertake; it is merely to consider.

KATERINA: [*A bit subdued*] Yes.

ZODITCH: Yet many things are finally arrived at which,
at first, were but considered.

KATERINA: [*Her hopes picking up*] Yes. Yes.

ZODITCH: As you know I am by nature and by inclination a bachelor. However, since the death of my dear
mother who was constantly by my side these past
thirty-five years, I have had the inclination to seek
another who might be equally solicitous of my welfare. One who might be concerned to see, as it were,
the proper socks laid out in the morning, the stove
lit fifteen minutes before awakening, the washbasin
filled with water neither too hot nor too cold and, as
it were, et cetera, et cetera, et cetera. In brief, one
who might so conform her life to mine that we become
a single entity of one mind, of one direction. I, on the
other hand, shall, as it were, seize the helm of our
mutual fortunes and guide the ship all safely into harbor. A man can do no less than to captain his ship, a
woman can do no more than obey. Nothing less is
correct; nothing more permissible.

KATERINA: Is it then to be so nautical? What of love,
Mitya?

ZODITCH: What of love! On the sea of marriage love is
understood.

KATERINA: [*Taking his hand and stroking it*] Our love,
Mitya?

ZODITCH: Our love! Any love! There is no need to bring
up superfluous topics. We must proceed logically. The
disorganized mind is the handmaiden of cupidity.
[*Pulls a sheet of paper out of his pocket. From this*

point on she slowly but surely begins making physical overtures.] Now. My bill of assets. What you may expect in terms of physical property. [*Places the paper before her. She leans close.*] Three pairs of shoes. Two in excellent condition. One in used condition, though without holes. Seven pairs of black socks. The wash, therefore, must be done no later than the sixth day of the week. [*She puts her hand on his ankle.*] There is no need to inspect the socks at this time. Everything is as I will state it. [*Proceeds with the inventory. She moves in on him by degrees as he recites his list of assets.*] Three suits: one black, one brown, one gray. Eighteen pieces of undergarments. In undergarments I am particularly fortunate, having received twelve pieces in total settlement of my late cousin's estate. Five shirts, four cotton white, one Egyptian cotton striped. A wool overcoat, full-cut, with imitation pearl buttons. A malacca cane belonging to the estate of my late father, still in the process of settlement, but to which I have indisputable right; a Persian rug, nine by twelve, purchased for me by my departed mother in Constantinople; bedding supplies consisting of two sheets, two pillowcases, one pillow, and a six-inch-thick Siberian goose-down comforter.

KATERINA: And your heart, Mitya?

ZODITCH: [*Pulling out a bank book*] A bank statement, listing monetary assets in excess of one hundred seventeen rubles.

KATERINA: And your heart, Mitya? Your heart?

ZODITCH: What are you talking about? We are itemizing now!

KATERINA: [*Grown increasingly amorous*] I must have love. Love. Love.

ZODITCH: There is no place for love in an itemizing of particulars. Where is your list of physical property?

KATERINA: [*Grabs his hand and places it on her heart.*] Here is my physical property. Feel it beating.

ZODITCH: Where is your bill of purchase for the house?

Your list of bank holdings? Your movables? Your tangibles and intangibles?

KATERINA: My dogs, Mitya, what of my dogs?

ZODITCH: Superfluous. To be gotten rid of. I am not piloting a doghouse.

KATERINA: Be my pilot. Mine. [*Shoves some fudge practically into his mouth.*]

ZODITCH: Show me the bills of purchase. How many horses are in the stable. I don't want any fudge. [*She puts the fudge halfway into her mouth and begins to crawl all over him. She wants him to take the other half in his mouth. He retreats along the couch until there is no room to retreat. She literally begins physically overpowering him. She presses the fudge against his mouth until he starts biting it. His conversation until he devours the fudge runs something like:*] What are you doing? Why are you touching me? You're pushing me. Listen. Don't. Wait. How much is your bank balance? What are you doing? Don't come any closer. You're hurting me. Let me up. Up. Up. Up. [*When he does take the fudge from her mouth into his, he starts chewing it up furiously. Now she does the talking.*]

KATERINA: We will have our honeymoon in the house. We will stay in the bedroom. There will be no need for you to work. No need to ever leave the house. We will raise the rents. [*She grabs his head and forces him to kiss her.*] Don't kiss me so hard, Mitya, not yet, not yet. I want to make love to you. Yes. Oh, make love to me always. Always. Never leave the house. Patience, Mitya, not yet. Wait until we are man and wife. Be sweet. Be gentle. Never leave the house.

ZODITCH: Let me go. For the love of God. You're crushing me. I can't breathe. You're crushing me.

KATERINA: Kiss me, Mitya. Put your arms around me. Crush me. Crush me.

ZODITCH: Get off. Off. [*He suddenly frees himself from her embrace and flees to his desk. Lights out on the* couch. *He stands shakily by his desk trying to catch his breath. Suddenly, from down below there comes the voice of* KATERINA PROLOMNAYA *in the midst of the barking of dogs.*]

KATERINA: [*Shouting*] If you're coming down, Zoditch, come down! I haven't all night to spend waiting for you! [*Followed by wild barking.*]

ZODITCH: [*Wildly to himself, almost tearfully*] Yes. Yes. Good-bye, Miss Grubov. Good-bye. [*Out loud*] Yes. Yes. I'm coming, Katerina Prolomnaya. I'm coming. [*Runs over to the closet and slips into the gray trousers.*] Coming. Coming. [*Throws on the coat, grabs the diary and some official papers. He stamps them with a seal.*] With a seal. Official. [*Starts to read as he runs out.*] I'm coming, Katerina Prolomnaya. Coming. [*Light dims on* ZODITCH's *room but does not go out. Lights up on* CHULKATURIN *standing in the entrance to the* OZHOGIN *living room.* KIRILLA *is warmly welcoming him. He rushes up and puts his arms around* CHULKATURIN.]

KIRILLA: Ah, my friend, you have come. In spite of everything you have come. [*To* VOLOBRINA] Bring some tea for our guest. Quickly. [*Embraces* CHULKATURIN *again as* VOLOBRINA *heads for kitchen.*] Come in. Come in. Let me take your coat. [*Helps* CHULKATURIN *off with his coat.*] Here, by the fire. Soon winter will be down upon us. You are well?

CHULKATURIN: Yes.

KIRILLA: Good. Good.

CHULKATURIN: And you and Madam Ozhogin?

KIRILLA: [*Opens his hands as a form of silent reply meaning, "As well as might be expected."*] Well.

CHULKATURIN: And Liza?

KIRILLA: Ah. How quickly the summer has gone. How quickly youth vanishes. Smoke, that is all it is, dear Chulkaturin, smoke and expectations. This is a different household you have come into.

CHULKATURIN: You mustn't blame yourself.

KIRILLA: But they blame me, all of them, Anna, the servants. You see what ingratitude is? Could I tell what a snake he was when he came into this house? Is it every snake that walks around and says he is a snake? But he never fooled you, my dear friend. You knew him from the start. I saw no more than the show of things, but you saw into the heart. You saw the snake in the man.

CHULKATURIN: Has he written to her? [KIRILLA *shakes his head.*] That is to be expected. It is just as well.

KIRILLA: [*Slowly nodding his head*] Yes. Just as well. Oh, my friend, what can I say to you? You fought, you risked your life to save my daughter from him and only received contempt in return. What can be said to you?

CHULKATURIN: Your friendship now is all I desire.

KIRILLA: You have that, my friend, from the bottom of my heart.

CHULKATURIN: And to bring Liza happiness.

KIRILLA: Ah, if that were only possible. If I could believe that you could find forgiveness for her.

CHULKATURIN: It is possible. I do forgive.

KIRILLA: [*Sinking into his chair. He is almost in tears.*] What irony. Bitter bitter irony. The whole town condemns her and you who have every right . . .

CHULKATURIN: I do not care what fools condemn. [*Sinks to his knees by* KIRILLA'*s side and touches his hand.*] You understand? She is not of less value to me because of fools.

KIRILLA: She is a young girl. She made a mistake. The judgment of the young is not foolproof.

CHULKATURIN: Yes. As you say. If she will have me even now I will marry her. I will take her to Lambswater. She will be loved as no woman has ever been loved. She will be respected. I swear that to you.

KIRILLA: [*Speechless*] Respect? Is it yet possible?

CHULKATURIN: Believe what I say, my friend. If you

142

believe nothing else of me, believe that. Let the past be done.

KIRILLA: [*Practically bursts into tears as he hugs him.*] You have her. You have her. I don't know what to ... You have her! Go to her. She is alone in the garden. ... Go, my son. Take her. [*He releases* CHULKATURIN.] Your coat. Don't catch cold. [*Gives* CHULKATURIN *his coat.* CHULKATURIN *stands in the doorway leading to the garden.* KIRILLA *flees the living room.*] Anna! Anna! [*Lights out on* CHULKATURIN. *Lights up on* ZODITCH *in the apartment of* KATERINA PROLOMNAYA. *She stands before a meat grinder, grinding meat. In the background we hear the intermittent growling of her dogs.*]

ZODITCH: Katerina Prolomnaya, what is loneliness? Did not the Roman poets tell us, "Lupus pilum mutat, non mentem," meaning we are all thrust alone on a dark sea. [*Pauses expecting a response. There is none. He goes on.*] A dark sea! A sea without light. A sea of gigantic waves. In life, Katerina Prolomnaya, the wind blows. The wind blows! [*Pauses for a second to wipe his forehead with a handkerchief.*] And what is the effect of this wind? It pushes us along. We do not know where we have sailed from. We do not know where we sail to. We sail! [*Again he pauses, but still she continues grinding.*] No man can say, "No, I will not sail. No, I will remain where I am safe." This he cannot say because the wind blows. That is the substance of it all—the wind. And what is the effect of this wind when we sail in the darkness, Katerina Prolomnaya? Who's to say how many of us are blown over the edges of the world. Which is to say without metaphor, how many of us come to bad fortune because he ... or she ... sailed alone. To sail alone is to vanish alone. And this is the answer to my question, Katerina Prolomnaya.

KATERINA: You have received the extra coal and oil I sent?

ZODITCH: [*Nervous. Wiping his forehead again*] Yes, yes, thank you. We see that what is loneliness is to be alone and to vanish alone. [*Softly, as if trying to remember a set speech*] To vanish alone. [*Then a bit too loudly*] Loneliness must end! How is loneliness to end? Loneliness ends when a light is lit.

KATERINA: [*Suddenly shouting at the dogs*] Shut up!

ZODITCH: [*In a moment of sudden fright* ZODITCH *knocks a small piece of meat off the table. He instantly bends down to pick it up.*] Excuse me. Excuse me. [*Puts the meat back on the table. He continues, nervously.*] And what power do we have to strike such a light? Mutual feeling . . . mutual regard, but even more than this, love. Love is a light. When two boats come together they make a light. This is the holy light of marriage. Now we must ask, what is marriage? Marriage is a sacrament, and by a sacrament the Church means a sanctity and a union of spirits; therefore, marriage is not based on material possession. Oh no, Katerina Prolomnaya, it is not a contract of assets and liabilities. The Church does not intend us to inquire into the number of houses owned, the number of horses in the stable. Love is above these things. It makes a harmony from separateness. It makes joy. It is above rings and rubles. [KATERINA *has stopped grinding the meat and now stares directly at him. He has grown very nervous.*] It is the light that moves above the darkness of the sea. It is the star and moon. It is the refuge, the shelter, the roof against the wind. [*Suddenly taking her hand. She continues trying to grind the meat. He continues trying to get her to stop. A silent grinding.* ZODITCH *is dismayed. Nevertheless he continues.*] Know, dear Katerina Prolomnaya, that it was not for nothing that your extra coal to me was given. Know that such seeds of generosity, of goodness, did not fall on barren ground, but that they found their way to this heart that even now illuminates with respectful fondness.

KATERINA: Now that you have been advanced in your position you will pay me two extra rubles a month for coal and oil.

ZODITCH: To you, Katerina, I offer this hand of marriage, this hand of spiritual bondage, this hand . . .

KATERINA: I cannot marry you. You are too old, too . . . [*Looking him up and down*] short. [*Lights slowly fade out on* KATERINA PROLOMNAYA.]

ZODITCH: [*Turns and faces the audience.*] Too old? *I* am too old? It is *I* who am laughing, Katerina Prolomnaya. [*Laughs a dry hollow laugh.*] I laugh to think you can laugh at me. It is you who are the wrinkled fish here. [*Cups his hand to his ear.*] Is that so? Is that so, madam? Well, it is I who stoop to consider marriage to you. I laugh in your face. I withdraw my offer. . . . When I marry Miss Grubov your tongue will hang out to come to the wedding. [*As he climbs the stairs leading back to his apartment, somewhere in his mind comes the sound of* KATERINA *laughing.*] You keep your dogs away from me, Katerina Prolomnaya. Your tongue will hang out to be invited. Get away, you filthy beasts. Get away. [*He begins kicking at invisible dogs.*] To a man of my position your assets are nothing. I am not interested in your buildings and your rents. I am a man of sensibilities. A man interested in love and feelings. Get away from my legs, you bitches. I'll kick your heads in. You think I didn't know the coal was given just to raise my rent? Keep your coal and kerosene. [*Laughter breaks out again.*] What did you expect for a husband? A giant? Jack and the beanstalk? A ten-foot monster? There is no golden goose for you. You are no princess of the pea. Get away. Leave me alone. I'll kill you, you bitches. I'll kill you. Gregory! Gregory! Madhouse. Madhouse. Madhouse! [*Lights dim on* ZODITCH *frozen in a scream. Lights up on* LIZA *and* BIZMIONKOV *in the garden.* CHULKATURIN *stands half unseen in the archway.*]

LIZA: How brown the garden has become. How dry.

BIZMIONKOV: Perhaps the captain will yet write.

LIZA: You think so? [*Catching herself*] No. It is done. He will not write. Ivan Petrovich has gone to Petersburg and he will not write. Shall I dig up these flowers, do you think, and bring them inside? They will die in the first snow.

BIZMIONKOV: Let them die, Liza.

LIZA: Papa must have taken the spade inside. I cannot seem to find it.

BIZMIONKOV: What of Chulkaturin?

LIZA: [*Suddenly stops looking for the spade. She speaks with scorn.*] That one? How hateful that name sounds to me. [*Touching some flowers*] These petals are still soft. I can save these flowers.

BIZMIONKOV: He has not left yet.

LIZA: Ah. Still he waits. For what does he wait? To forgive me? I do not need his forgiveness. Better that he had never known my brother. Better that the door to this house had remained forever shut against him.

BIZMIONKOV: He is in love with you.

LIZA: His love is nothing to me now! I cannot forgive him. What did he want here? Did he come all this way to stand alone at dances? To throw flowers to no one? To shoot Ivan? For what did he come?

BIZMIONKOV: [*Slowly*] I think Nikolai Alexeevich Chulkaturin came all this way to love you.

LIZA: [*There is a pause in which she looks at* BIZMIONKOV *for a long time, as if seeing him for the first time.*] How good you are. You are an angel. What should I have ever done without you?

BIZMIONKOV: Is there nothing then for Chulkaturin?

LIZA: I have forgotten him. [*Raising her hands to his face*] My friend, if you love me, knowing all, I will do as you ask. I will become your wife. [BIZMIONKOV *embraces her, slowly, tightly.* CHULKATURIN *lets out a short cry.*]

CHULKATURIN: You, Bizmionkov? You?

ZODITCH: No, Miss Grubov! Not Pandalevski! [*Lights*

go out on BIZMIONKOV *and* LIZA. ZODITCH *and* CHUL-KATURIN *are left facing each other across the stage.* ZODITCH *grabs the manuscript in his hand.*] This is a story of lies! You are a liar! You distort! Do you see what I am doing? I reject this manuscript! I reject you! [*Writing across the face of the manuscript.*]

CHULKATURIN: And I stood in the garden dumb and dark with hedges, stood as if the winds of a thousand centuries might wash upon me and find me standing yet. And for all of it, the roses shut in books, the crowns of May, the duels, the summer dances, what for all of it, if, at the last, to say, "Bizmionkov, is it you?" [*Extends his arm to* ZODITCH.]

ZODITCH: Liar! I am the one that is loved! That is the ending. I am loved! [*There is a pause in which* ZODITCH *and* CHULKATURIN *stare at each other. When* ZODITCH *speaks the anger has been replaced by anguish.*] What do you want of me? [CHULKATURIN'*s arm falls. Lights out on* CHULKATURIN. ZODITCH, *with rage, throws the diary violently away.*] I am the one that is loved. There is no other ending. [*He begins curling himself up into a hard ball as if suddenly very cold. Lights out.*]

VOICE: And when I had passed through the antique marketplace of Samarkand, through the cries and fevers of the merchants, the monkey's hand fell within his cage, and there was nothing further to the matter.

CURTAIN

The
Ceremony
of Innocence

A Play in Two Acts

For Alan Markman

Turning and turning in the widening gyre
The falcon cannot hear the falconer;
Things fall apart; the center cannot hold;
Mere anarchy is loosed upon the world,
The blood-dimmed tide is loosed, and everywher.
The ceremony of innocence is drowned;
The best lack all conviction, while the worst
Are full of passionate intensity.

W. B. Yeats

The Ceremony of Innocence was first presented by The American Place Theatre in New York City, on December 14, 1967. It was directed by Arthur A. Seidelman; the scenery was by Kert Lundell; costumes were by Willa Kim; and the lighting was by Roger Morgan. The cast, in order of appearance, was as follows:

CAST
(*In Order of Appearance*)

FIRST MONK . . . . *Robert Shattuck*

SUSSEX . . . . *Dolph Sweet*

KENT . . . . *William Devane*

BISHOP . . . . *Ralph Clanton*

ABBOT . . . . *Peter Bosche*

ETHELRED . . . . *Donald Madden*

ALFREDA . . . . *Nancy R. Pollock*

EMMA . . . . *Olive Deering*

THULJA . . . . *Sandy Duncan*

SWEYN . . . . *Ernest Graves*

EDMUND . . . . *David Birney*

THORKILL . . . . *Howard Green*

MONKS, SERVANTS: *Oliver Lewis Bachellé, Lee J. Caldwell, Anthony T. Casco, Jr., Edward Galardo, Davidson Lloyd, Lou Prudenti, Jeffrey A. Rasi, Ronn Ridgeley, James Robiscoe, Walter Skolnik*

ACT I

The events take place in a monastery on the Isle of Wight, Christmas Day 1013, and in the castle of King Ethelred the previous winter.

ACT II

King Ethelred's castle, late summer and fall 1013, and then the Isle of Wight, Christmas evening 1013.

ACT I

PLACE AND TIME: *A monastery on the Isle of Wight, Christmas Day, 1013. Later, scene shifts to* KING ETHELRED's *castle in London, November 1012.*

SCENE: *A room in the monastery.*

ON RISE: *The stage is dark. A procession of* MONKS, *chanting and carrying lighted candles, crosses the stage and exits. After a few moments there is a steady pounding by someone on a heavy door, followed by a voice within the monastery calling out loudly,* "The door! There is someone at the door!" *The pounding continues as the lights come up. A* MONK *comes to the center of the stage. He stands looking and listening for someone to come and answer the door. When no one does, he shouts, again, and this time enraged.*

MONK: There is someone at the door! Whose business is is it to open the door! [*The pounding continues.*] It is not my business to open that door! [*When nobody comes or answers his shout, the* MONK *gives out a deep cry of rage and then exits right to open the door. When he returns it is with three men, each thoroughly chilled from the cold. One of the men,* AELFHUN, THE BISHOP OF LONDON, *whispers something to the* MONK. *The* MONK *nods, kisses the* BISHOP's *ring, and exits. The* EARL OF SUSSEX *impatiently waits for the* MONK *to leave. He is fairly bursting with what he wishes to say. The third man, the* EARL OF KENT, *stares at* SUSSEX.]

SUSSEX: I come for the king this once and then I come no more. I am not a man that begs. If he will not of his own return with us, then I have done with him.

KENT: Really?

SUSSEX: [*Emphatically*] Once I have done, I have done.

KENT: And having done with him, what will you do, Sussex? Return to your shire?

SUSSEX: I will defend my shire. I will do as my men expect of me.

KENT: Then I take it your men expect to die.

SUSSEX: If it comes to that.

KENT: Oh, rest assured, my dear Sussex, it will come to that. You will not keep the Danes out of your shire three months.

SUSSEX: Then I will not keep the Danes out three months!

KENT: [*To the* BISHOP] Listen to the logic of this.

SUSSEX: I am a soldier.

KENT: Your military credentials are always in our mind.

SUSSEX: The thought of death does not frighten me so much that I am content to grow blind imagining Ethelred will return. I come this once for the king, and then no more. If he will not defend his lands, then let the Danes have them. When they come to Sussex, they will find the land burnt beneath their feet.

KENT: Wonderful.

SUSSEX: No Danish plow will ever furrow my land.

KENT: Brilliant. [*To the* BISHOP] Sussex imagines that once his imperial skull has hit the earth the entire universe shall wind down. The spring will not come round again. The rain will not fall again. Birds will of a sudden develop black tongues and fail to offer seasonal twitterings. [*To* SUSSEX] Well, you may burn your land as you will, but the land will be washed clean again, the spring will come again, and the Danes will plant your land, eat at your table, and if they

find your bed sufficiently comfortable they will lift
their dirty boots upon it and sleep in it.

SUSSEX: No man sleeps in Sussex's bed, but Sussex!
Before they touch what is mine it will be burnt to the
ground.

KENT: [*To the* BISHOP] There you have it, Your Grace,
the military mind in all its pristine intricacy. Chop
down the trees. Poison the wells. Fire the crops. [*To*
SUSSEX] Burn less and keep more! I do not find spite
so delicious that I am willing to substitute my possessions for it.

SUSSEX: Then let Ethelred act. Let that goddamn marsh-
mallow quit this monastery. I am ready to fight. I am
ready to kill these bastard Danes.

KENT: Yes, Sussex. Yes! Yes!

SUSSEX: We waste our time coming here. Place is colder
than an Irish tit. [*Walks a few feet away. The* BISHOP
speaks to KENT.]

BISHOP: There is a monastery at Jarrow like to this one,
a place where for want of leather to make shoes the
monks go barefoot, or if they are fortunate, they find
a piece of cloth and cord and bind them about their
feet. All the winter long the wind blows along the
floor freezing the stones you kneel upon, icing even
as you pray.

KENT: Pray for what?

BISHOP: The death of the man who prays beside me, for
when he dies I shall steal his blanket, yea, and if they
think to bury him in his woolen habit, to cheat me,
to rob me of my expectations, I pray they die as
well, or that Christ gave me the cunning to steal the
wool from out the grave. I never saw a monk die at
Jarrow, but that the brothers stripped him naked
and thought themselves blessed to fall into such a
profit of clothes.

KENT: Then you are well out of such a place.

BISHOP: I have grown used to serving God in London.
Though saints and fanatics may think otherwise, I

have never served God better than I do today with pitchy fires burning in the sacristy and velvet padding stuffed beneath the kneeling rail. I pray Ethelred remembers his comforts as well.

SUSSEX: [*Overhearing some of the conversation*] Or maybe Ethelred'll sit with his ass against a stone wall and a blanket hanging over his head. That's more likely, isn't it?

KENT: You think so, Sussex? Well, with a little patience we'll find out, won't we?

SUSSEX: The son of a bitch never had the guts it takes to pull a herring out of the water.

KENT: The trouble with you, Sussex, is that you tend to judge people by the size of their mouths. I should assure you that there are some men smaller than their mouths. As a matter of fact, I should assure you that there are some men who, if they did not vent upon the void a steady stream of foul air, we should be in great danger of losing sight of entirely.

SUSSEX: You saying something to me, rosebush?

KENT: Nobody ever really says anything to you, Sussex. Haven't you ever noticed that?

SUSSEX: What's that supposed to mean? [KENT *in exasperation raises his eyes to the ceiling.* SUSSEX *imitates him.*] What's that supposed to mean?

KENT: Nothing. Absolutely nothing.

SUSSEX: What's nothing supposed to be? Some kind of philosophy? [*Raises his eyes again.*] You talking to somebody in the woodwork? [*Stares at* KENT.] Well, you can take your philosophy and piss on some flower with it, Kent. You and Ethelred make a real pack. You know what I mean, Kent? A real pack. Two fuddies without enough piss in their skirts to water a geranium.

KENT: If you'll bring your face over here, I'll water that.

BISHOP: I think it would be best if we found a way to be less argumentative.

SUSSEX: Then tell him to shut his mouth. [*Returns to*

his corner of the room.] Half the men in my shire are dead because of him and that pansy-bush of a king.

KENT: They're dead because you marched them to Grimsby without any orders.

SUSSEX: They were my men, not yours, not Ethelred's. What were we supposed to do? The truce was violated. The Danes were at Grimsby. Were we supposed to wait until they walked into London? Where were you and Ethelred when we were fighting one man to six at Grimsby? Where were you when we were dying? [*To the* BISHOP] They were sitting on their ass in London. That's where they were.

KENT: You don't look any the worse for it.

SUSSEX: [*Deeply enraged; his voice grows ominously calm.*] Sometime, Kent, when your back is to the wall, call for me.

KENT: As a matter of fact, it strikes me as somewhat odd that you have come back from Grimsby at all. Half his men lost at Grimsby, but Sussex, sworn by a blood oath to stand by these men to the death, somehow, miraculously, returns. Miracle of miracles.

SUSSEX: I could not save them.

KENT: Of course.

SUSSEX: I would have given my life to save those men.

KENT: Doubtless. [SUSSEX *moves toward* KENT. *The* BISHOP *steps between.*]

BISHOP: There is no man here, Sussex, that doubts your courage in the face of death. You have proven yourself too many times for that. [*Kent turns away. They stand for a moment in silence until* ABBOT OSWALD *enters. He goes over to the* BISHOP *and kisses his ring.*]

ABBOT: Your Grace. [*Turning to* KENT *and* SUSSEX] My lords.

BISHOP: How does King Ethelred fare today, Abbot Oswald?

ABBOT: He holds to his cell, Your Grace.

SUSSEX: [*With overt sarcasm*] At his prayers?

ABBOT: He remains at confession.

SUSSEX: So much to confess? Is there so much to confess?

ABBOT: His Majesty finds it so, my lord.

SUSSEX: Well, we find it extraordinary. Those of us closest to Ethelred have always found him so full of grace and piety that confession always seemed more a matter of form than necessity.

ABBOT: Nevertheless His Majesty is still in confession.

SUSSEX: Well, let him get done confessing. The Danes don't give a damn about him confessing.

KENT: The military situation is delicate, Reverend Father. The Danish fleet sits at Grimsby waiting only a favorable turn in the weather to sail up the Humber. Once that is accomplished England lies split in two. If the king does not move the army north within the week, King Sweyn will be in London before spring. The Danish king will take the throne of England.

SUSSEX: Then we'll all be out on our ass. Even those of us fingering beads in monasteries.

ABBOT: What you say may be true, my lords, but I cannot alter these military matters. This island sits of itself in the ocean, and we within the confines of the monastery sit walled within our devotions. We may not concern ourselves with political disputations.

SUSSEX: You may not concern yourself with political disputations? Well, you may. You may! What the hell else does the Church concern itself with if not political disputations?

ABBOT: What is it you wish of me?

KENT: Access to the king. We must speak with him.

ABBOT: He will not quit his cell, my lord; beyond the confessor he permits no one to enter.

BISHOP: Reverend Father, will you tell the king that we have come upon matters most urgent, and that we are content to wait until it pleases him to see us? We do not desire to interfere with his confession, save only that the needs of England . . .

SUSSEX: Now! We have to see him now! Tell him now!

ABBOT: I will do what I can. [*Bows to the* BISHOP *and* EARLS.] Your Grace. My lords. [*Exits.*]

SUSSEX: [*Imitating the* ABBOT] We may not concern ourselves with political disputations.

KENT: [*Violently angry*] Why don't you shut your mouth?

SUSSEX: Who the hell do you think you're talking to?

KENT: You! I'm talking to you! Save your brilliant retorts for your horse. I'm sure your horse lives for them.

BISHOP: [*Futilely*] We quarrel too much. [*They both stare at the* BISHOP. *Lights out. Lights up on a cell in the monastery. Except for a cone of light coming through a small window high up in a wall, the cell is in shadows and darkness.* ETHELRED *lies in a bed, his covers wrapped about him. He tosses restlessly. The sound of* MONKS *chanting as they go by causes him to stop moving. There is the sound of a door opening and closing.* ETHELRED *sits up. The* ABBOT *comes into the cone of light.*]

ABBOT: Your Majesty, the Bishop of London and the Earls of Kent and Sussex have come. [ETHELRED *merely looks at the* ABBOT *and wraps the blanket tighter around himself.*] Do you wish for light, Your Majesty? Shall I have candles brought to you?

ETHELRED: Is it so late?

ABBOT: The sun will be down in another hour, Your Majesty.

ETHELRED: I had thought it earlier. I had thought . . . I thought Edmund was a child again, and I took him to hunt with me. My son always liked to hunt. I remembered a day when the woods were barren. All living creatures dead. Then the hounds which had not halloed all that day began halloing. Edmund running after them. He did not wish the game to escape. "Hurry, Father, hurry." The snow so deep upon the ground I could scarcely pull my boots free. Ice caking at the top of my boot, sliding down like broken glass against my skin. "Hurry, Father, hurry. Here are the hounds. They have brought the game down." The fawn, her belly ripped open, still moved her legs in the bloody snow, little running movements. The doe, heaving her sides while the hounds tore at her throat. I would have thought she would have found a noise to make, but there was no noise. Edmund thought it a fine catch. The broken snow was like a field of crystal red dye. [*Sharply*] You have set the windows in this monastery too high. No man could ever see out of them. The monk you sent to take my confession . . . I do not wish to see him anymore.

ABBOT: Shall I send another confessor to Your Majesty?

ETHELRED: No. I have no wish for another confessor. The monk was too much traveled. Too much here and there. Where did the brothers go, the ones that passed by my door?

ABBOT: To chapel, Your Majesty. We celebrate the festival of Christmas this evening.

ETHELRED: Christmas. Again, Christmas. My son was born on Christmas Day. A cold month to be born into. [*Gets out of the bed.*] Is it a mystery, do you think, that our Lord was come into the world in such a dark month?

ABBOT: I do not know, Your Majesty.

ETHELRED: [*Disturbed*] I think it was to a purpose. Had He wished, He might have been born to a better linen, to a better time. [*Calming*] Perhaps this December birth was a way of telling us that out of darkness may come joy; that out of despair we may yet come to a new life. I have heard men who chart the heavens say that in the dead of this month, the very dead of this December month, the winter itself has already begun to die a little. That the sun which has all this time shrunk lower and lower upon the horizon now, somehow, begins to rise in its new season toward the center of the sky.

ABBOT: This astronomy may be true, Your Majesty, but I have no precise knowledge of it.

ETHELRED: No, of course, you do not have precise knowledge of it. There were men in England, scholars I brought into England, that had precise knowledge of it, but the war has chased these men out, they would not stay where the wars were constant, so now I am left with men who have no precise knowledge. No precise anything beyond the length of their battle instruments. What did my earls say to you? Were they angry?

ABBOT: They wish you to quit this monastery.

ETHELRED: And were they angry?

ABBOT: I think they be honest men. The war has made them plain in their speech.

ETHELRED: We have all become plain. An English virtue. Did they not also tell you that if I do not return and march the army north to the Humber it will go badly for England? [*The* ABBOT *nods.*] England. If I press them to it they will say not badly for England as much as badly for me. They threaten me with that: King Sweyn will come to London; the Danish king will take your throne. As if all those men rooted out of their English homes to die along the frozen Humber shall die only that I might remain squatted upon the English throne. And if I pressed further, if I drew by force of reason their arguments down to marrow, I would find, by reason, that their concern lies not with England or with England's king. Let the Danes allow them their shires, their castles, their meat and furniture, and they would not have come here this once for me. I might sit upon this island forever like Icarus in some sky-high tower counting feathers.

ABBOT: Your Majesty does his men wrong to doubt their loyalties. There is no man in England who does not serve you. Were they not loyal they would not have come.

ETHELRED: [*Looks at the* ABBOT *for a moment and then begins to laugh.*] Loyalty? It is the army they want released and only I can do that for them. That is why they have come. This is what loyalty among men is— self-seeking, illimitable, infinite, self-seeking. Forgive me, Father, I do not laugh at you. I laugh that I have come to the end of my reason and I see in front of me . . . an abyss. An abyss without end. I flattered myself thinking reason was men's joy, that reason was not madness. Reason is madness. To know reason is to know madness. Here, take your hands . . . [*Grabs* ABBOT's *hands and forces them together.*] pray for us, pray because we are dogs, pray because we do the things dogs do. Lord, forgive us our acts.

ABBOT: And so He shall, Your Majesty. Though what we do be darker than the grave, still He shall come to us lovingly.

ETHELRED: [*Dropping the* ABBOT's *hands.*] I do not wish to know that though I slew half the world yet at the end I should come to redemption. Shall I be redeemed because at the core of this skull is madness? Shall I be redeemed because this mind that teaches me I am not a dog also teaches me I cannot control myself any better than a dog. Am I God's dog? Is the King of England God's dog?

ABBOT: God never held men to be dogs, Your Majesty.

ETHELRED: How is it dogs love so to hunt? How is it with them in their kennels when their master approaches to set them loose, how eagerly they thrust their necks against their chains as if in their anxiety to be at the throats of their prey they cared not if they tore their own necks asunder? Did you not mark my earls when they spoke to you? Did they not move about the room as hounds within a kennel?

ABBOT: They moved as men move.

ETHELRED: Nay, nay. I think they moved as dogs. Even as dogs.

ABBOT: When the winter is past, events will take on a brighter coloration. Often it is this way. The season weighs upon us more heavily than the events themselves.

ETHELRED: If once I return to England there shall be many a man now living who shall never see the spring. Yet I must give my earls an answer. I must not procrastinate. This very evening at your Christmas dinner I must let them know whether I will return or hold to this monastery. They will not have it otherwise. I must learn to accustom myself to these demands.

ABBOT: Your Majesty cannot contemplate remaining here?

ETHELRED: May not a king find sanctuary where beggars are taken in? I have a feeling that these that stay locked within these walls are out of the way of God.

ABBOT: What place can be free of God?

ETHELRED: Only the ghost of God moves through these stones. Only the shadow of Him who made me moves through this mortar. Shadows of Him, shadows of others. [*As the* KING *turns and stares off into the darkness, a light gradually comes up on the motionless figures of* KENT *and* SUSSEX. *As the* KING *speaks he looks at them.*] All the faces of all the living and the dead, so many faces, and yet, as if in a dream, no, as if in a death, I have seen all the faces before. The world moves forward day by day while time moves backward memory by memory through me. [*We hear the sound of* SUSSEX's *voice coming out of the darkness of another time. The lights dim out on* ETHELRED *and come up full in his London castle.*]

SUSSEX: I cannot believe this treaty to be honorable. What answer do you have to that?

KENT: I believe the treaty to be honorable.

SUSSEX: Where is there honor for us when we sue for

peace by the payment of tribute money? Is it honorable to pay tribute money to these Danes?

KENT: If you and the army cannot prevent these Danish raids, then I believe it honorable to buy them off and have them gone.

SUSSEX: This cannot be honor.

KENT: Then think of it as sensible.

SUSSEX: I do not wish to think of it as sensible. I would not lose my honor for all the sense in the world. Why should the Danes abide this rag paper of words? Why should they not take the money we have given them and when it is safely put away find cause to strike at England again?

KENT: [*Grown increasingly exasperated*] Because their daughter will be held hostage, here, in England, here!

SUSSEX: Listen to me. I like you not, but we are English. Talk sense. This Danish daughter is nothing to them. The Danes do not love as we love. Their daughters are spewed out on the countryside like hot flies upon the cattle. Ask King Sweyn of his daughter next year and he will say to you, "Daughter? What daughter? I have left no daughter in England."

KENT: And do you say this of your own children?

SUSSEX: I do not put my children out to pawn. That is the difference between these Danes and us. This pledge of peace we have obtained from them is thin. At the first wind of trouble they will find cause to sacrifice her to their profit. I know this Sweyn. The man is cunning. He will come again upon us. Every week that passes he will say to himself, "There is England. There are the cowards that pay us money. What keeps us from them? Let us be at them."

KENT: What pledge of peace satisfies you?

SUSSEX: No pledge. There can be no pledge made that will end these wars.

KENT: These wars must go on and on, then? You see no end to them?

SUSSEX: Eventually we will achieve victory.

163

KENT: There is no end to this "eventually." For two hundred years we have waited for this "eventually."

SUSSEX: Had you a better knowledge of military matters you would know that victory is closer now for us than it has ever been.

KENT: How closer? I see no diminishment of these Danish raids. There is no less burning of our cities this year than last.

SUSSEX: They argue for peace. That they are willing to hostage their daughter to us for tribute money is an indication that they grow weary. Pay them off and they will take new heart; deny them this treaty, renew our defense, and they will flag. We will be in a position to carry the war into Denmark.

KENT: We are being destroyed by these wars. Can't you understand that?

SUSSEX: We are destroying them, that is what I understand. Where are the ships they struck at England with last year? Gone. Sunk. Down at the bottom of the channel.

KENT: Where is the cathedral at Canterbury? Burned.

SUSSEX: [*More or less mumbling to himself*] A minor loss.

KENT: Where is the port at Sandwich? Burned.

SUSSEX: No military significance.

KENT: Where is the harvest in Dorchester?

SUSSEX: A minor loss.

KENT: Burned. What satisfaction do you find in the destruction of twenty Danish ships that so outmeasures these losses?

SUSSEX: We drowned the crews of these boats. There was not a Dane that made it back to shore alive.

KENT: This is our compensation?

SUSSEX: Yes. We drowned them all. All drowned. [ETHELRED *enters and stands for a moment in the archway looking at* KENT *and* SUSSEX. *His face seems flushed, exalted. In his hand he carries a rolled-up parchment.*]

ETHELRED: [*Coming forth and holding out the parchment*] Done, my lords, done. Though at every moment a thousand arguments threatened to break forth . . . signed. England is at peace. [KENT *takes the document.* ETHELRED *walks a few feet away and sits down in his chair.*]

KENT: [*To the* KING] Then England has done well for itself.

SUSSEX: [*In an angry whisper to* KENT] There are those that think otherwise.

KENT: [*To* SUSSEX] There are always those who think otherwise.

SUSSEX: [*To* KENT] Then give us less reason to think otherwise.

ETHELRED: Sussex.

SUSSEX: My liege?

ETHELRED: In the courtyard you will find King Sweyn's animals. See to the loading of our silver upon them. [SUSSEX *angrily bows and exits.*] Kent.

KENT: Yes, Your Majesty?

ETHELRED: Go to King Sweyn's daughter and bid her fair welcome to England. Say to her England's king has now a daughter. [KENT *exits. The light in the room begins dimming until only the figure of* ETHELRED *is seen. In the dark we hear the voice of the* QUEEN MOTHER, ALFREDA. *As she speaks the lights come up on her.*]

ALFREDA: Kill the Danes, my son. If you do not kill the Danes, they will kill you.

ETHELRED: Will you still speak to me of killing?

ALFREDA: Kill the Danes, my son.

EMMA: [*As* QUEEN EMMA *begins to speak the light illuminates her, and then gradually the entire room*] I have heard, husband, that you intend to take further money out of the treasury to rebuild the shires of Cambridge and Bedford.

ETHELRED: What the Danes have laid waste to, I will rebuild.

EMMA: Who will rebuild our treasury when you have
made paupers of us all? My husband is of a mind to
teach the entire population to read and write their
language. He would put writing instruments in the
hands of farmers whose mental facilities are already
stretched beyond belief in the apish drawing of a
straight furrow across the land.

ALFREDA: It is impossible that farmers be taught beyond animals.

EMMA: If the Almighty intended these farmers for ought
else than plowing their land and obediently paying
the Church and crown their tithes, their foreheads
would not bulge out beyond their skulls nor their
tongues loll out of their mouths like the very oxen
they sleep with.

ETHELRED: You mistake the nature of men, Emma.

EMMA: Do I? I think I know the nature of men well
enough. When the Danes came to Normandy, my
father stuck poles upon the beach and every Dane
he caught within his land he strapped to a pole and
set afire. The fur coverings burnt off them with the
stink of slaughtered pig, and the smoke billowed out
in clouds across the channel. A pity none of the
stench of victory reached England. It might have
taught us better how to deal with enemies. From the
distance you would have thought the Danes candles.

ETHELRED: I am ever mindful that your father's inclina-
tions were more to the slaughterhouse than to reason;
butchery better suited his instincts than ruling.

EMMA: My father was the Duke of Normandy, husband, and he defended the borders of his domain,
and he paid no tribute to any man. But England's
king melts into religious shapes. In time Englishmen
will fight their women for a place in front of the fire
to draw out skeins of wool, or else they will put on
monks' cowls and go about vapid business through
the countryside.

ETHELRED: Neither, madam. It is only you who finds courage compassed by brutality. Let God's commandment to injure no man fall upon England. I will have this.

ALFREDA: Are you then in preparation for holy orders, my son?

ETHELRED: You give me cause to envy the Church its quiet.

EMMA: Well, there is no quiet. There is no quiet anywhere. What would you have England do? Shut itself up inside a monastery? We are loosed in a world of wolves. The fox is at the chicken, the wolf is at the fox, the Dane is at us. Is it left for the women of England to lecture their men on duty?

ETHELRED: I know what my duty is. I need no woman to tell it to me.

ALFREDA: Kill the Danes. Take our money back before Sweyn reaches the sea.

ETHELRED: The agreement is signed.

EMMA: I do not care that the agreement has been signed. This agreement is nothing to us. This is Kent's agreement. I know what mouths are at your ear. I know who is the instigator for this.

ETHELRED: Enough! The truce will not be violated.

EMMA: When the time is right, King Sweyn will take your crown and stuff it on his head. You will find your burgeoning moralities sorry comfort then. [EMMA *exits*.]

ALFREDA: We do well to keep what is ours. Though your wife be a bitch and her father a butcher, still a king may learn from them. What profits you to be reasonable, always reasonable? The state stands on your convenience. Discipline your reason to your convenience and when it no longer serves your uses, why then farewell to it and find another skin. These promises you have made to the people are good promises. Good *promises*. The people are ever in love with talk of betterments and it is wisdom to ever tell the people what they love to hear, but as you ever made promises you must ever find cause for delay.

ETHELRED: And what delay pleases you?

ALFREDA: War. War is ever the cause for delay. The cause by which all rulers come to keep their crowns and the people's contentment. Let a war stand between the promise and the fulfillment and the people will never mind it. Tut, they will thank you for it. They will think you great because you have thrust them into great wars. Not a father in England but that he will be proud to see his son come home from these wars, an arm lopped off in defense of his country. Know this or be damned for a fool: it is the people who love these wars; they will serve no man who will not give them war.

ETHELRED: I have grown sick of this counsel, madam; I do not see it thus.

ALFREDA: Neither did your stepbrother, Edward, see the knife that pierced his side, though that thrust sent him, nevertheless, to heaven. You were ever slow at seeing.

ETHELRED: Better I had been stillborn than you found cause to murder that saint.

ALFREDA: And so you cried. Ten years old and so full of tears. [*She touches* ETHELRED, *who winces and moves his arm away.*]

ETHELRED: Do not touch me. I have asked you never to touch me.

ALFREDA: Tears all morning. Tears all afternoon and night. Even when I took a candlestick and beat you till you fell to the floor, still those endless soppy tears. Edward would not have cried so much for you.

ETHELRED: Edward would have had you executed.

ALFREDA: But Edward was not my son.

ETHELRED: Nor am I, Mother. I was freak born unto you. Something found in a chamberpot thrust between your legs.

ALFREDA: [*Angrily strikes at him with her cane.* ETHEL-

168

RED *knocks the cane aside.*] Do not so quickly disavow your birth. You may yet find honest kinship of more value than pious imbecilities. You think you have found an ally for yourself in the bishops of England? It was they who saw to it that Edward was crowned and not you. It was they upon Edward's death that had to be dragged to the Cathedral to anoint you, and that was done only under the greatest duress.

ETHELRED: Did you expect them to rush to the cathedral with the son of a murderess!

ALFREDA: I expect nothing of them save that they serve the cause of their own interests. They are lackeys to every wind.

ETHELRED: They are in agreement with me. There is no bishop in England who does not support this truce.

ALFREDA: No! They are not your men though you tattooed your name on their skulls and branded the seal of England to their ass. Oh, they will support this truce as long as it is convenient for them to do so. Why shouldn't they? What you aren't giving away to the Danes in tribute, you're giving to them. They wouldn't care if we were reduced to shelling clams in a mud hut if they could get a single spire on their cathedrals out of it.

ETHELRED: [*Pulling* ALFREDA *very close to him.*] You will grow old, Mother, and older, and you will sicken and you will die, and still there will be no war in England. And when you die I will bury you in some orchard newly planted and in the turning of the slow seasons you will feel the sound of fruit dropping upon you and you will know that as you saw the world and hated it, there was once in England a king found who would not have it so.

ALFREDA: Fool! [ALFREDA *exits. Lights dim down on the* KING, *and then, blackout. Lights up on King Sweyn's daughter,* THULJA, *talking to* KENT.]

THULJA: What I really like to do is swim. I can swim

for . . . oh, about a mile. I'm probably the best swimmer among my sisters. I have five sisters. We're all girls in my family. No boys. My sister Emily was supposed to be a boy. A lot of the witches and stargazers said that, but then my mother bumped into a female goat before Emily was born and so she turned out to be a girl. You have any girls?

KENT: I have a daughter.

THULJA: She as old as I am?

KENT: She's fourteen.

THULJA: I'm fifteen. I should be getting some marriage offers soon.

KENT: I would imagine so, Thulja. You're very pretty.

THULJA: Do you really think so?

KENT: Yes.

THULJA: I don't know. I was under consideration last year by a German baron, but it didn't work out. I think he wanted somebody fatter, somebody with jowls. He kept pulling my cheeks to see if they would puff out, and when they wouldn't he got very angry and started spitting into his beard, and my cousin, Thorkill, who doesn't like the Germans very much, hit him in the face with a fruit bowl. There was a bad argument after that, I can tell you. Everybody was sticking their knives into the table. I really lost my chances there, I can tell you.

KENT: I wouldn't be too disturbed about it, Thulja. I think it's always wise as a matter of policy to reject the first offer that comes along.

THULJA: Yes, I think so. I agree with you very much. I'll show you something. [THULJA *goes over to her trunk and pulls out a variety of clothes. She finally comes to a gray wolf fur.*] This is a wolf fur. You put it on your feet and no matter how cold it gets your feet stay warm. My father gave it to me. [*Returns to her rummaging.*] This is muskrat. You wind it around your neck to keep the wind out. Your daughter have a fur like this?

KENT: No.

THULJA: What does she use to walk out with, then?

KENT: She doesn't walk out much. My daughter's been ill for some time.

THULJA: Oh. I'm sorry for that. What's her name?

KENT: Catherine. [THULJA *looks for a few moments at her muskrat, and then, impetuously, thrusts it forward to* KENT.]

THULJA: I give her this. Tell her Thulja says hello to Catherine and wishes her to be well. [KING SWEYN *enters.*]

SWEYN: I think we are not much liked in this court, daughter. I have not entered a room today but that some one or two English quit it.

KENT: There are some not yet reconciled to the treaty, Your Majesty. In time they shall be brought to an understanding of it.

SWEYN: Yet I think there be many earls in England who have not signed this truce, earls brought to the conference table by your king to sign who would not sign. Perhaps when time or occasion gives them opportunity they think to turn their silence into blacker shape.

KENT: Then I pray there be no occasion. We have all dwelt long enough within the slaughterhouse.

SWEYN: So pray all of us and yet war follows war. This money given by Ethelred for partial settlement of our claims against this island, though somewhat generous, is still little welcomed by many of my countrymen. They urge me, even as they pack their saddlebags with English silver, to give over any monetary settlement with England. "Return the money," they say. "What shall we do when the spring comes and we wish to fight the English? What good shall money do us when we cannot fight?"

KENT: What good shall money do them when they are dead? Let these men, these always angry warriors, learn to be content with less than killing, or if nothing less than killing will satisfy them, why then let them find a place so barren, so inimical to life that no living creature will touch it, and there let them hack each other to pieces. Let them do what they will with one another, save that the rest of us are free of them. I think we are not so well off, none of us, that we can afford stupidity forever. Somewhere we come to the end of it, somewhere stupidity runs out.

SWEYN: If it be so, let it be now. I have put my signature to these peace instruments and my daughter's life lies pledged to them. Another time shall not suit me as well. Make no mistake, my lord, if in spite of these earnest declarations war comes again, none of us shall see the end to it. Hatreds will have grown only the more violent for this treaty having been made and our pledges lost. [*Putting his arm around* THULJA] Our dearest pledges.

KENT: I wish Your Majesty safe voyage home. [*Exits.* SWEYN *looks after him.*]

SWEYN: [*Almost to himself*] I think though England's king signed this document the better part of it lies in that man. I had not thought the English so rich. [*Directly to* THULJA] They speak well, those English, the ones that choose to speak.

THULJA: I like those English I have spoken to, Father. The Earl of Kent has a daughter who is my age. Her name is Catherine. She's been sick for a long time and because of the sickness she can't go out much. I think I will probably become very friendly with Catherine. What will probably happen is that she will come visiting me here, or if she can't do that, what I will probably do is visit her. She shouldn't sit alone. Not having any sisters, she's probably left alone too much. I will have to see that something is done about that.

SWEYN: Thulja, do not become . . . [SWEYN *finds it difficult to express some of his thoughts to* THULJA.] too . . . too quickly involved with these English. Be a little less ready to pour, as it were. I don't know how to say this to you. You tend to pour yourself too quickly into things. You understand what I'm saying?

THULJA: No, father.

SWEYN: Here, sit down beside me for a moment. I am leaving you with the English for a while not because the English are giving us money for a truce, though that's part of it because we have just claims against the English and they must be satisfied, but that is not the main reason. The main reason is that many of our countrymen have settled in England and up until now the English have not treated them very well.

THULJA: Why, Father?

SWEYN: Because they were foreigners here, and foreigners are never treated very well. In a hundred years these Danish families will be more English than the English, but meanwhile we must remember that they are still Danes and that they must be protected in this new land. King Ethelred has agreed that he will respect these countrymen of ours and put them under the protection of English law, if I agree to this treaty, which I have done.

THULJA: Will I stay here a long time?

SWEYN: Three years. Do you think three years is a long time, Thulja?

THULJA: I will be eighteen years old.

SWEYN: Yes.

THULJA: That's pretty old.

SWEYN: It will not seem so to you, Thulja, when you are eighteen.

THULJA: They didn't want to take anybody else?

SWEYN: Only another of my daughters. Should I have taken another?

THULJA: I'm the oldest. I guess the oldest was the best choice.

SWEYN: I thought so.

THULJA: If you took Margaret or Emily they would have cried all the time. They're terrible criers.

SWEYN: Then I have made the best choice?

THULJA: Yes. I agree with you.

SWEYN: Good. Now I want to tell you some things about the English. When you meet them, you must always remember their names and their titles. There is nothing the English love so much as their names and titles. If you have any trouble remembering them, be sure to get a little book and write them out. Now, when they talk to you, do not be in too much of a hurry to part from them. Find out what they want. You understand what I am saying? [THULJA *nods her head, but* SWEYN *is not convinced.*] What I'm saying is find out what they're saying behind what they're saying. When you were in Denmark it was all right to smile and be pleasant, but this is not Denmark. The English do not understand pleasantness the way we do. Too many smiles and they will begin to think you are being cunning about something. I know you are not a cunning child, but they do not know this of you. This does not mean you should not smile. There is nothing better for a young girl than to be seen smiling, but not smiling too much, just now and then, appropriate smiles, that's what I'm saying, appropriate smiles. You, on the other hand, must not confuse their habit of blunt speech as a sign that they are not concealing something. When people prize bluntness as a virtue they soon learn to conceal things bluntly. Now, at confession do not confess too much. Some of the bishops do not always remember that they were anointed by God. They remember better that they were appointed by the king, and between what some remember and others forget sometimes a word trickles out. [*Looks at her a moment.*] You do not find this too much at one time?

THULJA: No, Father.

SWEYN: Good. [*Pulls out a piece of paper.*] From your

mother: Keep your hair free from all animal grease
in that such grease has a tendency to become rancid
after a few days. Keep your teeth clean especially
mornings and evenings . . . well, there's no use reading this, I will leave it for you. [*Gives her the paper.*]
When you return to Denmark I shall have something
very good for you.

THULJA: What?

SWEYN: What would you like most?

THULJA: Furs.

SWEYN: Something better than furs.

THULJA: What's better than furs?

SWEYN: A husband.

THULJA: [*Not too happy*] The German ask me to wife
again?

SWEYN: Not the German! This time you will have your
choice. Whoever pleases you.

THULJA: I don't want anybody with a beard.

SWEYN: Then you will have somebody without a beard.
Somebody just to your liking. I promise you that.
[*Takes her hand.* THULJA *lifts her* FATHER's *hand to
her cheek.*] You are the best of all my daughters,
Thulja. The very best. [KENT *enters.*]

KENT: Your horses have been brought onto the road,
Your Majesty.

SWEYN: I must leave now, Thulja. Remember all that
I have told you. [*Hugs her.*] God be with you. [*Quickly
exits. For a long moment* THULJA *just stands looking
after her* FATHER.]

KENT: If you look out the window, Thulja, you'll be
able to see your father leave. [THULJA *slowly goes
over to the window, more out of a desire to obey
than to wish to see the departure.*] Do not be too
sad. We are all of us, in life, parting from each other,
sometimes for hours, sometimes for years. But even
after the longest time we find each other again, and
are made the more joyful for having been separated
and having been found.

THULJA: [*Staring out the window*] The snow is so deep now. The horses move so stiffly, I cannot tell which horse carries my father. All the men and horses look the same to me. The wind and snow blows upon them so heavily. [*Turning to* KENT] Can you see my father, Lord Kent? [*Kent looks out the window.*] Do you see which horse he rides upon? [EDMUND, KING ETHELRED'S *son, enters unseen. He is armed and wears the clothes he has hunted in.*]

KENT: They are all gone into the snow, Thulja. I cannot see them anymore.

EDMUND: Then let them be gone. It would seem King Sweyn, unlike some of the lilies in this court that bloom and bloom long after their perfume has become offensive, knows best instinctively how to open with dispatch and fold timely upon profit. [*He looks at* THULJA *for a few moments. She smiles.* EDMUND *smiles back.*] Is this Danish flower to be an annual, my lord?

KENT: The tribute payment to the Danes will be renewed each three years, my lord, Edmund.

EDMUND: Then I pray we are most fertile in England so that we will be able to afford this plant that is now to blossom upon us every third year.

KENT: We shall be fertile enough to meet our obligations.

EDMUND: For I fear if our English soil becomes sucked dry in the feeding of it, we shall be forced to find some new blood to water it. Tell my father I have returned from my hunting, Lord Kent.

KENT: As you wish. [*Starts to exit.*]

EDMUND: Not as I wish! As my father wishes. We do in England what my father wishes . . . while my father be king. [KENT *has turned around to face him.*] Though England today has lost forty-eight thousand marks of silver to the Danes, yet we all consider ourselves in great fortune having gained . . . what is it we have gained, Kent?

KENT: Peace.

EDMUND: Yes. Peace. I noticed the change immediately upon entering this room. There is an air of peace thickly laid throughout. No doubt in time we shall all grow dizzy in the breathing of it. [KENT *exits.* EDMUND *again stares at* THULJA. *He smiles.* THULJA *returns the smile. The smile drains from* EDMUND'S *face as quickly at it came.* THULJA *becomes uneasy.* EDMUND *smiles again, the grin distorted, artificial.*] Is that chest a present to the English court?

THULJA: It's mine.

EDMUND: But I think it must not be. I think as your father has taken a chest from my father, a very heavy chest, like as not he intended this chest as a tangible exchange.

THULJA: It's only my clothes.

EDMUND: And yet it looks to be very heavy. Undoubtedly there is something of value for England in it. May I see what's in it? [THULJA *hesitates for a moment and then opens her chest.*]

THULJA: This is a wolf fur for the feet. You keep it on your feet and they stay warm.

EDMUND: Do they?

THULJA: Yes. I have also brought some very good shoes for the summer.

EDMUND: Did you?

THULJA: Yes [THULJA *starts digging into her trunk for them. She pulls out her shoes and hands them to* EDMUND.] My sister, Hilda, made them for me. They're sewn very well. You can see how straight the stiches are. [EDMUND *calmly, deliberately, begins ripping them.*] Don't do that! What are you doing? [*She tries to get her shoes back, but* EDMUND *keeps them out of her reach as he continues ripping them.*]

EDMUND: I don't think they're made well at all. I think they're very cheap. [*He throws the shoes away.* THULJA *runs after them.*] I think everything you've brought us is very cheap. [*He sticks his hand in the chest and begins ripping and throwing her clothes all over the room.*] This is cheap. And this is cheap. And this is cheap. You have taken our money and left us cheap merchandise. [THULJA *keeps running around the room trying to gather up her clothes.*]

THULJA: What are you doing? Leave my clothes alone. Stop it! Stop it!

EDMUND: Everything here is cheap! Cheap! Cheap! [ETHELRED, *followed by* BISHOP AELFHUN *and* KENT, *enter.* THULJA *runs over to* KENT. ETHELRED *grabs* EDMUND'*s arm.*]

ETHELRED: Stop it! [EDMUND *in a deliberate show of strength slowly forces his arm free and then calmly, contemptuously drops the piece of clothing.*] Are you a madman? Do you do what you do in some nightmare?

EDMUND: She gave me cause to be provoked.

THULJA: I did nothing. I gave him no cause.

ETHELRED: What cause? [EDMUND *says nothing.*] What cause did she give you to be provoked?

EDMUND: I have forgotten it now. Perhaps in a while I will remember it again.

KENT: [*To* ETHELRED] My liege, shall I take the girl to her room? [ETHELRED *nods and* KENT *begins leading* THULJA *out.* THULJA *looks over to her trunk.*] Leave the trunk here, Thulja. [*They exit.*]

ETHELRED: [*To* EDMUND] Give me a cause! Or have you grown so malignant you can no longer find reason for what you do?

EDMUND: Her nose seemed crooked to me.

BISHOP: This is not a reason, my lord.

EDMUND: And yet I think it is a reason. When I entered the room her nose began to grow. It appeared to grow longer and longer until the tip of it curved upward against the ceiling. I was appalled that God should make a foreign nose so arrogant that it should be forever pointed at an English ceiling.

ETHELRED: Do not be overcunning with me, Edmund. I have grown weary of overcunning speech.

EDMUND: Directly after you instructed the lord treasurer to bring the tribute money into this room where it would be handy for the Danes to get at, I encountered him here. "Where would it please Your Majesty to have the money set down?" he said to me. His voice seemed to be coming from the edges of the world. I could hardly hear him. I did not answer. Again, this time coming closer, "Where would it please Your Majesty to have the money set down?" Again I failed to hear him. A third time, "Where shall the money be set down?" "Why, by the throne, Lord Treasurer, by the throne." And all the time a little word kept rising up in my thoughts, but, by my *honor,* I could not bring myself to remember what this word was. It was a little insect of a word no bigger than a flea's prick into the blood. A sort of word a soldier might with *honor* find bloodied about on the battlefield. And I thought: no matter, when I see it in England again I will remember it. "Is all the money here, Lord Treasurer?" "Yes, my lord." "Not a mark missing?" "No, my lord." "Why then, I shall remember you this day for honesty."

ETHELRED: Where is the honesty in your speaking, Edmund? You give too much honesty and none. What would you have me do?

EDMUND: Stuff the bodies of forty-eight thousand lord treasurers into that box before honor sold for so cheap a price.

ETHELRED: Do not belabor me with hyperboles. What would you have me do?

EDMUND: I would have the Danes die, or shut all the rainy puddles and skies of England in that box that I might chop off the hand of the thief that reached for it.

BISHOP: There has been too much chopping, Edmund. We are approaching a time of less chopping.

EDMUND: [*To* BISHOP] Be cunning or be dead. There is no kindness among nations. [*To* ETHELRED] Sweyn has fed on our blood, and now moves away, but in a little while he will grow hungry remembering where he feasted last. He will come back again, he will take this realm and have you dead that his spawn may lay their eggs upon my inheritance.

ETHELRED: I am not of your mind.

EDMUND: I know what mind you are of. It is a mind that keeps to books and beds and between the pages of one and the sheets of the other no man can give you the limits. You would sooner lolly in court belly-high with cowards than preserve by battle what is mine! [ETHELRED *in his momentary rage raises his arm to strike* EDMUND. EDMUND *does not move. He lowers his arm*.] Strike me! Strike me!

ETHELRED: I want these constant invasions by the Danes to end. If money will do it, then let money do it. We will replenish our treasury if there is peace, but if the wars continue all the soldiers in Christendom will not save this land.

EDMUND: The old kings of England did not think so, nor did her old bishops think so. When the Danes gutted with fire the town of Canterbury and the cathedral there, when the Danes held the Archbishop of Canterbury for ransom of only three thousand marks, he chose to have his head bashed in rather than be so redeemed.

BISHOP: And so he died.

EDMUND: And so he died. Time was when no man in England was so finicky about death. Time was when the bishops and kings of England stood with her yeomen on the cliffs, swords back to the earbone, daring the world to set foot in this land.

BISHOP: You remember a time that is past.

EDMUND: Is it now not economically advantageous to have England's bishop down at the Dover cliffs with a drawn battleaxe?

ETHELRED: No. Nor is it wisdom to incur property damage in excess of a hundred thousand marks every time the Danes invade. I do not mention to you the wanton slaughter of our countrymen that is likewise averted, since you account vaunting words and military honor in far greater esteem than simple living.

BISHOP: Believe me, my lord, the act of staying alive in a land covered with frost and sickness deserves some consideration by the crown, if only because men are so easily made willing to squander their lives away for any adventure properly presented to them by those in power.

EDMUND: I do not think men squander their lives in defense of their land. I do not like the sound of that word.

BISHOP: Well, choose another word, Edmund, still death will be attached to it.

EDMUND: And what do you attach to *love* of this land?

ETHELRED: Death. Death. It always comes to death.

EDMUND: Then I think Death has become King of England, the fellow is never out of conversation. If death is all that concerns the living, then let's fold our palms up to God and pray for speedy funerals.

BISHOP: Be a little less hot, my lord. Excess is not a virtue for all occasions.

EDMUND: A soldier would think it so.

ETHELRED: [*Suddenly grown very angry*] Well, you are not a soldier! You are heir to the throne of England, and though you stood a thousand years upon the battlefield and took a hundred wounds you would not be a soldier. This crown serves England, not the battlefield. All your arguments are the arguments of a fool! [EDMUND *starts to leave.* ETHELRED *runs after and grabs his arm tightly.*] You listen to me! The Danish raids have reduced this land to barbarity. There is not a shire from Norfolk to Sussex free of famine and murder. Out of fear of the Danes kinsmen do not protect their kinsmen any more than they would protect a stranger. Fathers sell their sons into foreign slavery for a price; women caught alone in their own yards are set upon by men one after the other like dogs copulating in each other's filth. I do not have a bishop left in my country north or south of the Humber that can translate a simple Latin religious service into English. I have no men that can lay simple stone on stone, fix the simplest injury to a horse. I want these men back from the Continent. I want the cathedrals rebuilt. I want this country whole again. [EDMUND *pulls his arm free.*] You will help me hold this truce, Edmund. [EDMUND *exits.* ETHELRED *shouts down the hall after him.*] You will help me hold this truce! Edmund! Edmund!

END OF ACT I

ACT II

TIME: *A night in late August 1013.*

PLACE: KING ETHELRED'S *study.*

ON RISE: ETHELRED, KENT, *and* BISHOP AELFHUN *sit around a table littered with the work of a long day. A small model of a boat rests on the floor.*

ETHELRED: [*Reading a document*] I am aware of Abbot Taunton's desire for a new mill, Aelfhun. However, what I should like to see is Abbot Taunton made aware of needs other than the piling up of wealth for his order. The man and his monastery have the largest hoard of silver south of the Humber River. These continuous professions of his to poverty amaze me. I know of no other abbot in England whose common dinner plate is silver and who yet requires crown money before he will build a needed mill. [*To* KENT] How long before the scholar from Aquitaine will finish making these books?

KENT: By the spring, my liege.

ETHELRED: [*Signing the document*] No later than the spring, then. You may tell him that if I can find another scholar to help him I will. I would have these books finished and in use as quickly as possible. [*Gives the document to* KENT.]

BISHOP: I assure Your Majesty that the amount of silver held by the Sheffield monastery is nowhere near the sum commonly assumed.

ETHELRED: I know not what is commonly assumed, Aelfhun, but it would appear they have sufficient silver to commonly dine upon it.

BISHOP: It was only used for the occasion of your visit, Your Majesty. They thought to please you by a show of good service. Come upon them another day and you shall find them using wood.

ETHELRED: I hope so, Aelfhun. It is not pleasing to see a priest grown fat in the service of God.

BISHOP: Shall I say, then, to Abbot Taunton that he shall have his windmill?

EMMA: [*Entering in time to catch the* BISHOP's *sentence*] Shall you come to bed, husband?

ETHELRED: Within the hour, Emma. There is some work I must do.

EMMA: [*Coming forward to face the* KING] I am tired and would like to sleep.

ETHELRED: I shall come to you within the hour, as soon as I have finished what I am doing, Emma.

EMMA: If you have hopes of . . . speaking to me before we fall asleep, you will put this work by until another time. If once I fall asleep, I shall sleep without waking till morning.

ETHELRED: [*Looks at* EMMA *for a moment and then begins speaking to the* BISHOP. EMMA, *her anger mounting, listens for some moments, and then turns and leaves.*] You may tell Abbot Taunton that if he will set aside a fifth of his profits from the present mills and use them for the purchase of books for his monks that they may become as literate as they are plump, we will extend to him a goodly portion of his construction cost. And if he will set aside a small room within the monastery so that the farmers who use the windmills and pay the monastery for the use of those mills can receive some simple instruction in the addition and subtraction of numbers, we shall give to him an even larger amount toward the construction cost.

BISHOP: And how shall they obtain the full money for this windmill?

ETHELRED: Let them also teach these farmers how to write their names and read a bill of sale and I shall send enough money to Sheffield to cover the cost of the mill in its entirety.

BISHOP: They are not used to this. The monasteries have always kept for their own uses all the money earned from the farmers.

ETHELRED: Then let them become used to different practices. I wish the people who dwell within these shires to thrive as well as these monks. That is also important to me, Aelfhun. I do not wish to see Englishmen in their ignorance and hunger begging for food along the side of English roads. If English families continue to die of hunger what are the fruits of this peace, this dearly paid-for peace, to them? [*Becoming more gentle*] Come, Aelfhun, we have always been in agreement that if our people are to be helped, money must be set aside to do it. This you have said yourself.

BISHOP: I have spoken of crown money, Your Majesty. Secular needs must be met by the crown, not the Church.

ETHELRED: Food and the knowledge to keep from starving are not secular needs, Aelfhun. The Church cannot expect all these costs to be placed upon the royal treasury. Let the Church contribute a little and we shall contribute a little, and little by little we shall do all that we have set out to do.

BISHOP: We assumed that all the money would come from the royal treasury. [ETHELRED *just stares at the* BISHOP.] If Your Majesty will permit me, I should like to retire now. The day has been long.

ETHELRED: Yes, of course. Good night, Aelfhun.

BISHOP: Good night, Your Majesty. [*To* KENT] My lord. [*He exits as* ETHELRED *continues to stare after him.*]

KENT: Shall we go over the plans for the construction of Master Lombardi's boat, Your Majesty? The Florentine would like to secure his lumber no later than the end of this summer.

ETHELRED: [*Still looking after the departed* BISHOP] We pull apart from each other, Kent. [*Turning to* KENT] I know not how it is, but like some coil of metal cunningly wound about my foot, each step I would take to cure these ills of England becomes more difficult than the last. Though Aelfhun seems ever in agreement, he is ever not in agreement, so, too, my other lords. Each plan provokes a quarrel, each quarrel a delay. We are at peace in this land but we cannot bring it to profit.

KENT: Men are reasonable, my liege; they will choose the path of reason.

ETHELRED: I think reason teaches my nobles where self-advancement lies. They do what profits them. If they can keep within my grace, well, then, well; and if not, not. They give a kind of mouthed loyalty to what I would do and then stand like stone upon self-interest and their properties.

KENT: Then you must bend them until they are more serviceable. It is not fitting that any man disturb what you do by thrusting his personal advancement before it. We all bear to the commonwealth a duty. Let there be in England contempt for men who will not serve their country, they deserve nothing better.

ETHELRED: How sure you are. I am sure of nothing. Thirty-five years since my brother Edward's death, and I am still sure of nothing. [*Standing up and looking about the room*] They made this room for him that he might have a place to be alone when he was king. The books on the shelf are all Edward's books; this chair, this table, all Edward's. The window was cut for him when he was twelve because he loved what was beautiful and it pleased my father to please

Edward. All made for Edward when he would be king.

KENT: And now Your Majesty is king and in you all that Edward might have done is done. There is Edward's monument and England's victory: what was lost in a death is found again.

ETHELRED: Is it? They hated me, the bishops, they whose love for Edward was as nothing to mine. And what was my ambition? That I might fish with him in the sea caves of Cardiff? That through a summer's day I might hang upon his sleeve? That I might sleep by his side in the forest? That was all my ambition. They made him a saint only that I might be spited. Kneeling there in the cathedral, tears scalding my face, not yet ten years old, I heard a priest whisper, "Bastard," as the gold circled upon my head.

KENT: [*Coming forward and touching the* KING] This is old time, my liege. It is half a lifetime since Edward's death.

ETHELRED: Nay. Just now, he dies. Just now the knife scrapes the bone, the eyes come down, the body folds. Who would have thought so much perfection could die? [*Looking directly at* KENT] Come to me tomorrow. I shall find a good stand of oak for this Florentine boatmaker.

KENT: [*Kneeling*] Good night, my liege. [*Exits.* ETHELRED *covers his eyes with his hands and then, recovered, reaches for a small lodestone attached to a string. He spins it, almost idly, and watches as it comes to a stop. There is a noise in the hall.*]

ETHELRED: Who is that? Kent, is it you?

THULJA: [*Sticking her head into the room*] It's me, Thulja. (ETHELRED *gestures for her to come in. She hesitantly comes forward.*] I saw the light.

ETHELRED: Come in. Come in.

THULJA: Everybody else is sleeping.

ETHELRED: Yes, I would think so. It's very late. Why are you not sleeping?

THULJA: [*Shrugs her shoulders.*] I keep trying to sleep, but I can't stay asleep. I'm turning into a bad sleeper.

ETHELRED: [*Touching a chair near him*] Here, sit by me. [*She sits down.*]

THULJA: I saw Edmund this morning. He was throwing spears into a target. He's very good. He didn't miss a single throw.

ETHELRED: Did you speak with him? [*She shakes her head.*] Why not?

THULJA: Because he doesn't talk to me. I say "Good morning" or "Good afternoon" every time I see him, but he never says anything to me. He sneers a lot. That's what he does. He's a very good sneerer.

ETHELRED: I'm afraid you're right, Thulja, though nobody will mention it to him.

THULJA: Well, they should. He does it all the time. [*Giving a few sneers to bring home her point*] That's what he does. It's very difficult to talk to someone when they do that. [*Looking at the lodestone*] Is that the stone that always points to the north?

ETHELRED: Yes.

THULJA: How may a stone know one direction from another?

ETHELRED: I don't know, Thulja.

THULJA: Does Master Lombardi? [ETHELRED *shakes his head.*] What I think is that it's been charmed. In Denmark we sometimes get small fiends caught in things and then they do strange things when they want to get out. When they get trapped in a milk bucket because you put a lid on it too fast, you can hear them pushing at the lid after a while and if you don't let them out they spoil the milk. We get a lot of buckets of milk soured that way.

ETHELRED: You think Master Lombardi has put a little fiend in this stone of his?

THULJA: Maybe the fiend got trapped all by itself. They're always getting themselves into trouble like that. Usually it's in trees, though. They like to go in trees a lot because it's dark and nobody can get at them. I guess they don't care for people much. Is that Master Lombardi's boat?

ETHELRED: It's a model for his boat, Thulja. And these are the charts for it. If we hold to these specifications Master Lombardi shall build us a boat larger than any boat that has ever been built, her sails alone will blot the sun from my entire courtyard.

THULJA: What's he going to do with such a big boat?

ETHELRED: Sail the West Sea.

THULJA: The ocean? [ETHELRED *nods his head.*] The whole ocean?

ETHELRED: [*He reaches out to touch her.*] The whole ocean. He wants to put out from England and sail for as long as the flood of the sea flows below his ship.

THULJA: Well, the serpents won't let him do that.

ETHELRED: I think he thinks there are no serpents, Thulja.

THULJA: Well, there are. Even up in Denmark we have serpents. I can't tell you how many boats are sunk by them. And after the serpents, you come to the abyss where everything falls over. Even the sun falls over.

ETHELRED: And yet the sun comes back to us, does it not? So, too, we hope, shall Master Lombardi.

THULJA: I think if he goes out on the ocean he will die. Nobody·ever comes back from the West Sea. They all die there.

ETHELRED: Do you fear then so much for a man you have never met, Thulja?

THULJA: Yes.

ETHELRED: Then I think Denmark has surely sent us her gentlest daughter. I fear for Master Lombardi, too, Thulja. He sees, in his mind, lands where rivers flow against banks of gemmy diamonds, and common trees bend with branches of golden filament, and by his dreamings we are made all full of longing for what may be only dreams. Yet men have set out for causes far worse than this and in their determination accomplished good. We cannot always know the end of things. If the boat will do it, and if this stone be true as it appears, England may sail an ocean and take hold in strange lands. How good the time seems to me for all good things. [*Lights out. Deep rhythmic sound of a beating drum. Upstage, on a raised level, we see the figure of* EDMUND *dimly lit upon a bridge. In his hand he holds a large battle-ax. As he speaks, describing the events, he becomes engaged in combat with his foes. The light upon the scene is red now, and the action stylized into slow motion.*]

EDMUND: In my hunting I came upon a stream spanned by a footbridge so narrow only a single man might pass. As I made to cross, four Danes approached from the other side, four farmers who bore in their hands their staves and hoes. Though I had been first upon the bridge, they said I might not pass until it pleased them. They claimed the right to a first crossing because they were Danes and I English. They shouted at me that I was to return and wait their passing. I would not wait. I would not go back. And when I reached the other side one raised his hand as if to strike me. I slew him. And when the second rose against me I slew him, and he fell where the first had fallen. Where the others fled from me, I pursued. Though they sought to lock themselves within their houses, I would not let them go. I overtook them and in my rage that they had raised their hands against me, slew them. I severed their heads from their bodies. I broke their skulls. [*When* ED-MUND *is finished speaking, he stands alone amid the bodies of those he has slain. The drum stops. Lights out. A spotlight comes up on each of the ensuing speakers.*]

ALFREDA: This was well done.

SUSSEX: It was a kindness to allow those Danes who had settled in this land to remain. A kindness abused.

EMMA: My father would not tolerate any Danes in Normandy. Where he caught them, he burned them.

BISHOP: They had no weapons. They were farmers.

KENT: They were protected by treaty.

EMMA: Then let them not speak. Let them not stand by the bridges of this country and tell a king's son he may not pass.

EDMUND: I was first to the bridge. I was midway upon my crossing.

ALFREDA: [*Going to him and addressing him*] And so you should have been first to cross.

EMMA: [*Touching* EDMUND, *almost caressing him*] Had they been midway and you not yet upon the bridge, yet they should have turned and permitted you first crossing. They are an insolent people.

SUSSEX: They interpret the truce as a sign of English weakness. They grow bolder the more we grow reluctant.

ALFREDA: Once given permission to farm the land they conceived it a right. Once conceiving it a right, they learned to abuse all who crossed upon it. They thought their insolence safe within a treaty.

EMMA: [*To* EDMUND] Ever these Danes confuse good intentions with fear. When my father burned them they stunk like pigs.

BISHOP: Their death was too great a penalty for the offense. As they were but farmers . . .

ALFREDA: [*Turning on the* BISHOP] There were four of them. Four.

SUSSEX: [*To* BISHOP] If they did not wish to provoke a battle, they should not have raised their hands to strike.

ALFREDA: [*To* BISHOP] When farmers grow vindictive, what children shall they spawn upon us?

EDMUND: As he made to strike me, he brushed against me. The hard wool of his jacket infuriated me. Had he kept his distance, had he not brushed against me, I might have grown no more than angry. I drove my knife through his jacket and into his heart. The touch of him offended me.

EMMA: It would have gone well for them if they had not touched you.

SUSSEX: It is not for them to stand so near to us.

EDMUND: When the first had fallen, the second struck at my genitals with his staff. My groin burned with his blow. I drove my ax upon his skull. Like a white flower slit, I cleaved his skull.

EMMA: My father would not bury them.

BISHOP: If they are Christian, they should be buried.

KENT: Our honor was pledged to their protection.

SUSSEX: Let them stay in their own land. They should not have come to this land.

BISHOP: [*Becoming less charitable*] Sometimes these farmers have been insolent. Sometimes they farm the land and offer nothing back to the Church.

ALFREDA: To kill a Dane is not to kill a Christian. They pay nothing to the Church. Wherefore should the Church concern itself with them? Those who live like animals should not expect to be protected like men.

KENT: They were men.

ALFREDA: Unchristian, unmannered. They were something less than men.

EMMA: My father would not bury them. He hated the touch of them.

ALFREDA: They were dogs upon our land. When a dog dies he is left to be embalmed by the wind and rain. There are no special ceremonies over the death of a dog.

BISHOP: Lacking baptism, responsibilities are lessened. We are not truly obliged to see this as a Christian death. Their baptism is not clear. I have no knowledge of their baptism.

EDMUND: He fell against me. The weight of his body pitched against me. The others sought to flee.

KENT: And so you might have stopped.

EDMUND: I overtook them, and in my rage I slew them.

[*Lights out. In the dark we hear* ETHELRED *shout out:*]

ETHELRED: Do not justify murder to me! I will not listen to justification! [*Lights up full. Present, besides* ETHELRED, *are* BISHOP AELFHUN, *the* EARL OF KENT, *and* EDMUND.]

BISHOP: Your Majesty mistakes me if he conceives I justify the slaying of these Danes. My wish is only to ameliorate a quarrel already grown too sharp between himself and Prince Edmund.

ETHELRED: You justify these murders by your constant reminder to us that these deaths were not Christian deaths.

BISHOP: I merely wish to bring to His Majesty's attention that the Church does not consider the death of a non-Christian quite the same thing as the death of a Christian.

ETHELRED: How not "quite"? Give me an answer that if I meet a sane man in this world I might give it to him.

BISHOP: The murder of a Christian in possession of a soul causes injury to that soul, whereas a non-Christian, unbaptized and lacking a soul, receives injury to the body alone. Crimes against the body are crimes against what is mortal in us, crimes against the soul which God has placed within His Christians are crimes against what is immortal in us and therein crimes against the Almighty himself. The offense involved in killing a non-Christian can therefore in no ways be measured as heavily. To do so is a mockery of God.

ETHELRED: This is a plague of words. Murder made reasoned. Reason made murdered. I will not be reconciled to cunning.

BISHOP: What will reconcile Your Majesty to his son? If we do not yoke ourselves together, our discord will only serve to Danish advantage.

ETHELRED: [*Pointing an accusing finger at* EDMUND]

Let that homicide be contrite. Let him be set to public acts of penance that we may come before Denmark with our hands clean of murder.

EDMUND: No! You will not shame me before them.

ETHELRED: Wherefore did you kill farmers, homicide?

EDMUND: That they might not kill me. Should I have bowed to them and backed off the bridge? Is this what Englishmen are set to in their own country?

ETHELRED: Yes. Yes. Better that you had backed off a thousand bridges, than brought us to the point of war again.

EDMUND: [*To the* BISHOP *and* KENT] There is the fright behind these whining postulations of contrition. The coward's fear of war. It is not that Edmund has done wrong but that this peace, this female peace, stands endangered. [*To all of them*] Well, I am not in love with the bitch.

BISHOP: Your Majesty, it will be contrition enough upon England's part to offer good compensation for these deaths. As we would pay a peasant a just amount for the death of his wife or his livestock by a member of the nobility, so we will offer these Danish widows what is their due. To go beyond this in our desire to maintain peace is to cast more guilt than is necessary upon our cause. In what we say to the Danish ambassador we must look to the future. Should war come it will be an intolerable burden for Englishmen if they are forced to the battlefield having heard public acknowledgments of crime fall from our tongues.

ETHELRED: Murders have been committed. Do not deny me these murders.

BISHOP: Nations are not free to admit murders; they are not private men that they may acknowledge guilt. What your son has done was done as a prince of this realm and we must stand to it. Our concern now lies not with the fine exercise of justice, but with the greater needs of the commonwealth. Another day shall see us more punctilious in our justice.

ETHELRED: Shall I have this commonwealth without justice? [*There is a moment of silence.*] So silent, Kent? What say you to this?

KENT: Where the needs of England and justice are the same I would England be just.

ETHELRED: And where they are not? [KENT *hesitates.*]

KENT: Then I must be English. For England's need let these deaths be an accident. Prince Edmund met four Danes in the woods and in an accident slew them. [*Lights down. A voice in the dark seems to answer* KENT.]

THORKILL: Wherein may we call this an accident? King Sweyn bids me ask, "Wherein may we call this an accident?" [*Spotlight on* THORKILL.] We sit on the bench in Denmark and watch the snow come down upon our boats. We build small fires with seawood. We drink our liquor and spit into the fire while men gather. If we do not find satisfaction we will find war. If we rub our knives upon whatever stones we find, sharpening, always sharpening, we will find a war to use them. We would do ill where ill has been done. What Edmund has done to our kinsmen we would do to Edmund. What is justice if not giving injury to those who injure us? Wherein may we call this meeting in the woods an accident? King Sweyn bids me ask you, "Wherein may we call these deaths an accident?" [*Lights up full on the scene. All present as before.*]

KENT: We consider it an accident, my Lord Thorkill, in that there was no intent.

BISHOP: Prince Edmund believed himself to be attacked. There was no further intent beyond his own defense.

THORKILL: [*To* ETHELRED, *though he talks to the others as well*] You conceive this meeting at the bridge to be a chance occurrence?

KENT: [*The* KING *says nothing.* KENT *is forced to answer.*] We do, my lord.

BISHOP: We are pleased that King Sweyn takes this opportunity to assure himself that upon our part there was no intent to provoke renewed quarrel between our countries. If these Danish widows will take compensation for the death of their husbands, they shall find us most generous.

ETHELRED: [*Suddenly interrupting*] Where there is wrong we shall make right. We wish nothing in this to be thought of as a cause for war.

BISHOP: As we have placed by treaty these farmers under protection of English law, so their death is a matter of concern to us as it is to Denmark. Often out of misfortune bonds between nations are strengthened. We pray this present adversity shall give way to yet a firmer peace.

THORKILL: Upon our part we welcome these expressions of good faith and wish to give our assurance to England that we shall not strain an accident into a cause for war. We are no less resolved than you to see this peace maintained. [*Directly to* ETHELRED] With Your Majesty's permission, before we go into the bills of compensation, King Sweyn bids me receive answers to certain questions. [ETHELRED *nods.* THORKILL *pulls out some papers.*] Was my Lord Edmund aware that in crossing the bridge he was entering upon land set aside by treaty for the farmers?

EDMUND: I followed a deer I had wounded.

BISHOP: The stream at this point, my lord, wanders in and out of the Danish land. It is difficult to know at any moment whether the boundary line has been crossed. My Lord Edmund naturally assumed he was on the English side.

THORKILL: In following this deer, my lord, were you not aware that you were crossing upon Danish land?

EDMUND: I followed the deer.

BISHOP: I think we may agree that the trespass was accidental.

THORKILL: [*Persisting in his question*] Did you initially wound the deer on the English side of the stream or on the Danish side?

EDMUND: I wounded the deer by a tree.

THORKILL: Do you recall which side of the stream this tree was on?

EDMUND: One side or the other.

THORKILL: The Danish side?

EDMUND: I know not what side.

THORKILL: Then I will put down that the crossing was accidental and without knowledge of trespass.

EDMUND: Will you?

THORKILL: Shall I put that down or no, my lord?

EDMUND: You may put down what pleases you.

THORKILL: It pleases me to know the truth; if you give me the truth I will write it down.

EDMUND: Write down, then, that in the middle of an English wood I was set upon by four Danes, and cowards that they were I slew them.

ETHELRED: [*In anguish that* EDMUND *will not allow the situation to be soothed over*] My son thought he hunted upon English land. He was not aware of his trespass.

THORKILL: [*To* EDMUND] Was my lord aware that the farmers were unarmed?

EDMUND: They seemed armed to me.

THORKILL: In what way armed, my lord?

EDMUND: In iron helmets. They had upon their heads thick iron helmets.

THORKILL: Their heads were uncovered.

EDMUND: I think you be mistaken. I took them for armed. If they were not armed they would not have spoken to me as they did.

THORKILL: How did they speak to you, my lord?

EDMUND: In a manner I liked not.

THORKILL: What manner like you?

EDMUND: I like not your manner.

BISHOP: If it pleases you, my lord, direct your questions at me. Let me answer these questions.

EDMUND: He may as easily direct his questions at me. I do not mind answering questions.

ETHELRED: We will answer to these questions!

EDMUND: I do not mind answering questions! I will find answers to satisfy him.

THORKILL: I am not here to be satisfied, my lord, but that King Sweyn be satisfied.

EDMUND: Then let him be satisfied with what he is ever satisfied with—money. We have offered him money, let him take it. Do not question a prince of this realm as if he were some plowman to be taught obeisance.

ETHELRED: [*To* EDMUND] Be still!

THORKILL: My Lord Edmund mistakes me for an unarmed farmer.

EDMUND: I mistake you not. [*Holding some money out in a purse*] Take it. [THORKILL *doesn't move.*] Take it, Danish bastard. Take it! (THORKILL *turns to exit.* EDMUND *hurls the purse at him and then runs at him.* THORKILL *whirls about and stabs him.*]

THORKILL: I meant not this.

EDMUND: Give me your knife, Father. I still may stab him with it. [*Dies.*]

ETHELRED: [*Falling to his knees in anguish*] Edmund. Edmund! [*Blackout. Lights up on an area behind the Cathedral of London.* THULJA *sits on a small stone bench listening to the faint sounds of music coming from the cathedral. She draws her cloak about her and then stares up toward the top of the cathedral. The sun is very bright and she is forced to shade her eyes. After a few moments the* EARL OF KENT *enters.*]

KENT: The services are almost over, Thulja. They will be out soon. Are you ready to leave?

THULJA: Yes. I wish only to say good-bye.

KENT: [*Sitting next to her and taking her hand*] Thulja, speak as you will to His Majesty, but do not be forward to the rest. Say nothing to them unless they bid you speak. I would not have you give them the slightest cause for anger. Edmund's death has filled them with hatred they little care to conceal.

THULJA: Am I to stay with you and Catherine from now on?

KENT: Yes.

THULJA: Is it too dangerous for me to stay here? Is that why I have to leave?

KENT: We think it would be best, at least for a time, Thulja, if you did not stay in London.

THULJA: I have given them no cause for hatred. I have ever wanted their friendship. I wanted Edmund to like me in spite of what he did when I first came.

KENT: I know, Thulja.

THULJA: He didn't hurt me ripping up the clothes. If he really didn't like me he could have struck me instead of just ripping up my clothes. I thought about that after a while. I'm sorry he's dead. I'm sorry he killed the farmers. I wish nobody had to die. I wish Queen Emma would like me if she could. I wish Queen Alfreda would like me. I wish . . . I don't know. I miss my sisters a lot now. I miss my father. I feel so different now than when I came last winter. I should have been older when I came. I should have found something to say to Edmund. I think I could have found something to say to Edmund.

KENT: What, Thulja? When no man ever found words to say to Edmund, what should you have said to him?

THULJA: I would say good morning to him when we met and he would turn away. For no cause he would turn away. No matter how often I gave him greeting he would not answer, and yet in leaving him I think his eyes turned upon me. I think had I once looked back I might have found him standing upon a word and from a word if we could not become friends, perhaps we might have become something less than enemies. [*Stands up and looks at the top of the steeple.*] The steeples glare so in the sun. The ice has made them seem like crystal in the sun.

KENT: I've written to Catherine and she's very excited having you come. She demands that I put you in the room next to hers, if you would like that.

THULJA: Yes. I would like that very much. I want to be very close to Catherine.

KENT: [*Noting that* THULJA *persists in looking up at the steeples*] What do you see up there, Thulja?

THULJA: The light. The light of the sun upon the ice. How high they have built the steeples, as if they should touch only upon the clouds. [*Looking at* KENT] I saw them leave this morning with Edmund's body. So many people walked with him to the church, and when they come out he's going to be alone. Always from now on he's to be alone.

KENT: Put your mind to other thoughts, Thulja. So the church will be English, Edmund will be content to lie in it. As I have loved King Ethelred and he has lost a son, I mourn his death, but no further. Though Edmund was valorous in war, in peace he was somewhat murderous. We do wrong if we do not keep a remembrance of what the dead have truly been.

THULJA: I would not have had him die. I would not any of us be dead. You told me when I first came to England that though men lose each other yet in the end they come upon each other again. I think some of us are lost and are not found again. I think some die and are lost to us forever. [QUEEN ALFREDA *enters followed by* KING ETHELRED, QUEEN EMMA, *and* BISHOP AELFHUN. *They all kneel to the* BISHOP *as he silently offers a prayer.*]

EMMA: [*As she kneels by the* KING's *side.*] Why is that girl still walking about?

ETHELRED: Be still, madam, be everlastingly still. I like it not that you are ever at my ear.

EMMA: You will not shrug me off.

ETHELRED: Be still!

EMMA: [*Angrily*] Wherefore am I to be still and she free to speak? Because her kinsmen have murdered Edmund, do you find cause to set her loose? [*To* ALFREDA] He will reward these murderers. He turns her loose.

ETHELRED: She is not turned loose.

EMMA: She is! She is! Edmund is dead and he turns her loose!

KENT: Truly, madam, she is not turned loose. She but leaves London.

EMMA: Where do you take her?

KENT: I may not tell you that, madam.

EMMA: [*To* ALFREDA] You see what they do? [*To* THULJA] Where do they take you? [THULJA *looks at* KENT *and* KENT *shakes his head, indicating that she is not to answer.*] Where do they take you?

THULJA: I know not what to say to you.

EMMA: [*Standing up*] Do you speak more easily with men? Do you find your tongue more liquid with men? I've seen you swagger through this court. Day by day grown more used to eating our food, sleeping in our beds, drinking our water, taking what is ours. [*As the* BISHOP *exits, the others, one by one, stand.*]

THULJA: [*Holding out her hand to* EMMA] Should we not give you food and a place to sleep if you came to Denmark?

EMMA: Stand back from me. I do not wish to be touched by you. I would lie on stone before coming into a Danish bed.

ETHELRED: Kent, leave now. I would not have this continue.

THULJA: Do not hate me, madam. Truly, I have sought no injury to you.

EMMA: I can't stand the smell of you. Your hands move the way an ape's hands move; you walk the way animals walk.

ETHELRED: Leave with Lord Kent now, Thulja. I will find another time to give you a better good-bye.

EMMA: [*To* ALFREDA *and then to the rest of them*] You see how eager they are to offer their ears to her tongue? It flatters them when young girls bend to them. Old stallions in perpetual spring imagining themselves young.

ETHELRED: Be still! I will not have this, Emma.

EMMA: [*To* THULJA] Do you Danes love as we English love, or do you merely copulate as animals do? We English have been given to understand that Danish men mount their women as beasts do. That they enter them from behind. Have you required this of my husband?

ETHELRED: [*Loses control and, grabbing* EMMA, *begins to strike her.*] Enough! Enough! [EMMA *under the blows seems to receive a certain pleasure in provoking* ETHELRED *to physical violence, as if in the violence was a confirmation to her of something.*]

EMMA: You have all lain with her! All of you! She has gone down on her back to you! Animals! Animals! Bouc! Bouc! Bête!

(KENT, *who is leaving with* THULJA, *passes by* QUEEN ALFREDA. *As* THULJA *goes by, she is suddenly stabbed by* QUEEN ALFREDA. THULJA *falls to her knees.* ALFREDA, *almost mechanically, continues to stab at her.* ETHELRED, *absorbed in his own violence, fails to hear* THULJA's *cry. Lights out momentarily, and then up full. We are in the dining room of the monastery at Wight.* KENT, SUSSEX, *and* BISHOP AELFHUN *are seated about a table. For a moment there is silence and then* SUSSEX *begins drumming his fingers on the table.*]

SUSSEX: Does he come or do we wait? Eh? Eh? Wait for what? Eh? [*He gets up and looks down the hallway leading into the dining room. He returns to the table, and when he speaks his voice is full of sarcasm.*] You think we'll leave the way we came? You think the ocean'll stay flat until it please us to cross?

You know what the wind is doing to the ocean? I've got seven hundred men in my shire waiting for me to tell them what to do, but I'm not going to be able to tell them what to do if I'm down at the bottom of the ocean. If I'm down at the bottom of the ocean sucking fish, I'm not going to be able to tell them what to do. I'll tell you this: if this be not the last meal he takes in this place, it be the last table I sit down to with him. I'm done eating with him. I have no patience for this.

BISHOP: Be patient, my lord, he will be here.

SUSSEX: I am not a patient man.

KENT: Are you not patient?

SUSSEX: I am not a patient man. Shall I be the one to speak to him? [KENT *opens his arms to indicate* SUSSEX *can do as he pleases.*] I care not whether I speak or another.

KENT: I care not whether you speak or not.

SUSSEX: Shall I speak? [*Looking at the* BISHOP.]

BISHOP: [*Looking at* KENT] It would be best if we decided who is to speak. What we have to say should be said in the most effective manner.

KENT: Then let Sussex speak. His mouth is ever effective.

BISHOP: I think it would be best if you spoke.

KENT: I cannot see that it matters who speaks. We are all of one mind here. In spite of different paths we have come to this common fork. [*Joining his fingers together in a sarcastic gesture to the* BISHOP.]

SUSSEX: You have been most allied to him. He will listen best to you.

KENT: Then I will speak.

SUSSEX: So you speak bluntly and to the point. I would not have Ethelred think that any fawning words in this speaking come from my part. [ETHELRED *enters unobserved and stands silently listening. The* ABBOT *is with him.*]

KENT: What fawning words?

SUSSEX: If it please Your Majesty; if Your Majesty so desires; with Your Majesty's permission.

KENT: You conceive these fawning words?

SUSSEX: Yes. They fawn.

KENT: In what way do they fawn?

SUSSEX: I know not in what way they fawn. They fawn!

KENT: Then you shall speak.

SUSSEX: I am content that you shall speak save that there be no fawning words.

ETHELRED: My lords. [*They turn around, surprised. They stand, and then kneel.*]

KENT: My liege.

BISHOP: Good evening, Your Majesty.

SUSSEX: Your Majesty. [*When* ETHELRED *speaks to his* LORDS, *his staring look implies more than his casual questions. As he speaks to them he raises them to their feet.*]

ETHELRED: [*To* KENT] Did you have a good crossing, Kent?

KENT: The sea was calm, my liege. We had no trouble.

ETHELRED: [*To* BISHOP AELFHUN] How fare you, Aelfhun?

BISHOP: I am in good health, Your Majesty.

ETHELRED: And you, Sussex? Are you in good health?

SUSSEX: My health is good, Your Majesty.

ETHELRED: [*Still looking at* SUSSEX, *though he addresses* ABBOT OSWALD] Will your monks share this dinner meal with us, Abbot Oswald?

ABBOT: If Your Majesty wishes.

ETHELRED: And if they could find a song for this holy season, Reverend Father, I would have it. [ABBOT OSWALD *exits as* ETHELRED *and the rest take their seats. They are silent.* ETHELRED *looks at one and then the other.*] So silent, my lords? We have not at other times been so silent with one another.

BISHOP: Your Majesty is in good health?

ETHELRED: I have not slept well this past week, Aelfhun. I thought I saw in the burning seawood of my grate last night the shadow of my stepbrother, Edward.

BISHOP: A dream, Your Majesty?

ETHELRED: I know not if it was a dream. This shadow spoke strangely to me, saying, "Listen, brother, I live in a cave by the Cardiff Sea where the mackerel boil up like a million silver ribbons and nobody ever comes." And as I watched, the shadow grew smaller and smaller like some little thing the universe was swallowing up. I thought Edward meant to have me follow him.

SUSSEX: The Danes continue to bring boats ashore at Grimsby.

ETHELRED: What means my dream, Sussex?

SUSSEX: I do not read dreams. I am a soldier.

ETHELRED: Do you understand this dream, Kent?

KENT: [*Looks at* ETHELRED *and then holds out to him a scroll.* ETHELRED *does not take it*] If Your Majesty will take the field against King Sweyn, these English lords will put their fortunes to it. If Your Majesty will not take the field they will acquiesce to Danish rule.

BISHOP: There is a great will among these earls to fight for your cause, Your Majesty. They wish only to be led.

ETHELRED: I would have my Lord Kent say something of my dream.

KENT: What shall I say, my liege?

ETHELRED: Say what you will, so that you say it.

KENT: There is no meaning to dreams. In war we put dreams by.

ETHELRED: Say more, Kent. I would have you say something further to this dream.

KENT: England's needs are war, Your Majesty. There was a peace, the peace is done.

ETHELRED: Then we will not talk about peace or dreams. We will talk about Master Lombardi.

SUSSEX: The boatbuilder?

KENT: He is gone.

ETHELRED: How gone?

BISHOP: Of his own will, Your Majesty. He has gone back to Florence.

ETHELRED: And when shall he come again? [*They look at* ETHELRED *but make no answer.*]

SUSSEX: This is not what we have come to discuss.

ETHELRED: Then we will discuss the scholars I have sent to the northern monasteries.

SUSSEX: There are no scholars at the northern monasteries. There are only Danes at Grimsby. We have come to discuss the Danes at Grimsby.

ETHELRED: All come to discuss the Danes at Grimsby? All? [*Looking from one to the other.*]

BISHOP: The resolution to this war is common, Your Majesty.

KENT: If you do not challenge this Danish assault upon you, Sweyn will take the throne of England by midsummer.

ETHELRED: There was a time you were wont to speak to me of peace. Fair peace. Sweet peace. Not a morning but that you bent upon my ear tales of ancient cities whose peoples found greatness when their rulers found peace. Not an evening but that you thrust upon my eyes visions of old Greece. Where now these tales? Where now these visions?

KENT: We are into war. In war visions are put down. For the common welfare we put down our visions until the time is better.

ETHELRED: The time is never better. We are ever in a war, out of a war, preparing for a war, finishing a war.

BISHOP: If Your Majesty could only return to England and see how eager his subjects are for the defense of his crown and the slaughter of the Danes. Not a man in England but he will put his sword to this quarrel.

ETHELRED: I would that they would draw back from this quarrel with half the eagerness they draw into it,

or that some among us found it as just to do right to
our enemy as to do wrong.

SUSSEX: What right?

BISHOP: Of what right does Your Majesty speak?

ETHELRED: The right they come upon. We have slain
their daughter. We have murdered the innocent. If
after long years of war I should meet King Sweyn
upon the ruins of some field and he should say to me,
"Wherefore did my daughter die? Wherefore did I
give her to you and you slew her?" what shall I say
to him?

BISHOP: If it please Your Majesty, you may say nothing.
There is no obligation held to do right to our enemy.
There is only an obligation to England.

SUSSEX: As he will strike you upon the field, so you will
strike him. This is what men do.

ETHELRED: Are we in a dungeon? Is this world a dungeon wherein men in their chains strike one another?

KENT: Yes! Though you would not have it. Yes! We
are in a dungeon. You speak of dreams, they come
to show you vacancy; you speak of visions, they will
show you voids. In the morning I went out and the
sky was full; in the evening I came back and the sky
was down. I saw a cow on Monday; on Tuesday I
saw a carcass set upon by flies. At thirteen my daughter ran, at fourteen I strapped slabs of wood to her
legs that she might stand. Oh, we have spoken each
to each of antique realms and justice, but that was
each to each, that was not now. Now we have come
upon a rat's den where walls slime and men find
gillyflowers to piss upon. Do you see justice here? I
do not see it. No, I do not see it. I see accident here:
in the joy of my hunting I came upon a man and I
slew him because he would not let me by. I see decay
here where dead men are robbed for wool and priests
singing of paradise fight for cloth to bind about their
feet. I see futility here. I see despair here. I see distortion here: I'm sure another day shall find us more

punctilious in our justice, but now to the war, by the cross of our Lord, to the war that we may be fixed into our killings, or die. [*Directly, suddenly, to the* KING] Resolve yourself to it. We are now fixed into these killings or else become bystanders to England's extinction. We are set to our duty though the cause be rotten.

ETHELRED: Then you are mad. No peace? No justice? Though the cause be rotten I am to be driven into a war for it? Well, I will not be driven into a war for it. I will not add to injuries, nor will I leave the quiet of this house for a war. The girl is dead. That is the end to these injuries. I do not care that you find it easier to achieve purpose in your war than in my peace. Let there be a war and you tell me not a man in England but that he will know what he must do. Though his wife be cut down by the plague and his child limp with disease, still when the drum is struck he will fall to and strike the man who bids him find cause to keep from it. If this be so, then we have come to hell and know it not. I think it must be by some dog's instinct that you love your violences. Not a cry of war in the air but that you sniff upon it as if smelling an old friend, but place peace before you and like some dog turning upon its tail you turn upon your confusions. I have seen men in war furl out their banners and throw themselves upon the pikes of their enemies with such dispatch a half-crazed savage would be startled to watch it, and yet give these same men land and a sometimes peace to live a saner life, and they yawn at the heavens and turn sick. I see that I have been in error. I sought to find a dozen men to plant an orchard while all about me nature bloomed a thousand lunatics ready to chop it down. Well, madmen, the girl is dead and that is the end of these injuries.

BISHOP: [*Grown very angry*] They injure us! As they have lost a daughter, we have lost a son. In the eyes of God and men the death of one cancels the death of the other. I cry victory to us, death to them!

SUSSEX: Victory to us! Death to them! [*At this point the singing of the approaching* MONKS *becomes audible.* SUSSEX *stands up and, stiffly angry, walks out of the room. After a few moments* BISHOP AELFHUN *follows.* KENT *is the last to leave. He kneels to his* KING *and then rises and leaves.* ETHELRED *stares at the empty chamber enveloped now only in the rising sound of song.*]

CURTAIN

The Poison Tree

A Play in Two Acts

For Jamie and Elana, who will grow up
in a new century,
perhaps free of old poisons

The Poison Tree by Ronald Ribman was first presented at the Ambassador Theatre, New York City, on January 8, 1976. The play was produced by Emanuel Azenberg, William W. Bradley, Marvin A. Krauss, and Irving Siders; directed by Charles Blackwell; settings by Marjorie Kellogg; lighting by Martin Aronstein; costumes by Judy Dearing; production manager, Henry Velez; general manager, Jose Vega.

CAST

(In Order of Appearance)

ALBERT HEISENMAN	*Danny Meehan*
WALTER TURNER	*Daniel Barton*
OFFICER LOWERY	*Gene O'Neill*
OFFICER DI SANTIS	*Peter Masterson*
SERGEANT COYNE	*Robert Symonds*
OFFICER LLOYD	*Charles Brown*
OFFICER ROLLOCK	*Pat McNamara*
OFFICER FRIEZER	*Arlen Dean*
WILLY STEPP	*Cleavon Little*
BOBBY FOSTER	*Dick Anthony Williams*
CHARLES JEFFERSON	*Northern J. Calloway*
BENJAMIN HURSPOOL	*Moses Gunn*
SMILING MAN	*Dennis Tate*

ACT I

Scene 1:
   The Adjustment Center, a maximum security area
Scene 2:
   Sergeant Coyne's office

ACT II

ACT I

Scene 1

The Adjustment Center, a maximum security area inside the prison.

ON RISE: *The stage is dark. In the dark a match is struck, and as the lights come up we see a white prisoner,* ALBERT HEISENMAN, *lighting his cigarette.* HEISENMAN, *except for the occasional movement of raising the cigarette to his lips, stands motionless, staring out of the front bars of the "strip cell," a four-by-eight cubicle. The strip cell has a hole in the floor used as a toilet, a three-foot-wide plank of wood covered with a blanket used as a bed, an electric light that burns constantly overhead, and nothing else. The cell adjacent to* HEISENMAN's *is occupied by a black prisoner,* WALTER TURNER. TURNER *is a large, powerful man. Except for the blanket he holds about him as he stands, he is naked, his body trembling in the cold. Several yards away, seated behind a desk, is the guard on duty,* OFFICER LOWERY. LOWERY *is a pleasant-looking young man who might be in his mid to late twenties. He is trying to work out a mathematical problem while a somewhat older guard,* OFFICER DI SANTIS, *looks on. After some moments a prison bell sounds.* OFFICER DI SANTIS *checks his watch and, patting his friend on the shoulder, exits. For perhaps half a minute there is silence and then a single clear note of a musical instrument is struck and the* BLACK PRISONER's *head begins to move, shaking*

214

from side to side. The struck note gradually blends into the sound of other notes from the same instrument. The blanket falls. Muscle by muscle, as if freeing himself from great pain, the body of the PRISONER *begins to move. A kind of dance is begun, a stretching out of limbs, a bending of the spinal column, the silent lifting and placing of feet, at first almost spastically and then in rhythm to the instrument. As the music picks up in tempo and intensity, the movements of the body follow, faster and faster, freer and freer. The* PRISONER *begins making sounds in his dance, sounds below the level of language, yawps of rage and freedom, his feet striking hard against the floor.* OFFICER LOWERY, *hearing the sounds, turns and stares at the* PRISONER. *For some moments he sits watching, and then, his slide rule still in his hand, walks over to a position in front of* TURNER'S *cell. He stares into the cell, for a time almost stunned, unable to believe what he sees.*

LOWERY: Turner? What's the matter with you? Turner? You hear what I'm saying to you? What are you doing? What's the matter with you? [*The music and dance have built to a crescendo. The* PRISONER *is totally oblivious to anything outside of himself. The* GUARD *moves forward, placing his head against the bars of the cell.*] Turner? Turner?

(*Suddenly the* PRISONER *grabs the* GUARD *around the neck and begins to strangle him. The* GUARD *fights back, clawing at the* PRISONER'S *face. The slide rule falls to the floor. The fight is desperate, furious, filled with anguished cries of pain. For a long time the* GUARD *fights back. He calls "*DI SANTIS, DI SANTIS,*" over and over again, until, with a final jerk of his arm, the* PRISONER *breaks his neck.* DI SANTIS *enters in time to catch the falling body of the dead* GUARD. TURNER *emits a scream of exaltation and flings himself high up on the bars. The* OTHER PRISONER *con-*

*tinues to stare straight forward, smoking his cig-
arette.)*

LIGHTS OUT

Scene 2

ON RISE: *A pool of light slowly comes up to reveal*
OFFICER DI SANTIS *standing downstage left of center.
He stares blankly forward as the voice of* SERGEANT
COYNE *shouts at him from the dark.*

COYNE: You want the truth of it straight, Di Santis? I'll
give it to you. Lowery didn't have to get killed. He
got himself killed because he was negligent. Sloppy
and negligent. [*Lights gradually begin coming up on
the entire scene.* SERGEANT COYNE *sits behind a
paper-strewn desk at stage right. Seated near the
desk, to his left, is* OFFICER LLOYD, *a new guard, who
is black.*] He sat on his behind reading his goddamn
college books when he should have been keeping his
eyes on his cages. One week on rotation duty in the
Adjustment Center and we lose a man who's been
in our section five years. For what? For nothing.

DI SANTIS: [*Deeply angry*] He did his job.

COYNE: You think so? Well, I'm telling you he didn't
do his job.

LLOYD: [*Starting to get up*] Maybe I oughtta wait outside, Sergeant Coyne.

COYNE: Just sit where you are, Officer Lloyd. Di Santis
here will tell you all about the man you're replacing
—Mr. St. Francis of Assisi.

DI SANTIS: You got no call saying that.

COYNE: [*Rising and pacing stage right*] Oh, don't I?
Lemme tell you something about your buddy. He
came to work here in a zoo, a zoo filled with some of
the most stinking vicious animals that ever ended up

216

in a cage, and he wouldn't buy it. I told him that, you told him that, everybody he ever worked with in here told him that, but he wouldn't buy it. Oh no, he was gonna be the one guard in here that was gonna be different—Mr. St. Francis of Assisi.

DI SANTIS: What is that? Some kind of dirty word? What are you blaming him for? For trying to be a decent human being? For trying to make something outa his life besides working in here?

COYNE: That's right. You got it right on the button, because you work in here there's no room for college books, or slide rules, or anything else but keeping your eyes on your cages. [*Crossing to* DI SANTIS *at left of center*] He saw that con was giving him trouble, he should've called as many guards as he needed to subdue that man. He should've fixed it so that man wanted to buck the system, he couldn't even crawl outa that cage. But no, he hadda wing it alone. As far as I'm concerned he wanted to be St. Francis of Assisi, he should've gone to work in a monastery. Somewhere you make a mistake they don't cut your heart out.

DI SANTIS: Is that what you want me to tell his wife?

COYNE: Yeah, you tell her how you're sloppy in this place you end up a pair of broken shoelaces and a badge, you tell her what happens to great human beings in this place. You tell her, tell her what you want, he was your friend. [*Crosses to his desk.*]

(OFFICER ROLLOCK *enters stage left, followed a few paces behind by* OFFICER FRIEZER. FRIEZER *holds a clipboard with some papers, and* ROLLOCK *a laundry bag filled with personal belongings of the dead guard.*)

ROLLOCK: Hi, Sarge.

FRIEZER: [*Crossing to* OFFICER LLOYD *at desk.*] Hey, buddy, how ya doing? Lloyd? You get settled in yet?

LLOYD: No, not yet.

COYNE: Is that it, Rollock?

ROLLOCK: [*Putting down the laundry bag*] That's it.

FRIEZER: [*Handing a sheet of paper from the clipboard to* SERGEANT COYNE] Here's a checklist.

DI SANTIS: [*At left of* ROLLOCK, *staring down at the laundry bag*] What is this?

ROLLOCK: Lowery's stuff.

DI SANTIS: I know it's Lowery's stuff. What did you put it in, a laundry bag?

ROLLOCK: Sure, I put it in a laundry bag. What did ya want me to put it in, a cardboard box? [*Offering up a small laugh.*]

DI SANTIS: [*Suddenly grown even more angry*] No, not a cardboard box. I expected you to put it into something that shows his wife some respect—a valise, a suitcase. Is this what you want me to dump on his front porch—a laundry bag?

COYNE: Take it easy, Di Santis.

DI SANTIS: No, I don't feel like taking it easy. What is this? Some kind of joke? I ask him why he puts Lowery's belongings in a laundry bag, and he asks me if I want it put in a cardboard box?

ROLLOCK: [*Turning around to the* OTHERS *for support*] That's what they gave me in supply. I asked them to give me something to put his stuff in and they gave me a laundry bag. That's what they always give me.

DI SANTIS: You got a man's personal belongings in there, Rollock, it's not a load of wash.

FRIEZER: [*Crosses to right of* DI SANTIS] Hey, man, take it easy. He knows it's not a load of wash.

DI SANTIS: Does he? [*To* ROLLOCK] What would you do if they gave you a paper bag from the A&P, put it in that?

FRIEZER: It's just routine, man. What are you getting so excited about?

DI SANTIS: [*Pulling some unfolded clothes out of the bag*] I'll tell you what I'm getting excited about,

Friezer. You didn't even pack it. You just dumped his stuff in here. A man you worked with for five years gets killed and you just dump his stuff in a laundry bag without even packing it.

ROLLOCK: That's the way I put everybody's stuff in.

DI SANTIS: Well, not this time, Rollock. This time you're gonna take everything outa there and pack it. You understand me, Rollock? [*Pointing down at the laundry bag*] Pack it!

LIGHTS FADE OUT

Scene 3

The traveler opens to reveal a cell inside the general prison population.

The cell is defined by the grouping of the cell furniture, which consists of two single cots and one double-decker bunk. There are no walls. The grouping of the beds will form a cell almost triangular in shape. One single cot at stage right of center will form the stage right side of the triangle. The double-decker bunk laid end to end with the other single cot will form the stage left side of the triangle. The only entrance into the cell is above the stage right cot. The corridor outside the cell runs in a half circle from the stage right no. 1 entrance to the stage left no. 1 entrance. A curved tier rail at stage right runs at an angle along the stage right side of the corridor. The upstage end of the tier rail meets with a tier wall which runs across the stage, upstage of the cell.

The stage right cot is WILLIE STEPP's. *The lower bunk of the double decker is where* BOBBY FOSTER *"lives."* CHARLES JEFFERSON *is in the upper bunk, and* BENJAMIN HURSPOOL *is in the stage left cot.*

ON RISE: VOICES *shouting in the dark.*

VOICE 1: What's black all over, got a head made outa steel wool, and rhymes with jigger?

VOICE 2: I don't know. What's black all over, got a head made outa steel wool and rhymes with jigger?

VOICE 1: Nigger. Nigger. Nigger.

(*A chorus of* VOICES *joins in.*)

VOICES: Nigger. Nigger. Nigger. Nigger. [*Lights up on a cell containing four black men, each engaged in an activity that has now come to a stop. The first man,* BOBBY FOSTER, *in his late twenties, is writing a letter; the second,* WILLY STEPP, *about the same age, is reading a newspaper; the third man,* CHARLES JEFFERSON, *in his early twenties, is polishing his shoes; and the fourth man,* BENJAMIN HURSPOOL, *older, in his fifties, is reading a weight-lifting magazine. The cries of the* CHORUS *grow as more men pick up the chant. Someone has begun beating out a rhythm with a steel bar on a steel pipe.*] Nigger. Nigger. Nigger. Nigger. Nigger. Nigger. [*And then the* CHORUS *begins dissolving as* VOICE *after* VOICE *quits and then there is silence. One by one the* MEN *in the cell return to their activities.*]

STEPP: [*On cot right*] There's an interesting item here in the society page. "What is eighty-seven feet long and white all over? Mrs. Arthur Cunningham's scrumptious yacht, that's what. Word has it that the Cunningham yacht is being busily refurbished in time for the upcoming marriage of daughter Patricia—Poo Poo to her friends—Cunningham to you know who of the French diplomatic set. It would seem that the cool and elusive Poo Poo has finally fallen in love after spurning the attention of such divine catches as Tony Kirkland of the Wilmington, Delaware, Kirklands, and Brian Morgendecker of the New York

banking Morgendeckers. Whirling into town yesterday, draped in an ostrich feather boa and a delicious
white point d'esprit gown designed for her by Carlos
DiGras, the lovely Poo Poo was not denying her
former suitors were crying from St.-Tropez to Acapulco." [VOICE 1 *calls out again*.]

VOICE 1: We're coming down to string you up, niggers!
You hear me? We're coming down to string you up!

(FOSTER *leaps out of his bed and runs through the
open cell door onto the cell block corridor to the
tier rail*.)

FOSTER: [*Shouting up at the* VOICES] Come on, Whitey!
Come on down! [*The chorus of* VOICES *starts up
again, joined in by the banging of the steel bar on
the pipe*. JEFFERSON *suddenly covers his ears with
his hands and bends his head forward*.]

VOICES: Nigger. Nigger. Nigger. Nigger. Nigger. Nigger.

FOSTER: I'll kill every one of you! Come on down!

VOICE 1: [*Shouting over the* CHORUS] We're gonna get
you, nigger! [*The* CHORUS *continues for a few more
moments and then dies away*. FOSTER *returns to his
cell*.]

HURSPOOL: [*On cot left*] I sure do admire the way the
veins in your neck stand out from all that terrible
shouting. You is a fierce man, Bobby Foster. You is
a terror to behold in your righteous anger. [*Listening
for a moment to the silence*] I do believe you have
terrorized them into silence.

FOSTER: You better watch your mouth, Hurspool.

HURSPOOL: Yes, sir. I'll sure do that. All you young
brothers are terrible to behold. You can see what all
this terrible shouting has done to the young brother
over here. [*Pointing to* CHARLES JEFFERSON, *who still
sits with his hands over his ears*] It has unglued him,
I do believe.

FOSTER: [*Goes over to* JEFFERSON *and gently lowers*

his hands from his ears.] They ain't gonna shout no more, Charles, so you just keep workin' on your shoes.

HURSPOOL: That's right, Charles. You just keep workin' on your shoes so you can have them nice and polished when you see the parole board. Ain't nothin' them gentlemen likes to see so much as a pair of nicely polished shoes.

FOSTER: [*Sitting, lower bunk*] You shut your mouth, Hurspool, or I'm gonna bring my fist right upside your head.

HURSPOOL: I sure didn't mean nothin' by what I said, Brother Bobby. [*Rises.*] I was just thinkin' what with Brother Charlie here going up before the parole board tomorrow he is certain to be walkin' the streets 'bout this time next month. [*Crossing right to* STEPP] Ain't that right, Brother William? Wouldn't you say that's a certainty? [*Turning back to* FOSTER] Of course, Brother Bobby here one of these days will be makin' his fifth appearance before the parole board on account of the fact they done turned him down the last four times, but what I always say is the fifth time is luck. Yes, sir, Brother Charlie, you remember that. The fifth time is luck. [FOSTER *suddenly swings at* HURSPOOL, *knocking him down. They scuffle as* STEPP *pulls* FOSTER *away to stage right.*]

STEPP: Leave that ignorant bastard alone, brother. Leave him alone. He just wants you to get caught fighting with him, that's all. Now leave him be.

FOSTER: I'm gonna kill you one of these days, Hurspool! You remember what I tell you!

HURSPOOL: [*Slowly getting to his feet and wiping the blood off his mouth*] You keep on fightin' this way, Brother Bobby, and you is bound to get caught. You is just naturally gonna be removed to the Adjustment Center for some adjustments. Maybe they even gonna have to carry you out in a box like they carried Brother Turner, unless'n of course you is willin' to do some crawlin'. A man's willin' to do some crawlin' they just naturally assume he's made the right adjustment. Ain't nothin' the man likes to see so much as a dumb nigger crawlin'. You gonna crawl, Brother Bobby? You gonna give old Hurspool here the opportunity to see you crawl? I surely hope so.

DI SANTIS: [*Offstage sound of* DI SANTIS *singing as he comes along the cell block corridor.* DI SANTIS *enters, right no. 1 entrance, crosses up center.* ALL THE PRISONERS *with the exception of* BOBBY FOSTER *have returned to their previous activities.* FOSTER *offers up a small laugh, which* DI SANTIS *overhears.* DI SANTIS *pauses, turns around, and enters the cell.* FOSTER *sits on lower bunk.*] How come you boys are just sitting here? You looking for a good laugh you oughtta go into the television room and watch some television. They got a big Superfly kind of movie comin' up on NBC in about ten minutes. Superfly's gonna spend ninety minutes doin' nothing but kicking in white ass. "For every drop of black blood shed, a white man dies!" How about that? Man, he really tells it like it is.

[DI SANTIS *turns his back and starts to leave the cell.*]

FOSTER: No shit.

DI SANTIS: [*Immediately spinning around to confront them again*] Listen, if you guys hurry now, there's probably a seat or two still vacant on the Malcolm X memorial couch. You know the one I mean? With the cheap plastic covers and the stuffing coming out of it, the one in the back of the room. Or is that the Honorable Elijah Muhammad memorial water fountain I'm thinking about. I never can get them straight. Which is it, Stepp?

STEPP: I think you got them mixed up. You're probably thinking about the Richard M. Nixon memorial toilet bowl, which is right next to the Ronnie Reagan memorial urinal. I get them mixed up myself. [FOSTER *crosses down right and sits on foot of* STEPP's *bunk.*]

DI SANTIS: [*Stares at* STEPP *for a few moments and then*

turns to JEFFERSON *on upper bunk.*] Getting your shoes all shined up for the parole board, Jefferson?

JEFFERSON: That's right.

DI SANTIS: "That's right, sir"! [JEFFERSON *jumps off bunk and moves left.*] You facing a parole board tomorrow, Jefferson; you expect to get outa here you gotta con the man into believing that word's part of your permanent vocabulary. How many times you meet those people?

JEFFERSON: Once before.

DI SANTIS: You leavin' something out, Jefferson. You leavin' something out again.

FOSTER: [*To* DI SANTIS] Get offa him, man.

DI SANTIS: [*Ignoring* FOSTER *for the moment*] Respect for the law, Jefferson. That's what you're leaving out. Respect for the people of this state you spent half your life stealing from and are still willing to give you another chance on parole. I think you're gonna be sticking around for a while. You ain't learned everything yet, Jefferson.

FOSTER: Nobody's got nothin' to learn from you, man, so why don't you just take that shit and peddle it upstairs to the crackers?

DI SANTIS: [*Turning his attention back to* FOSTER] Now you take Foster here. Couple of months Foster is gonna be heading up for his fifth time. Now ordinarily he shoulda been outa here. Yes, indeed, Foster shoulda been long gone. Trouble is, Foster got a big mouth and a rep for bein' a bad ass. Thing about bein' a bad ass, though, is that it's like having a load of horseshit piling up on your back. Pretty soon it gets to weighing you down and you don't know what next you're supposed to do with yourself anymore. You start out usin' your fists and then after a while that just ain't enough to keep your rep going. Right, Foster? You got a monkey on your back. You wanna keep your rep goin' you gotta move up. You gotta pick up a blade, man, and when that ain't bad ass enough you gotta get yourself a piece. You ain't got a piece and use it on somebody you just ain't bad ass enough. You know what I see when I look at you, Foster? A two-bit punk with a piece shaking in his hand, wondering how it ever got there. That's about the way it was when they picked you up at the gas station, wasn't it? Too scared of your rep not to carry a piece and too scared of the man to pull the trigger. The way I heard it that cop just walked up to you and took the gun right outa your hand.

FOSTER: [*In cold anger*] Someday, honky, you and me is gonna meet outside this place. Just you and me.

DI SANTIS: [*At center*] Why don't you come on out now, bad ass? Come on! Come on! [STEPP *intervenes between* DI SANTIS *and* FOSTER, *silently talking to* FOSTER *and preventing him from moving toward* DI SANTIS] Why don't you try to do to me what that lousy nigger friend of yours did to Lowery? Come on! Come on! Whatta ya waiting for? I don't have a wife and three kids? [DI SANTIS *has totally lost control of himself.*] I'll give you the same thing I gave Turner! I'll split your lousy skull open! I'll . . . [*Suddenly catching himself and realizing he's said more than he intended.* STEPP *crosses to* DI SANTIS *at center, stares silently at him, then moves to his bunk and sits.*]

STEPP: Nobody's movin', man. We're just sittin' here nice and easy. Anybody comin' for you, they ain't comin' for you on your terms.

DI SANTIS: [*Still out of breath, still angry*] Always the smart ass, aren't you, Stepp?

STEPP: That's right, Mr. Di Santis.

DI SANTIS: Well, you just sit there nice and easy because you're gonna get old and gray sittin' there nice and easy. Ain't that right, Hurspool?

HURSPOOL: Yes, sir, that sure is right.

DI SANTIS: Always agree with the man, don't you, Hurspool?

HURSPOOL: Yes sir, I do.

DI SANTIS: Why don't you go watch some television? All I got is a twelve-inch black and white, but the state buys you boys a nice five-hundred-dollar color set, you oughtta watch it.

HURSPOOL: [*Crossing right*] Yes sir, that's just what I was fixin' to do. [*Exiting no. 1 right exit*]

DI SANTIS: [*Calling after him*] You just keep doin' that nice imitation of an Aunt Jemima, Hurspool, and you're gonna fake everybody out . . . [*Softly, to those in the cell*] . . . but me. Nice guy, Hurspool. If he wasn't in for throat-slashing a little ten-year-old black boy who wouldn't do a number on him, he'd be outa here by now. Maybe he'll even be outa here anyway, if he continues improvin' the way he is. Man likes to see improvement. Like you, Stepp, always readin', always improvin'.

STEPP: That's right.

DI SANTIS: [*Picks up one of the books on* STEPP's *bed, leafs through it.*] That's good. I'm gonna tell Sergeant Coyne you're improvin' and then maybe one day when nobody's in the cell with you we're gonna come around and take a look at this improvement. [*Tosses it back on the bed.*]

STEPP: Yeah, you do that.

DI SANTIS: I'm gonna let you in on a little secret, Stepp. Sergeant Coyne's got a bad impression of you. He's got the impression you're turning yourself into some kind of Commie troublemaker. Jesus, now ain't that crazy?

STEPP: Yeah, that's crazy. [*To* FOSTER, *who is sitting on foot of his bed*] What do you think, man? You think that's crazy?

FOSTER: Yeah, I think that's crazy.

DI SANTIS: That's what I said to Sergeant Coyne. That Willy Stepp's no Communist; a drug pusher, a cop shooter, a part-time pimp, but he's no Communist. But you know Sergeant Coyne. When it comes to a con, he don't believe shit, unless it's that they spend all their time braggin' about how they're gonna pull down a white woman they get outa here. Any of you boys ever had a white woman? [DI SANTIS *looks from one to the other, and when he looks at* FOSTER, FOSTER *replies.*]

FOSTER: Yeah.

STEPP: [*To* DI SANTIS] Have you?

DI SANTIS: [*Continues to stare at* FOSTER *as he speaks to* JEFFERSON.] Jefferson, that true first thing you get outa here you gonna pull down a white woman? [*Crosses left to* JEFFERSON.]

JEFFERSON: I ain't gonna pull down no white woman. What you talkin' about?

FOSTER: [*Walking to right of center*] You ain't gettin' yourself a nice piece of white meat?

JEFFERSON: No. I ain't doin' with no white meat.

FOSTER: Shit. First thing I do I get outa here I get me some of that. Ain't nothin' better than havin' a white woman doin' for you. Ain't that the truth, Willy?

STEPP: Yeah, that's the truth.

FOSTER: Sure is. You got yourself a nice white woman doin' for you you don't have to do nothin' yourself, 'cept maybe gas up some nice peach-colored pimpmobile the bitch done bought for you.

DI SANTIS: [*Stares at* FOSTER *for a moment as he crosses to center, smiles, and then, cocking his thumb and forefinger into a representation of a pistol, clicks it at* FOSTER's *stomach.*] You're dead. [*Exits down the corridor to right no. 1 exit, continuing with his song.*]

FOSTER: [*Looking after* DI SANTIS] That mother is outa his head, shootin' off his mouth about Walter Turner, walkin' around singin' to himself. [*Sits on lower bunk.*]

STEPP: What makes you think they got anybody in here in his head? That mother was good he first come here, you know that. You think white milk ain't gonna turn sour same as chocolate milk you keep it in here long enough? [*Lies down on his cot.*]

227

JEFFERSON: [*Shouting down the corridor after the departing* DI SANTIS] I ain't pulling down no white woman I get outa here!

FOSTER: [*Rises.*] Then what you gonna do, Charles?

JEFFERSON: I got someplace to go.

FOSTER: Where you goin'?

STEPP: Where you think he's goin', man? He's goin' home.

JEFFERSON: I ain't goin' home. I ain't never goin' back there no more.

FOSTER: Then where you goin'?

JEFFERSON: Tratmore School.

FOSTER: Tratmore School? Whatta you talkin' about? That ain't no school. That's a reform school.

JEFFERSON: It ain't no reform school! It's just a school, that's all.

STEPP: What do you want to go there for, Charles?

JEFFERSON: See some people about a job, maybe.

FOSTER: [*Moves to* JEFFERSON.] What's the matter with you, man? You ain't been there since you was twelve years old. There ain't no people there you know anymore. [*To* STEPP] This cat's outa his head. First thing he wants to do he gets outa one prison is go work in another one.

JEFFERSON: I told you it ain't no prison. It's just a place, that's all.

FOSTER: Yeah, it's just a place all right, only thing is you wanna get outa it for the weekend you gotta climb over a twelve-foot fence with barbed wire strung up on it.

JEFFERSON: Ain't no barbed wire strung there! All they got's some hedges and trees so you know where you's supposed to walk!

FOSTER: [*Crossing to* JEFFERSON] Hey, man, I'm just doin' a little funnin' with you.

JEFFERSON: Well, you ain't got no call talkin' like that 'cause you ain't never been there! You ain't never been in a place where they give you three meals a day and you still hungry they let you go down to the kitchen and eat what you want. You ain't never been in a place like that! Shit, I got more food to eat there than you ever seen in your life, and it was good food, too. You was probably scraping around your kitchen lookin' for something your mamma left over to eat while I was holdin' out my plate and gettin' seconds.

STEPP: Sounds like a nice place, Charles.

JEFFERSON: You wanna play some basketball or somethin', they got it right there, and that ain't no dinky little playground court. They got a real court! You wanna go out and play any game you can think of, they got it there. Man, they even had a place you wanna learn yourself somethin' about animals 'cause you wanna run a farm or somethin' like that, they got that right there. They even put a swing up there for us, not no little swing neither, but one they put in a tree! So don't you go tellin' me 'bout goin' back to some prison 'cause that school was the nicest place I ever been to in my whole life! [*Crosses and jumps up on his bunk. After a long pause in which* FOSTER *paces and* JEFFERSON *returns to polishing his shoes,* FOSTER *crosses to bunk.*]

FOSTER: You got a good enough polish on your shoes, Charles. Why don't you take it easy, find Smilin' Man, play some dominoes?

JEFFERSON: I ain't got the time now, you know that. I gotta get these shoes polished by tomorrow.

FOSTER: Those are prison shoes, man, they ain't never gonna take a shine! [*JEFFERSON just stares at him.*] All right, you just keep polishin' your shoes. [*Walks away and lies down in his bed, muttering to himself.*] Polishin' your shoes while you watch your life go by.

STEPP: [*Returning to his article*] Now where were we with the cool and elusive Poo Poo?

FOSTER: What the hell's the sense in readin' that crap, man?

STEPP: That's where you're not thinkin' right, brother, 'cause we gotta do what Madame Defarge did. We gotta remember. We gotta remember what they're doin' out there with their lives while we're doin' in here with our lives. [*Reading from the article*] ". . . the lovely Poo Poo was not denying her former suitors were crying from St.-Tropez to Acapulco. After what promises be to the most fabby fabulous honeymoon of this or any other season, the bride and groom will set up residence in the newly decorated thirty-eight room Cunningham maison adjoining the Bois de Boulogne." [*Lowers the newspaper und, carefully tearing the article out, begins to paste it into a scrapbook he keeps.*] Now that's an interesting piece of information to remember, Brother Bobby. Who knows but that one day you or I might be walkin' in the Bois de Boulogne and just happen to run into the cool and elusive Poo Poo. [*Crossing up to* FOSTER *and sitting right of him.*] It wouldn't do to pull her into the bushes without complimenting her first on her fabby fabby honeymoon.

FOSTER: The only one I wanna pull into the bushes is Di Santis.

STEPP: That's where you're wrong again, brother. You don't wanna do Officer Di Santis at all, because Officer Di Santis is as stupid a jackass as we are. When you develop the true revolutionary consciousness, you will see that Officer Di Santis is merely the pig hireling for the over-pig. [FOSTER *rises and crosses down right.* STEPP *follows.*] Now you kill off the pig hireling and whatta you got? Shit. That over-pig just looks down from where he's at and sees his pig hireling bleedin' away in the dirt and says to himself, "Motherfucker, they killed off one of my pig hirelings. I just better open this here wallet of mine and buy me ten more." [FOSTER *sits at the foot of* STEPP's *bunk, laughing.* STEPP *sits with him.*] Now, you wanna destroy the over-pig, then you gotta destroy the institutions that keep him in power. You destroy his institutions and that is a different story. Yes sir, that is a different story altogether. [*Rises and takes stage.*] Then you gonna witness the coming of the Apocalypse, my brother. All the evil forces of the earth rising up against each other in a final battle of the dinosaurs: the pig hirelings rising up against the over-pigs, one over-pig slayin' another over-pig, grindin' each other into the ground until they are just naturally dust blown away by the wind. And on that day we're gonna stand there and say, "Let it die! Let it all die!" And on the evening of that day the oppressed of the earth are gonna own the earth. The brothers that work in the mines are gonna own those mines, the brothers bendin' over in the lettuce fields are gonna own those fields. In no time at all that Mrs. Poo Poo is gonna have to give up her new maison in the Bois de Boulogne and start takin' in wash to make ends meet. [*Lightly punching* FOSTER *on the arm.*] Hey, my man, ain't that gonna be the day!

FOSTER: I ain't never gonna see that day, Willy.

STEPP: Sure you are. We both gonna see that day. All the brothers are gonna see that day.

FOSTER: You just druggin' yourself, Willy, druggin' yourself with your mind. Like you talkin' all the time about Africa, about how wonderful it is and how that's supposed to be our heritage, and how we're all gonna go there someday. And then I fall asleep imaginin' I'm there walkin down some road or something with some black woman who ain't never had her head put down. That's what you make me imagine, Willy. Some proud black woman who ain't never had her head put down, maybe dressed in nothin' but some jewelry, her hair cut short, proud of herself, lookin' up at you like she's been waitin' a lifetime for you. And then the lights come on and it's mornin', Willy. The guard comes down the corridor and it's mornin'!

STEPP: [*With great belief, sitting with* FOSTER] We're gonna see that day! We're all gonna see that day!

FOSTER: They ain't never gonna let us out of here, Willy! I'm gonna be twenty-nine years old this September. That's eleven years I been in here, eleven years for stealin' thirty dollars outa a gas station. [*Rises, crosses up to his bunk.*] You pullin' time with a sheet on you like we got, they ain't never gonna let you go, so I ain't foolin' myself about that anymore. You hear me talkin' when I come in here about how I'd be outa here in a year? I was sayin' to myself, "Well, a year of a nigger's life is worth thirty dollars to them." Well, that was just shit, man, 'cause now I got it down to less than three dollars a year and I still ain't goin' nowhere. I got it into my head one of these days one of those dogshits is gonna come in here and tell me my life ain't worth nothin' to them. Well, I ain't foolin' myself about that anymore. All's I got to do is sit in here and hate those motherfuckers, hate those motherfuckers till I die! [*Sits on his bunk.*]

STEPP: Well, maybe they give you somethin' you ain't even thought about.

FOSTER: They give me nothin'.

STEPP: Now you listen to me, my brother. I tell you they gave you somethin'. You got somethin' now you ain't even begun to think about before they put you in here. You tell me quick: you hate the man before you was in here?

FOSTER: Shit. [*Lies down.*]

STEPP: [*Crossing up to* FOSTER] Well, now you do. That's progress. You have moved from not givin' a care about anythin' 'cept yourself to hatin' the man and that is precept number one of revolutionary progress. Now maybe your brain is so besotted with all this imprisonment that you don't think hatin' the man is a step forward in any direction, but let me disencumber you of that notion right now. It is. It surely is. You have become a thorn in their side. You are piercin' their flesh day and night. You are festerin' up their life and they don't know what to do with you. That's why they put you in here. They have disillusioned themselves into thinkin' they are goin' to club you into submission, but you ain't about to be clubbed into submission. You too busy festerin' and festerin' with a poison that is like to kill them. You know what we are, brother? We are a tall black tree full of poison from which they ain't about to recover no way. [*Someone in a cell on the tier above begins to scream.*]

VOICE: I wanna go home! I wanna go home! I wanna go home! [*As soon as the screaming begins,* JEFFERSON *covers his ears with his hands.*]

JEFFERSON: Shut up! Shut up! Shut up!

VOICE: Mama! Mama! Mama!

LIGHTS DIM OUT

Scene 4

The GUARDS' *locker room.*

There is a urinal just right of center, left of center a row of lockers. Downstage of the lockers, a wooden bench.

ON RISE: HURSPOOL *stands right of the urinal, occasionally flicking the ashes of his cigarette into it.* DI SANTIS *is changing into his uniform by the lockers.*

DI SANTIS: Ever been in the guards' locker room before, Hurspool?

HURSPOOL: No, sir, I been workin' down the laundry.

DI SANTIS: You like working there?

HURSPOOL: Well, sir, I figure if that's the job they give me, why then, that's the job that's best for me.

DI SANTIS: Why is it whenever I talk to you, Hurspool, I get the feeling somebody is dumping a load of cotton on my head?

HURSPOOL: I don't know what you mean, Mr. Di Santis.

DI SANTIS: I ask you an honest question, why don't you give me an honest answer? Working in the laundry must be a pretty lousy job—all that heat and chemicals and everything.

HURSPOOL: Yes sir, I guess it is.

DI SANTIS: Sure it is. Now a man had a job in here all he'd have to do is mop up the floor a couple of times a day, give the toilet bowls a few swishes around with the brush. After that he could sit on his behind for the rest of the day, far as anybody cared. You like to have a job like that?

HURSPOOL: Yes sir, I would. [*Dropping his cigarette butt in the urinal.*]

DI SANTIS: Sure, it would be a lot better than the laundry. How long you been in here, Hurspool?

HURSPOOL: Twenty years.

DI SANTIS: When you figuring on getting out?

HURSPOOL: The last time I spoke to the man he said three, four years.

DI SANTIS: You're a lucky man being sentenced way back then. Nowadays the court could have given you an indeterminant sentence like Foster and Stepp. We can keep them in here as long as we like, one year to life depending on how we feel they shape up.

HURSPOOL: Yes sir, I'm sure lucky.

DI SANTIS: [*Looks at* HURSPOOL *for a moment, and then begins to laugh.* HURSPOOL *joins in.*] You know, Hurspool, in all the eight years I've been in this prison, that's the first time I ever heard you make a joke.

HURSPOOL: I don't have too much to joke about, Mr. Di Santis, not after twenty years.

DI SANTIS: No, I guess not.

HURSPOOL: Maybe when they let me outa here I'll remember what's funny.

DI SANTIS: You get out you're liable not to recognize anything.

HURSPOOL: Well, I'll sure do my best to start rememberin'.

DI SANTIS: Thing is a man gets close to getting outa here, he gets nervous, he makes a mistake, something happens and he's right back where he started from. He could go on that way forever. Could even die in here from old age, I suppose.

HURSPOOL: I ain't gonna make a mistake, Mr. Di Santis. I ain't made a mistake in fifteen years.

DI SANTIS: Yeah, I know that. I keep forgetting everybody tells me you've been rehabilitated. You're smart, Hurspool. Smarter than Bobby Foster, smarter than Willy Stepp, smarter than the parole board. Ain't nothing gonna stop you from getting out here, unless maybe it's me, 'cause you give me some reason.

HURSPOOL: I ain't never gonna give you no reason, Mr. Di Santis. You know that.

DI SANTIS: [*Has finished changing, crosses to left of* HURSPOOL.] Yeah, I know that. Well, that's all, Hurspool. [*As* HURSPOOL *starts to exit left no. 2 exit*] Oh, Hurspool, by the way . . . [*Fishing through his pockets and finally pulling out a toothbrush sharpened at one end into a knife point*] You ever see this before?

HURSPOOL: [*Stopped at left end of bench, staring at the outstretched knife*] No sir, I never did.

DI SANTIS: You know what this is? It's a knife. [*Turning the brush around so the bristles are visible*] It's a toothbrush somebody made into a knife. Somebody just sat down and filed the end of this brush until he made himself a knife. Now I bet you can't tell me where this knife was found?

HURSPOOL: [*Moving into center*] That's right, Mr. Di Santis.

DI SANTIS: Well, I'm gonna tell you, and this is gonna surprise the hell outa you. This morning while all you boys were downstairs working at your daily labor and laughing to each other about what a big man Brother Turner was for murdering a guard, a guard who never did anything but his job, I did a little reconnoitering around the cell block and this is what I came up with. What bed are you in, Hurspool? The top bed or the back bed?

HURSPOOL: The back bed.

DI SANTIS: Now this is the thing. For the life of me I can't remember which bed I found this knife in. Was it your bed or was it the other bed? Who's in that other bed anyway?

HURSPOOL: Jefferson.

DI SANTIS: Yeah, that's right. Well, what I want is the toothbrush replaced where it was. Whichever bed, it don't make no difference to me. I just don't want to be accused of taking personal property.

HURSPOOL: It ain't my knife, Mr. Di Santis.

DI SANTIS: That's what I thought. Then it must belong in Jefferson's bed. [*Holding out the brush*] You'll see that he gets it, won't you?

HURSPOOL: I do somethin' like that, they're gonna kill me.

DI SANTIS: Who's gonna kill you?

HURSPOOL: Willy Stepp, Bobby Foster, Smilin' Man. It don't make no difference which. They're gonna know for sure and they're gonna kill me.

DI SANTIS: Why is it, Hurspool, those whose lives are worth the least are always the ones who want to hold onto it the most?

HURSPOOL: Why don't you do it yourself, Mr. Di Santis? It's just as easy for you as it is for me. [*Crosses below* DI SANTIS *to exit left.* DI SANTIS *looks at* HURSPOOL

*for a second and then angrily grabs him by the arm
and pulls him over to the latrine.*]

DI SANTIS: Come over here! You see that cigarette butt
you threw in the urinal? We don't throw cigarette
butts in the urinal here! Now stick your hand in there
and pick it up! [*As* HURSPOOL *bends down to pick
up the cigarette butt,* DI SANTIS *moves to center.*] You
see, Hurspool, you're the one that never makes mistakes.

HURSPOOL: [*Standing at urinal with the cigarette butt
in his hand*] I got three years left, Mr. Di Santis. Let
me be.

DI SANTIS: You still a homosexual, Hurspool?

HURSPOOL: I don't know. After twenty years I don't
rightly know what I am no more.

DI SANTIS: Talk is you got your eye on a little Mexican
boy we got over there in the Spanish section. He's
a cutie. I saw him myself. A cutie little pretty boy.
Bet he'd just love having you bed down with him.
Trouble is what with you over in your section and
him over in his that ain't likely to happen, unless, of
course, you were to be given a transfer. That happen,
you could be over there tomorrow night, just that
quick. [*Holds knife out to* HURSPOOL.]

HURSPOOL: They're gonna kill me I do what you say!

DI SANTIS: Not likely, Hurspool. You're jail-wise. I'm
sure you'll find a way to wriggle out of it.

[*For a long moment there is silence as* HURSPOOL
*stares at the knife and then he takes it and walks
toward the exit.* DI SANTIS *counters to right of center.*
HURSPOOL *stops at the exit.*]

HURSPOOL: Why Jefferson?

DI SANTIS: Oh, I don't know. Why not Jefferson?

LIGHTS FADE AND OUT

Scene 5

The GUARDS' *locker room.*

ON RISE: OFFICERS FRIEZER *and* ROLLOCK *sit facing each other on opposite sides of the locker room bench,* ROLLOCK *right,* FRIEZER *left. In between are two open lunch buckets.* ROLLOCK *has a small order book in his hand and is reading out his shopping list. As he places each order,* FRIEZER *drops the merchandise, glassine envelopes of heroin, into* ROLLOCK's *lunch bucket.*

ROLLOCK: Nickel bag, Foxy Lady. Nickel bag, Superfly. Nickel bag, Hopalong Cassidy. Nickel bag, Cisco Kid. That's it for the heroin. Now I got six for the Red Devils. [*A banging steam pipe sends* ROLLOCK *jumping to his feet.*]

FRIEZER: Sit down, Rollock. It's just the steam pipe. Who's for the Red Devils?

ROLLOCK: [*Sits.*] Rye Crisp, Sunsweet, Grape Nuts, Maxwell House, Mother Paul's . . . [*Sound of a door banging shut.* ROLLOCK *jumps up, shoving his lunch bucket into his locker.*]

FRIEZER: You're gonna give yourself a heart attack one of these days, you know that? [OFFICER LLOYD, *dressed in his street clothes, and carrying an attaché case, enters left no. 2 entrance.* ROLLOCK *moves a few feet away to stage right and finishes putting on his uniform.*] Hi there, buddy.

LLOYD: Hi.

FRIEZER: How's it going?

LLOYD: Okay. What's that smell in here?

FRIEZER: You still smell it, huh? Di Santis got sick. We were just sitting here talking and he got sick. He threw up in that urinal over there.

LLOYD: [*Going over to his locker, begins to prepare to change into his uniform.*] Where's he now?

FRIEZER: Lying down in the dispensary. I never seen him get sick like that before. I thought his insides were gonna come up. What I get are these migraine headaches. It's like somebody put my neck in a vise. You ever get anything like that?

LLOYD: No.

FRIEZER: Wait'll you been around here for a while. What'd you do before you came here? Law enforcement?

LLOYD: No. I worked for an insurance company. Claims adjustment.

FRIEZER: Hey, no kidding?

ROLLOCK: What company was that?

LLOYD: Sun Life.

FRIEZER: So what happened?

LLOYD: It didn't work out.

FRIEZER: How come?

LLOYD: It just didn't work out, that's all.

ROLLOCK: How come?

LLOYD: I just didn't get the hang of it.

FRIEZER: Well, it happens that way sometimes.

ROLLOCK: You ought to know, Friezer. Why don't you tell him about that chicken farm you had outside Texarkana, the one that got so dry all the chickens started blowin' away in the wind.

FRIEZER: Why don't you tell him about your hamburger joint, Rollock? The one where the health department ran you outa town for serving coyote meat.

ROLLOCK: That's not true. I got this idea about calling them Coyote Burgers, but they were ground beef, one hundred percent ground beef.

FRIEZER: Sure they were, the only thing was whenever a rabbit came by the damn things jumped right outa your hand. [FRIEZER *leaves out a long coyote howl*.]

ROLLOCK: That's funny, man.

FRIEZER: [*To* LLOYD] Listen, you're going to work out here just fine. [*Moving closer*] Listen, after a while

I'll put you wise to a lot of ways you can pick up an extra buck here.

ROLLOCK: There ain't any ways to pick up an extra buck in here, Friezer.

LLOYD: I'm not looking to pick up an extra anything here. I just wanna do my job and go home to my family.

FRIEZER: Sure you can do your job, but there ain't nothin' wrong in pickin' up a few extra bucks on the side. The state don't pay that much, you know. Start yourself off with some porno magazines, some grass, nothin' heavy, and then after a while . . . they got a guy on the gun tower got almost forty thou put away for his family in the last five years.

ROLLOCK: You know, Friezer, you got a big mouth.

FRIEZER: Why don't you eat my ass, Rollock?

ROLLOCK: One of these days that mouth of yours is going to get you in more trouble than you know what to do with.

FRIEZER: [Crossing to right to ROLLOCK, nose to nose] You wanna give me some trouble right now, Rollock? How about it? [For a moment it looks as if there might be a fight, but then ROLLOCK backs off. He pushes FRIEZER aside, crosses below bench to exit left. He slams down the money he owes FRIEZER on bench and walks out no. 2 left exit. FRIEZER smiles sarcastically. Picks up money.] You don't have to worry about that jackass. The guy you wanna watch out for is Di Santis. I mean he's an okay guy, don't get me wrong. There ain't a guy in here stand by ya quicker than he will. [Crosses to center as he pockets money.] It's just that he's gettin' kind of serious about everything here lately, dedicated, you know, like a missionary or something. And then that damn thing with Lowery the other night . . . the kid was always tryin' to get Di Santis to go back to night school. I dunno, after a while everything around here goes blah. I guess it's just the place, you know. It does things to you, you don't even think about. [*Looking directly at* LLOYD] Who do you think killed that con Turner, in the strip cell?

LLOYD: I don't wanna know about it, man.

FRIEZER: Take a guess. Go on, take a guess.

LLOYD: Look, I don't wanna get involved in this. I just wanna do my job, that's all. You understand me, man?

FRIEZER: It was Di Santis.

LLOYD: The way I heard it, he was resistin'. If Di Santis killed him, he was resistin'.

FRIEZER: Resistin', shit. When we got down to that cell, that black mother was holdin' on to those bars like somebody poured concrete over him. I ain't never seen anything like it. It was like he was in some kind of trance. Rollock was bendin' over Lowery, sayin' "My God! My God!" and Di Santis went flyin' into that cell with some of those regular guards they got down there like he had a ten-cent firecracker up his ass. They must've spent ten minutes bashin' in that con's head. I couldn't pull any of them off. That mother's head looked like a can of mashed-up blood-worms lying on the floor. I ain't never seen anything like that. There must've been an inch of blood all over that corridor before they got finished. I couldn't even lift my feet up without them stickin'. [*Crosses above bench to his lunch bucket on bench.*] Man, I tell you, I don't ever wanna pull rotation duty down the Adjustment Center again. [FRIEZER *stares inside his lunch bucket and pulls out an orange.*] Goddamn it! I don't know what's the matter with that woman. She give me an orange. I told her I wanted a piece of chocolate cake. Something sweet! [*Puts lunch bucket in locker, slams locker shut, and exits left no. 2 exit as:*]

LIGHTS FADE AND OUT

Scene 6

A cell.

ON RISE: *Lights up dimly. It is late at night and the* PRISONERS *are sleeping. All is silence for perhaps thirty seconds and then* VOICE *of* SERGEANT COYNE, *amplified over a bullhorn, screams out.*

COYNE'S VOICE: All right, hit it!

(*The lights of the cell block are flooded on with eye-shattering brilliance as an army of* GUARDS, *led by* SERGEANT COYNE, *descends on the* PRISONERS. *The* GUARDS *enter with a great frightening hullabaloo of shouts and commands. What we see in this particular cell is what is happening all along the tier:* GUARDS *bursting into the cells, stripping the* PRISONERS *naked, pushing them out into the corridor, searching them and their cells. The* GUARDS *involved with this particular cell are* FRIEZER, ROLLOCK, *and* LLOYD. SERGEANT COYNE *stations himself in front of the cell, using it as a command point to shout orders up and down the tier.*)

GUARDS: [*To the* PRISONERS] Let's go! Let's go! Let's go! Out of here! Out of here! Get out! Let's go! Let's go!

COYNE: [*Shouting to all the* GUARDS] Move! Move! Move! Move! Let's go! Let's go! Strip 'em down! Move 'em! Move 'em! Move! Move! [*The entire corridor is filled with the sounds of the* GUARDS *yelling and the* PRISONERS *talking back.* FRIEZER, ROLLOCK, *and* LLOYD *charge into the cell, screaming.*]

FRIEZER, ROLLOCK, and LLOYD: All right, let's go, let's go, on your feet, strip down, strip down, let's go, let's go, come on, let's go!

COYNE: Get 'em out into the corridor! Strip 'em down! Let's go! Move 'em! Move 'em! Move 'em! Move 'em! Hands on the bar! Hands on the bar! [FOSTER, STEPP, JEFFERSON, *and* HURSPOOL *are pushed naked out of their cell and shoved against the railing of their tier. They comply with the orders of the* GUARDS, *spread-eagling their legs and grasping hold of the railing.* JEFFERSON *seems lost, confused.*]

FRIEZER, ROLLOCK, and LLOYD: Spread your legs! Hands on the bar! Let's go! Let's go! Hands on the bar! Hands on the bar! [ROLLOCK *ends* JEFFERSON's *momentary confusion by slamming his hands down on the bar.*]

FRIEZER: All right, spread your cheeks!

ROLLOCK: Let's go! Let's go! Spread your cheeks! [*As* EACH *of the* PRISONERS *in turn spreads his buttocks open,* FRIEZER *and* ROLLOCK *go down the line inspecting for concealed weapons or contraband.*]

FRIEZER: [*As* EACH PRISONER *is finished with his examination*] Hands back on the bar!

COYNE: One on the prisoners, two in the cells! One on the prisoners, two in the cells! [*Shouting now to a* GUARD *down at the end of the tier stage left*] Keep that man's hands where you can see them! [*Charging off in the direction of the guard offstage left no. 2 exit*] Get that prisoner's hands on the bar! [ROLLOCK *has entered the cell and begun his search.* LLOYD *is prying* JEFFERSON's *legs ever farther apart.*]

FOSTER: [*To* LLOYD] Take it easy with him, man. [*For a split second* FOSTER *and* LLOYD *stare at each other as if there might be some kind of human response between them.* LLOYD *is somewhat taken aback, somewhat hesitant about what to do.* FRIEZER *comes to the rescue.*]

FRIEZER: [*To* FOSTER] You open your mouth again, Foster, I'm gonna shove this pole two feet up your ass. You understand me? [*To* LLOYD] You don't take any crap from them. All right, get in the cell and help Rollock. [LLOYD *goes into the cell.* ROLLOCK *is wildly throwing everything about in his search. After a moment,* LLOYD *begins copying* ROLLOCK's *search technique. Down the cell block a fight of some kind has broken out. A* PRISONER *begins to scream in pain.* OTHER PRISONERS *call out in his defense.*]

PRISONERS: [*Off left*] Why don't you leave him alone! He ain't doin' nothin'! Leave him alone!

COYNE: [*Off left*] Keep that man on the ground! Get that club under his chin! Under his chin! Now hold him there! Hold him!

ROLLOCK: [*Finding the toothbrush concealed under* JEFFERSON's *mattress*] Well, lookee, lookee, lookee, here comes cookie! [*Rushes out of the cell, holding up the toothbrush knife.*] Stickin' razor blades in the soap don't make it no more. Now they're grindin' down the toothbrushes. [*Shows the knife to* FRIEZER, *who takes it*]

FRIEZER: [*Calling out*]Sergeant Coyne! Sergeant Coyne!

ROLLOCK: Hey, whatta ya doin'? I found that knife, not you! Gimme that knife! You ain't takin' credit for what I find!

FRIEZER: What difference does it make who gets the credit?

ROLLOCK: It don't make any difference? Then gimme that knife! [*He pulls the knife back and shouts for the* SERGEANT.] Sergeant Coyne! Sergeant Coyne! [SERGEANT COYNE *enters.*]

COYNE: What is it, Rollock?

ROLLOCK: I found this in the cell, Sergeant Coyne. They made a knife outa a toothbrush. You see what they did to the end here? [COYNE *takes the knife.*] Watch it. It's sharp.

COYNE: [*To the* PRISONERS] All right. Whose is it?

ROLLOCK: It was really buried away. I was lucky to find it.

COYNE: [*Again to the* PRISONERS] Whose knife is this? [*There is no answer.*] Where did you find it, Rollock?

ROLLOCK: In that bed. It was stuck all the way under the mattress.

COYNE: Whose bunk is that? [ROLLOCK *doesn't know.* FRIEZER *does.*]

FRIEZER: Jefferson.

FOSTER: That boy ain't never touched a knife since he came in here, and you know it!

STEPP: You know that knife ain't his.

HURSPOOL: That's the honest-to-God truth, Sergeant Coyne. That boy ain't never had a knife.

COYNE: [*To* LLOYD] Put him in a holding cell. I'll sign the order for it. [*To* FRIEZER *and* ROLLOCK] Lock the rest of them up.

FOSTER: He went up before the parole board this morning. What's he need a knife for?

FRIEZER: [*To* FOSTER] You shut your mouth! I told you to keep your mouth shut! Now move! [*For a second* FOSTER *stands still and then he enters the cell.* ROLLOCK *grabs* STEPP *and* HURSPOOL *by the arm and leads them back into the cell.* STEPP *pulls his arm free.*]

STEPP: Take your hands off me, man.

HURSPOOL: That boy never messed around with a knife. [JEFFERSON, *seeing the* OTHERS *enter the cell, tries to enter.* FRIEZER *stops him.*]

FRIEZER: You just stay here, Jefferson.

JEFFERSON: I never had no knife. I never had no knife.

FRIEZER: [*To* SERGEANT COYNE] Talk to you a second, Sarge? [*Walks aside with* SERGEANT COYNE *to down right.*]

HURSPOOL: That boy ain't never had no knife. No sir. That boy ain't never done nothin' like that.

FRIEZER: [*To* COYNE] That boy don't carry a knife, Sarge. I been here five years, I know the knifers, that boy's all clean time.

COYNE: They're clean time till you catch them, Friezer. There's always a first time.

FRIEZER: Yeah, there's always a first time, but I don't think this is it.

JEFFERSON: [*To* LLOYD *and* ROLLOCK] I went up before the parole board this morning. What I need a knife for?

COYNE: Well, I go by the book, Friezer, and that book applies to the guards as well as the prisoners. Now you ain't askin' me to bury up the evidence, are you?

FRIEZER: No, sir, I ain't askin' you to do that.

COYNE: Then what are you sayin' to me?

FRIEZER: Lots of ways a knife can get into a cell. Know that boy a couple of years, Sarge. First year or so a little bad ass, maybe, but the last two years he's clean time.

COYNE: Well, maybe he reverted, Friezer. [*Holding up the knife*] 'Cause this don't look like clean time to me.

FRIEZER: You're the boss.

COYNE: That's right. I'm the boss. Now get him into a holding cell. [FRIEZER *turns away.*] Friezer? [FRIEZER *turns to face* SERGEANT COYNE *again.* COYNE *purposely speaks loud enough to be overheard by the* OTHER GUARDS *and the* PRISONERS.] When you gonna learn? They don't do things for a reason. They just do things. [*Shouting down the tier as he exits up and left no. 2 exit*] All right! Get 'em back in the cells. Move 'em! Move 'em!

FRIEZER: [*Crossing to* JEFFERSON *at tier rail*] Let's go, Jefferson.

JEFFERSON: [*Wildly looking about*] No. No. I ain't goin' nowhere.

FRIEZER: I'm sorry, man. I ain't got no choice. Now, let's go.

JEFFERSON: [*Grabbing hold of the tier bars with both his hands*] No. I ain't goin'. I been polishin' up my shoes. I ain't goin'. [FRIEZER *and* ROLLOCK *start to pull him and when he resists they grow more violent.*]

FRIEZER: Pull his hands off the bars.

ROLLOCK: I'm tryin'. The son of a bitch won't let go. [*To* JEFFERSON] Let go before I break your arm off!

JEFFERSON: Please let me stay here. Please, I went up before the man. The man's lettin' me out. The man's lettin' me out! [JEFFERSON *breaks away and runs into the cell and grabs hold of the bunk.* FRIEZER *tries to pull him off.*]

FRIEZER: [*Noticing that* LLOYD *seems to be just standing there without helping*] Whatta ya waitin' for, Lloyd? We need some help here! [*Both* STEPP *and* FOSTER, *as well as* FRIEZER *and* ROLLOCK, *stare at* LLOYD, *waiting to see what he does. When* LLOYD *enters the scuffle it is with a vengeance, as if his mind has suddenly become cleared of all doubt. He grabs* JEFFERSON *around the neck and furiously starts pulling him away from the bunk.*]

LLOYD: [*To* JEFFERSON] You hadda make a knife! You hadda prove what a big man you are!

FOSTER: Leave him alone! You're choking him! You're choking him! [FRIEZER *strikes out with his club, hitting* FOSTER *in the arm.* FOSTER *lets out a cry of pain as he pulls his arm back.* LLOYD *tears* JEFFERSON *away and drags him off.* FOSTER *calls out to* LLOYD.] You black pig! You black pig! They put a uniform on you and you don't care about your own people! You sell yourself out for a uniform and a lousy job?

JEFFERSON: [*Calling out as they drag him off*] Bobby! Bobby! Bobby! [*A chorus of mocking* VOICES *from*

the upper tier begins to join in the shout until JEF-FERSON *can no longer be heard.*]
VOICES: Bobby! Bobby! Bobby! Bobby! Bobby! Bobby!
[FOSTER *stares upward at the screaming voices.*]

LIGHTS FADE AND OUT

END OF ACT I

ACT II

Scene 1

A holding cell area.

ON RISE: *The stage is dark. In the dark* SOMEONE *strikes a match and as the lights come up we see a prisoner,* ALBERT HEISENMAN, *lighting a cigarette. In the cell next to* HEISENMAN *is* CHARLES JEFFERSON. JEFFERSON *paces back and forth. The* GUARD *on duty,* OFFICER LLOYD, *is seated in a chair, reading a newspaper.*

HEISENMAN: [*Coming to the front of his cell, staring angrily at* OFFICER LLOYD, *and then suddenly poking his finger through the bars and shouting at him*] I'll tell you what the story is, Turner! The fella that was in the punishment cell before you was a bad housekeeper!

LLOYD: [*Angered at an interruption in his reading that has been taking place, off and on, for some time now*] I don't wanna hear that anymore, Heisenman. I already told you Turner's dead. You ain't in the Adjustment Center anymore. Now you just take it easy. You'll be outa that holding cell tomorrow morning, then you can do all the talking you want.

HEISENMAN: You see that little toilet hole in the floor there? [*Pointing toward a drain.*]

LLOYD: There's no toilet hole in the floor, Heisenman. That's a drain.

HEISENMAN: That right? Well, sometimes he didn't get his do-do exactly into it, sometimes he missed the hole. He had the same trouble with his pee-pee. He

249

started peeing into the hole and then he started peeing on the floor because he didn't care. After that the food didn't agree with him so good so he started throwing it up on the floor. That's what you got there now: do-do, pee-pee, vomit.

LLOYD: There's nothing there, Heisenman.

HEISENMAN: That right? As far as I know that kind of stink may be your idea of what things should smell like, but when I stop smoking and the smell whiffs over it makes me nauseous. It makes me feel like I can't hold my food down. Now I want you to tell them to hose your cell down. You show them the proper attitude of contrition, they're gonna hose your cell down the same way they got all the other cells in this confinement wing hosed down.

LLOYD: You're not in the confinement wing, Heisenman. How many times do I gotta tell ya that? Now just shut up. Shut up!

HEISENMAN: You see what I got here, Turner? I got a nice blanket. I'm smoking a cigarette. Tonight they're gonna give you that rolled-up ball of leftovers that nobody can eat while I'm gonna have a nice fresh serving of dog tuna right outa the can. You continue the way you're going, you're gonna be heading for a bad cold, the night after that it's going to be pneumonia.

LLOYD: [*Going over to left of* HEISENMAN] Shut up, Heisenman, just shut up!

HEISENMAN: I'm almost finished with my cigarette, Turner. I don't get through to you polite, I'm gonna find another way of getting through to you.

LLOYD: Are you, man?

HEISENMAN: I'll tell you something about me. When I get annoyed I tend to destroy whatever I get my hands on. I push my hands right through the bars and just grab hold, then it's good-bye teaching seminars on Nietzsche. Good-bye Superman and Albert Camus. You know why I said that? I said that because I'm coming to the end of my cigarette. I don't know what I'm gonna do when I come to the end of my cigarette. [HEISENMAN *abruptly becomes mute and motionless.* JEFFERSON *has grown increasingly agitated, his pacing erratic, directionless. He begins uttering sounds, small cries.*]

LLOYD: [*Crossing back to his desk*] There's nobody out here but me, Jefferson, so you can just cut out that goddamn crap. I know guys like you. I've known guys like you all my life. Now shut up. Just shut up. You hadda prove something? You hadda prove you were a big man? You hadda prove you were as tough as the rest of them? You hadda make yourself a knife? Big man. Big shot. Now we'll see how tough you are. We'll see how you like goin' down to the Adjustment Center. You couldn't play it straight. Oh, no. That was too tough. You hadda prove you were a big shot. They don't have it in enough for us already. You hadda give them some more reasons. You hadda prove you were a real nigger. One son of a bitch like you in a cell block is all the excuse they want to take it out on the rest of us. But you don't give a damn about that. You're like all the rest of the niggers in this place. You don't give a damn about your own people. All you care about is yourself. Well, I'm sick of it. It's tough enough getting anywhere in this bastard world without having guys like you ruining it for the rest of us all the time. Don't you come to me for any help. I hope you rot in there for what you've done to us, you son of a bitch!

LIGHTS FADE

Scene 2

The GUARDS' *lounge.*

The traveler opens to full stage. At right a small table

*with a coffee urn, cups, sugar, etc. Right of center a
bridge table with chairs right and left of it. Up center
is a clothes tree. Left of center is a cot covered with a
blanket.*

ON RISE: SERGEANT COYNE *and* OFFICER DI SANTIS *are
hunched over a game of Scrabble.* SERGEANT COYNE *has
taken his shoes off.* SERGEANT COYNE *keeps rearranging
his playing tiles as* OFFICER DI SANTIS *stares at him in
mounting annoyance over the delay.*

DI SANTIS: [*On chair right, finally in exasperation*] You
gonna put down a word or what?

COYNE: [*On chair left*] I'm gonna put down a word.

DI SANTIS: When? Next Thursday? You've been shuffling those tiles around since a quarter to four. In
another ten minutes the sun's gonna come up.

COYNE: You want a word, huh?

DI SANTIS: Yeah, I want a word. There was a two-
minute hourglass that used to come with this game
until it mysteriously disappeared . . . along with the
rule book.

COYNE: All right, I'm gonna give you a word. [*Puts
down a word and spins the board around to* DI SANTIS.
DI SANTIS *stares at the word.*]

DI SANTIS: What the hell is that? [*Spelling out the word*]
T-O-M-A-I-N-E?

COYNE: Ptomaine. Ptomaine poisoning.

DI SANTIS: That's not how you spell "ptomaine."

COYNE: Sure it is.

DI SANTIS: Oh no. No no no no no.

FRIEZER: [*Enters left no. 1 entrance, carrying his lunch
bucket.*] You guys still at that game? Don't you ever
stop? [*He hangs his raincoat, cap, and baton on rack.
He keeps his lunch bucket. They totally ignore him
as he collapses on the cot.*]

DI SANTIS: You're not getting away with that! Ptomaine

252

is spelled with a *P*. Its *P-T*-O-M-A-I-N-E, not *T*-O-M-A-I-N-E.

COYNE: Bullshit!

DI SANTIS: No bullshit! That's the way the word is spelled! You must've picked up two hundred points in this game alone with phony spelling. You got "phlegm" spelled F-L-E-M, you got "faggot" spelled with one *G* instead of two.

COYNE: You wanna challenge my spelling go look it up in the dictionary.

DI SANTIS: I can't look it up in the dictionary! You took the dictionary along with the hourglass and the rule book.

FRIEZER: Jesus Christ, it's four-thirty in the morning! I gotta get outside in that lousy rain in half an hour. Lemme get some sleep.

COYNE: How do you spell "ptomaine," Friezer?

FRIEZER: [*Starting to spell the word*] T-O-E . . .

DI SANTIS: [*Rising and crossing to center*] Don't ask him how to spell "ptomaine." He's the worst speller in this whole prison.

COYNE: You don't accept his spelling?

DI SANTIS: No, I don't accept his spelling. I've been filling out his duty rosters for the last five years. He can't spell. [SERGEANT COYNE *starts adding up his score. Left to* COYNE] Whatta ya doing?

COYNE: Whatta ya think I'm doing? I'm adding up my score.

DI SANTIS: Oh no you're not. Not for that word you're not.

COYNE: [*As* DI SANTIS *walks to above* SERGEANT COYNE] The hell I'm not. I'm just going by the rules. The rules don't say nothing about me having to accept your spelling of a word without a dictionary. That's nine points for the word and it's a double word square so that's eighteen points, and fifty points for using all seven letters . . .

DI SANTIS: [*Pulling on the score sheet*] I don't accept this scoring.

COYNE: [*Holding down the sheet*] . . . so that's sixty . . . sixty-eight points and . . .

DI SANTIS: I don't accept this scoring!

COYNE: Tough nookies . . . and two hundred and seven from before . . . [DI SANTIS *starts pulling at the pencil.*] Whatta ya doing? Whatta ya doing?

DI SANTIS: Gimme that pencil! You ain't writing that score up! [*They begin fighting and struggling for possession of the pencil.*]

COYNE: The hell I'm not!

DI SANTIS: [*Gets pencil.*] The hell you are! [*Crossing left to below cot*] You've been cheating me for four years with this game, but you ain't cheating me no more! What happened to the hourglass?

COYNE: [*Following* DI SANTIS] Whatta ya think happened to the hourglass? [*They struggle for pencil.*]

DI SANTIS: You took it! You took it, you took the rule book, you took the dictionary! [DI SANTIS *gets away from* SERGEANT COYNE *and moves left and up around to above cot.*]

COYNE: [*Following to above cot*] Prove it! Why don't you try to prove it? Give me that damn pencil. [DI-SANTIS *grabs* COYNE's *genitals and* COYNE *jumps into the air, still holding on to* DI SANTIS. *They both topple down on the edge of the cot, sending them and* FRIEZER *sprawling onto the floor.* DI SANTIS *scurries after the pencil, finally grabbing it and holding it up in triumph.*]

FRIEZER: Jesus Christ!

COYNE: [*On the floor right*] You got me right in the nuts.

DI SANTIS: [*On the floor left*] My side hurts.

COYNE: Good for you. That's what you get trying to wipe out the old man.

FRIEZER: [*He has risen and has a piece of the broken cot.*] You broke the cot. Now we don't have a cot in here no more. It took me two years filling out requisition forms to get 'em to put a cot in here, and now we don't have a cot in here.

COYNE: [*As he crosses to chair left of bridge table*] Tell you what, Friezer, why don't you get Di Santis to fill out one of those forms for you? He's terrific with spelling.

FRIEZER: Very funny. [*Grabbing the mattress and moving to above broken cot.*]

DI SANTIS: [*Crossing to coffee urn at stage right*] Where you going with the mattress?

FRIEZER: I'm going to sleep. I'm gonna put the mattress down on the floor and I'm going to go to sleep. [*Which he does.*]

COYNE: [*Sitting, chair left of table*] You're gonna sleep your life away, Friezer. [FRIEZER *throws the covers over his head.*]

DI SANTIS: [*Pouring coffee*] Listen, before I forget, I wanna move that guy Hurspool outa the laundry and into the guards' latrine.

COYNE: Whatta ya wanna move him for?

DI SANTIS: I thought I'd give him a break. He's been pretty straight.

COYNE: Okay, take him out of the laundry. After all these years he's probably clean enough.

FRIEZER: [*Drawing the covers more tightly over his head*] Oh, Jesus!

DI SANTIS: [*Indicating* SERGEANT COYNE'*s cup*] You want some coffee?

COYNE: Yeah, okay.

DI SANTIS: [*Pouring* SERGEANT COYNE'*s coffee.*] I think I might as well transfer him outa that cell while I'm at it.

COYNE: Whatta ya talking about?

DI SANTIS: Well, the guards' latrine is by the Chicano block. Might as well put him close by it.

COYNE: You can't put him in with those Mexicans. They'll eat him up like a hot tortilla.

DI SANTIS: [*Crossing to right of table*] Come on, it's not gonna make any difference.

COYNE: [*Taking the coffee from* DI SANTIS] Since when do you start mixing the blacks with the Mexicans? You wanna kick up a riot, or what?

DI SANTIS: [*Sitting, chair right of table*] There won't be a riot.

COYNE: Whatta ya gonna do? Give a guarantee? Forget it. Keep him where he is.

DI SANTIS: He's gotta walk halfway around the prison to get to that latrine.

COYNE: So what? Let him walk. What else has he got to do with his time? [DI SANTIS *rises, walks away left to below cot, turning his back to* COYNE.] Whatta ya mad at me or something? I didn't transfer the guy, so what?

DI SANTIS: [*Turning to* SERGEANT COYNE] Look, I promised him. [*The covers slide away from* FRIEZER's *head.*]

COYNE: So you'll tell him it didn't work out. Tell him I didn't let it go through, that's all.

DI SANTIS: [*Crossing to left of* SERGEANT COYNE] He wanted to get outa that cell.

COYNE: What for? What's it supposed to be? The Honolulu Hilton? [DI SANTIS *crosses up and right to above table.*] He doesn't like the room so he wants another room? What are you talking about?

DI SANTIS: [*Crossing down to right of table*] He thinks maybe they're gonna blame him for what happened to Jefferson.

COYNE: Why should they blame him? [FRIEZER *sits up.*]

DI SANTIS: [*Becoming a little leery at* FRIEZER's *presence.*] I don't know why. You know the way they are.

COYNE: No, I don't know the way they are. You tell me.

DI SANTIS: What's the difference? Let's drop it.

COYNE: No, I don't wanna drop it. I wanna know what you're talking about.

DI SANTIS: Why don't you take your mattress and go sleep somewhere else, Friezer?

FRIEZER: No, it's all right, I'm comfortable here.

COYNE: [*To* DI SANTIS] I wanna know what you're talking about.

DI SANTIS: It doesn't matter.

COYNE: Don't tell me it doesn't matter. I wanna know what's going on here. I wanna know why you want Hurspool outa that cell.

DI SANTIS: He planted that knife on Jefferson.

FRIEZER: [*Standing up and crossing to below cot*] How do you know that?

DI SANTIS: You really want in on this, Friezer? Is that what you want?

COYNE: How do you know that?

DI SANTIS: All right. I gave him the knife. I figured Jefferson had some more time to do.

FRIEZER: Oh, boy, I knew it was a setup. Ten seconds on that corridor and I knew it.

COYNE: [*Rising*] You set a man up in my section?

DI SANTIS: You know the way the parole board is always letting them out before they're ready for parole. Hell, we're on the inside. We know what these guys are like. That's what you're always telling us about them yourself.

COYNE: Setting up a man? I've been talkin about setting up a man? I've worked twenty-two years in this prison and I never set a man up. You come along, I treat you like my own son, and you do that to me? You ruin a record of trust that goes back to the day I came into this prison?

DI SANTIS: It ain't just me!

COYNE: Don't hand me that!

DI SANTIS: There's plenty of others in this prison that think the same way I do.

FRIEZER: Where? Down the Adjustment Center, is that where you're talking about?

DI SANTIS: [*Crossing above the table to left and down*

to between COYNE *and* FRIEZER] That's right! They know you can't run a prison by the book anymore. You don't have the same kind of prisoners in there anymore. You start going by the book and they figure there ain't nothing they can't get away with. Look what they did to Lowery. He didn't get himself killed because he was reading his books. He got himself killed because there's no discipline left in this prison anymore. You got sections in here you can't even walk into without taking your life in your hands. You can't even walk down a cell block without listening to them laughing to themselves. The day after they murdered Lowery I'm walking down a cell block and they're sitting in there laughing to themselves. [SERGEANT COYNE *turns away from him and sits and starts putting on his shoes.*] Whatta ya gonna do?

COYNE: I'm getting that man outa that holding cell and then I'm bringing you up on charges.

DI SANTIS: For what? For trying to give some meaning to Lowery's death? For doing what you should have done if you had the guts? You're the one always talking about it being a zoo and them being animals. Goddamn it, what the hell was that all about?

COYNE: It's going by the rules. That's what it's about! You can't go by the rules you got no business working in here.

DI SANTIS: The law's the book, and the book is the law with you, huh?

COYNE: That's right.

DI SANTIS: Well, why don't you wake up, old man? It's not twenty years ago. What the hell do you think is happening out there? Every crazy with a gun thinks it's all right to kill a cop because he ain't nothing but a faceless pig in a uniform; every loony with a stick of dynamite thinks it's okay to throw it through a bank window and kill fifty innocent people because he has a cause! They've taken our country away from us and nobody has the guts to do anything about it.

[OFFICER LLOYD, *soaking wet in his raincoat, enters left no. 1 entrance and stands there unseen.*] And I'll tell you why. It's because they're minority groups, that's why. You're a minority group in this country and you got a free ride. You want anything in this country, you just ask for it. They don't wanna give it to you, you just take it. You're a minority group, it don't make no difference.

LLOYD: Sergeant Coyne? [*The* THREE MEN *turn to face him.*]

FRIEZER: [*Crossing to left to* LLOYD] Whatta ya doing here, Lloyd? You're supposed to be on duty down the holding cells.

LLOYD: [*Crosses right to left of center without paying any attention to* FRIEZER.] Sergeant Coyne?

COYNE: What is it, Lloyd?

LLOYD: I'm supposed to tell you to . . . to come down to the holding cells. The deputy warden wants to see you.

COYNE: What for? [LLOYD *just stands there.*]

DI SANTIS: [*Going over to* LLOYD *and speaking in a gentle tone of voice*] What's the matter, Lloyd? What happened down there?

LLOYD: Jefferson . . . he, uh, hanged himself. I was reading my newspaper, and it got late, I must've fallen asleep, I didn't think I fell asleep, and then I looked up and he was just . . . hanging there, he tore his blanket up and he was just hanging there.

DI SANTIS: Take it easy, Lloyd.

LLOYD: Are they going to blame me? I mean, is that what's gonna happen? I don't remember falling asleep. I was just reading my newspaper.

DI SANTIS: Nobody's gonna blame you. You ain't responsible for what a con does to himself.

LLOYD: I don't think I oughtta take the blame for this.

DI SANTIS: Don't worry about it. You did okay. [*Moving him toward left no. 1 exit*] Now go on back to the holding cells and tell the deputy warden Sergeant

259

Coyne's on his way. [FRIEZER *crosses right to* SER-
GEANT COYNE.]

LLOYD: [*Stopping down left*] I don't even think I fell
asleep. Maybe I was checking some of the other cages
or something when he did it. That's probably what
happened. I was checking some of the other cages
when he did it.

DI SANTIS: That's right. That's just what happened. Now
just keep your mouth shut until Sergeant Coyne gets
down there. He'll take care of it for you.

LLOYD: [*Exiting*] You just can't be everywhere at once.
You just can't.

COYNE: [*At chair left of table*] Meaningless. Absolutely
meaningless!

FRIEZER: [*To* DI SANTIS] How does it feel standing
around all this time arguing about a dead man?

COYNE: I've seen men die in the gas chamber, but that
was for something. But this . . . this was for nothing.

DI SANTIS: [*To* SERGEANT COYNE] Just like Lowery's
death, huh? No reason for no reason. [COYNE *crosses
up to rack to get hat.*]

FRIEZER: My God, what's happened to you?

DI SANTIS: You just better keep your nose in your own
business, Friezer. This ain't got nothing to do with
you.

COYNE: [*Crossing down to right of* DI SANTIS] Let's go.
You got something to say to the deputy warden.

DI SANTIS: For God's sake, it don't make a damn bit of
difference now! The man's dead! If you could bring
him back, okay, there'd be some point to it. But
there's no point to it now.

COYNE: Get out that door!

DI SANTIS: Look, maybe I rubbed your back up against
the wall, but you know I didn't mean anything by
it. Christ, we've been friends for years. Okay, so
maybe I made a mistake, but who the hell in prison
doesn't make a mistake?

FRIEZER: You didn't set that kid up out of a mistake. Maybe I made a mistake because I saw it was a setup down the cell block and I didn't push it; maybe Lloyd made a mistake because he's working a double shift and he got tired and fell asleep; but you didn't make a mistake. So don't try and hand him that garbage.

DI SANTIS: You wanna talk about garbage, Friezer? You so ready to sell out my life for one con? Why don't you tell him what you got in that lunch bucket? [*He crosses above* COYNE *and picks up lunch bucket from floor right of mattress.*] How about it, Friezer? Whatta ya got in that lunch bucket? [FRIEZER *crosses in and grabs bucket from* DI SANTIS.]

COYNE: What's he talking about?

FRIEZER: [*Exiting left no. 1 exit.*] Nothing. Nothing.

COYNE: [*Shouting after the exiting* FRIEZER] Whatta ya got in that lunch bucket, Friezer?

DI SANTIS: That's your specialty, isn't it? Ignorance. Ignorance of everything that's happening around here. Well, let me tell you something. It's not me who failed the law, or Friezer, or Lloyd—it's you! You know the way things are in this prison, but you don't wanna see it. That's negligence. What did you think negligence was?

COYNE: I've worked twenty-two years in this prison and I've never been negligent about anything! Where the hell do you get off accusing me of negligence?

DI SANTIS: Oh, come off it. You see them pushing dope in the yard, but you don't wanna see it. That's negligence! You see new prisoners being raped by gangs, but you don't want to see it. That's negligence! You see them beating prisoners to death in the Adjustment Center, but you don't want to see it. That's negligence! You cover it up like everybody else. You see a con you know never carried a knife being set up, but you don't get holier-than-thou about it until he hangs himself and it's shoved in your face. That's negligence.

COYNE: I didn't know about it until you just told me!

DI SANTIS: You didn't know about it? Bullshit! There wasn't a guard on that corridor didn't realize it was a setup. You just didn't want to see it! You just didn't want to get involved with it! I don't know what the hell you were like twenty-five years ago, but if there's anyone who hasn't been faithful to that fucking book of moron rules you live by, it's you, Sergeant Coyne, it's you! [COYNE *has slumped into chair.* DI SANTIS *grabs him by the arm and thrusts him part way forward*] Go on! You got something you wanna say to the deputy warden? [COYNE *moves left a few feet and stops.* DI SANTIS *stares down at the Scrabble board.*] What's the life of one con worth? What's the life of any of us in this prison worth? [*He folds the Scrabble board so the tiles fall toward the center, dashing against each other. Lights fade to reading. The following scene is an overlap and begins as lights fade.*]

Scene 3

A cell.

OFFICERS FRIEZER *and* ROLLOCK *are taking inventory of* JEFFERSON's *possessions.* ROLLOCK *calls out each item.* FRIEZER *marks the item down on a checkout sheet fastened to a clipboard. This scene is played down stage left. The lighting should be very tight and only the faces of* ROLLOCK *and* FRIEZER *should be seen. No props are used. In the remaining light on the previous scene we see* SERGEANT COYNE *walk slowly back to the chair left of the table, sit and take off his cap. On* ROLLOCK's *line* "That's it for regulation" *the lights on* DI SANTIS *and* COYNE *fade to out and the traveler will close.*

ROLLOCK: [*Offstage left*] One uniform, shirt.

FRIEZER: [*Offstage left*] Right.

ROLLOCK: [*Entering*] Pants.

FRIEZER: [*Follow on.*] Right.

ROLLOCK: [*In place*] Cap.

FRIEZER: [*In place*] Yeah.

ROLLOCK: Socks.

FRIEZER: Yeah.

ROLLOCK: Two T-shirts, two shorts.

FRIEZER: Yeah.

ROLLOCK: That's it for regulation. Personal items: packet of letters.

FRIEZER: Right.

ROLLOCK: Rosary.

FRIEZER: Yeah.

ROLLOCK: One book. [*Reading the title before he tosses it into the bag*] The Modern Farmer.

FRIEZER: Yeah.

ROLLOCK: Equivalency diploma.

FRIEZER: Yeah.

ROLLOCK: One picture, framed.

FRIEZER: Right.

ROLLOCK: Four pictures, unframed. [*Looking at the pictures.*]

FRIEZER: Right.

ROLLOCK: [*Holding out one of the pictures to* FRIEZER] How would you like to get into that?

FRIEZER: [*Ignoring the picture*] How would you like to eat my ass, Rollock?

ROLLOCK: That's the second time you said that to me.

FRIEZER: And I'm gonna keep sayin' it, Rollock . . . [*Pausing slightly, and then softly with a slight smile on his mouth*] . . . 'cause you're a prick. Now what's he got under the bed?

ROLLOCK: [*Bends down and pulls out* JEFFERSON'S *polished shoes.*] One pair of shoes.

FRIEZER: That's it?

ROLLOCK: [*Dropping the shoes into the bag*] That's it. [*He exits left no. 1 exit. We hear the sound of a hand-*

ball game. As the lights cross fade and the traveler opens and we segue into Scene Four, the Prison Yard.]

Scene 4

The prison yard.

The traveler opens to full stage. At stage right, on a line with the no. 2 entrance, hangs a body bag. Up center is a wooden bench. At stage left another wooden bench. This one set at an angle.

FOSTER *is sitting on the center bench lost in thought. On the bench at his left is* HURSPOOL's *shirt. On the floor just left of the bench is* STEPP's *shirt.* STEPP *stands left of the center bench exercising with a pair of dumbbells.*

As the traveler opens, FRIEZER *moves into the scene, crossing into center.*

Someone calls out from the court stage right.

VOICE 1: Hey, where you hittin' that ball?
VOICE 2: That's seven, six, mother. [*The ball bounces across the stage.* OFFICER FRIEZER *picks it up as he enters, and throws it back.* VOICE 1 *calls out.*]
VOICE 1: Thank you kindly.
FRIEZER: [*Crossing up left to* FOSTER] I wanted to tell you I was sorry about Jefferson. [FOSTER *ignores* FRIEZER *completely. He seems lost in his own thoughts.*]
STEPP: [*Moving down to left bench*] Yeah.
FRIEZER: [*Walking over to* STEPP] He was a good kid. [STEPP *just looks at* FRIEZER *without answering.*] No-

body figured on him hanging himself in the holding cell.

STEPP: You better drop it, man, 'cause we ain't interested in hearin' you talk about Charles Jefferson.

FRIEZER: I just wanted to tell you I wouldn't have put him in that holding cell if I didn't have to.

STEPP: That's right, man. You were just doin' your duty.

FRIEZER: Makes you feel any better, Stepp, you can blame me, you can hate my guts, don't matter to me. [Crosses right to exit.]

STEPP: I'm gonna tell you something, man. [FRIEZER stops right of center.] I don't hate your guts. Fact is I don't hardly think about you one way or the other. You are almost never in my head because you are just an ignorant motherfucker that don't know what he's doing one way or the other.

FRIEZER: [Crossing back to STEPP] You call me that again, Stepp, and you're goin' up for a 115 disciplinary report. I don't have to take that kind of shit from you. Now you know I got a job to do, and I do it, that's all.

STEPP: And you do a little extra shufflin' on the side, too, don't you, man? A little bit of grass, a little bit of horse?

FRIEZER: I do what's right by my own. I got a family to support.

STEPP: You ain't looking for my approbation by any chance, are you, Mr. Friezer?

FRIEZER: I ain't lookin' for nothin' from you.

STEPP: Well, that's good. [Putting down the dumbbell and crossing up to get his shirt] That's good, because I ain't got none of that to give you. [Crosses back down to left bench and lies down.] Now if you'll just step outa my light, I'm gonna get myself a suntan.

FRIEZER: You hold what happened to Jefferson against me, you're making a big mistake.

STEPP: [*Sitting up*] I ain't holdin' nothin' against you because I know the only reason the over-pigs let pig hirelings keep their balls is so they and their house nigger wives can copulate up some more pig hirelings to continue to carry out the work of the over-pig.

FRIEZER: What the hell are you talking about?

STEPP: I'm talkin' 'bout the fact that the over-pig needs a constant supply of labor for his industrial empires. Now in order to make sure he got this labor he has to keep raisin' his niggers. [*Stands.*] It don't make no difference to him whether those niggers are black, or those niggers are white—a nigger is a nigger to him. And when a nigger goes bad, when he gets it into his dumb head that the only reason he is allowed to exist is for the over-pig to use him to keep pilin' up his illegal, unnatural, unrighteous accumulations of wealth, that's when the over-pig requires the services of the pig hireling. The pig hireling hires himself out for money to keep the contaminated nigger away from the uncontaminated nigger. [*Crossing right to body bag*] He thinks he's supporting his family, but all he's doin' is suppressin' his brothers.

FRIEZER: You're gonna end up in the psycho ward, Stepp.

STEPP: [*At body bag*] The way I see it, Mr. Friezer, the only difference between you and me is that I know what they want my children for.

FRIEZER: I don't know what the hell you're talkin' about.

STEPP: [*Crossing back to bench*] I know that. I know that. That's why they is the over-pig and you is the pig hireling, and that is why I can't waste any more time talkin' to you . . . motherfucker. [*Stretching out on the bench.* FRIEZER *stares at him for a moment and then, angrily, turns his attention toward the handball court off right.*]

FRIEZER: [*Shouting*] All right, if you're not gonna play handball, get off the court! Go on, you heard me, get

off the court! [*As he starts to exit toward the handball court, a black convict known as "SMILING MAN,"
enters. He dribbles a little black handball past*
FRIEZER *as if it were a basketball. Someone calls out
from the court.*]

VOICE: Hey, where you goin' with that ball, Smilin'
Man? [SMILING MAN *just continues to do his act,
dribbling the ball in a circle around* FRIEZER *and
showing off his gleaming teeth in a fixed smile.*
FRIEZER *exits left no. 2 exit.* SMILING MAN *dribbles
his way over to* FOSTER *and* STEPP.]

SMILING MAN: [*Between benches*] What's the word on
brother Hurspool?

STEPP: They're moving him to another cell.

SMILING MAN: [*Dribbling the ball in a circle while he
does his reciting.*]

> No shit. No shit.
> They is movin' him about,
> They is movin' him about,
> 'Cause he is it,
> 'Cause he is it!

[*Suddenly catching the ball in his hand and holding
it.*] They keep that nigger under a gun tower twenty-
four hours a day we're gonna get him. Ain't no way
that nigger's got of stayin' alive.

STEPP: [*Sitting up on the bench*] Maybe the man don't
care about Hurspool stayin' alive.

SMILING MAN: What you sayin'?

STEPP: Maybe the man expects you to kill Hurspool.

SMILING MAN: After Hurspool's doin' for him. Shit.

STEPP: What's he need Hurspool doin' for him when
he got you doin' for him?

SMILING MAN: Hey, what you talkin' 'bout, Stepp? I
ain't doin' for him.

STEPP: [*Putting on shirt*] You kill yourself off, you ain't
doin' for him? They find a way to kill a brother off,
and what are you gonna do? You gonna kill off a
nigger gettin' even with them? You do that and you

tell me you ain't doin' for them. Shit. You doin' exactly what they expect you to do.

SMILING MAN: Then what you sayin' we supposed to do about Hurspool?

STEPP: [*Moves to body bag.*] I ain't sayin' nothin' 'bout what you're supposed to do about Hurspool. That mother ain't even alive no more. You see him walkin' around here, rubbin' his body all the time 'cause the laundry chemical is burnin' off his skin, and you think he's alive? You understand what I'm sayin' to you? The nigger is dead. They crawled up inside his head like they were maggots and they ate out his brain. The nigger is dead. They just ain't got around to noticin' it yet.

SMILING MAN: Then what you tellin' me we're supposed to do? All you been tellin' is what we ain't supposed to do. Now I wanna hear what we is supposed to do.

STEPP: I ain't tellin' you none of that either. How come you think I got answers for you all the time? How come you and the rest of the brothers never go find no answers for yourself?

SMILING MAN: [*Stares at him for a moment and then walks over to left of* FOSTER. *To* FOSTER] What you gonna do about Charles Jefferson?

STEPP: [*Crossing to right of* FOSTER; *protectively answering for* FOSTER] Don't you go askin' him 'bout what he's gonna do 'bout Charles Jefferson 'cause there ain't nothin' he can do about Charles Jefferson. Ain't nothin' nobody can do about Charles Jefferson no more. [*Moving with* SMILING MAN *to left bench*] You wanna find yourself somethin' to do, you think about who your real enemy is. And that real enemy ain't Hurspool, and it ain't even these motherfuckin' guards—it's the over-pig that puts them up to it. He sits there on top of his institutions feelin' safe and secure because he thinks he's got us believin' he's got a right to rule over us—that's who the real enemy is. Long as he's got those institutions between you

and him, long as he can make you believe he rules
by some kind of divine righteousness, then you ain't
never gonna be free. You're gonna have his hands
around your throat from the day you're born to the
day you die, and you ain't ever even gonna know
where those hands are comin' from.

SMILING MAN: Shit, I just cut those motherfuckin' hands
off.

STEPP: You ain't gonna cut nothin' off. You're gonna
spend your life slashin' and slashin' and the only
thing you're gonna cut is your own throat. Can you
understand that, Smilin' Man? You got a knife in
your pocket, all you're givin' them is a reason to
have a prison; you put a gun in your hand, all you're
givin' them is a reason to build an army. [*Crossing
right toward* FOSTER] There's only one way people
like us are ever gonna have a chance in this world,
and that's when we stop doin' what they expect us
to do, and start reachin' the minds of our own
people, and people like us all over the world. [FOS-
TER, *grown increasingly agitated by* STEPP'*s remarks,
suddenly turns on him as* OFFICER ROLLOCK *enters
left no. 2 entrance.*]

FOSTER: [*Rising*] Shut your mouth, Willy! Just shut
your mouth! [FOSTER *picks up* HURSPOOL'*s shirt,
crosses to left bench.* STEPP *crosses to body bag.* ROL-
LOCK *contemplates the outburst for a moment, looking from* FOSTER *to* STEPP, *and then he walks over
to* SMILING MAN.]

ROLLOCK: You sign out for that handball?

SMILING MAN: [*At his unctuous smiling best*] Yes, sir,
I sure did.

ROLLOCK: Then get your ass over to that handball court
and play ball.

SMILING MAN: [*Gives* ROLLOCK *an extra big smile and
begins dribbling the ball back to the handball court.*]
  Yes, sir, I'm gonna do that now,
  Yes, sir, I'm gonna move that ball,

Move that ball,
Move that ball,
Move that ball back to the handball court.

(SMILING MAN *exits left no. 1 exit.* ROLLOCK *gives* FOSTER *and* STEPP *a final lookover and exits.* STEPP *hits body bag and sets it swinging. Crosses to center bench and sits.* FOSTER, *sitting on ground at left bench, stares at the swinging body bag. The lights begin gradually dimming down and focusing on* BOBBY FOSTER, *and as they do the walls of the yard gradually become shadowed. As lights change,* JEFFERSON *enters left no. 2 entrance and stands at* FOSTER's *back.*)

JEFFERSON: I can't tell you how clever I was, Bobby. I did a clever thing.

FOSTER: And what was that, my man?

JEFFERSON: I took the end of the blanket they gave me and I tore it into thin strips and I made it into a rope. It was a good rope. You can see how well it's holdin' me up.

FOSTER: Yes.

JEFFERSON: I feel like I'm back in a playground again swingin' from a swing. You should have seen me in East St. Louis. I used to pump that old swing until my feet was kicking straight upwards in the air. I used to bend my neck back and let my head hang upside down watchin' the ground go backwards and forwards like some old clock. Shit, I knew nothin' could happen long as I held on. [*Pause.*] Well, I wanted to tell you how much I like all the brothers. I wanted to tell you I ain't afraid no more. I'm sorry I ever stole anythin'. I wish I was back in East St. Louis, swingin' from a swing, holdin' on as tight as I can and never lettin' go.

FOSTER: You hold on, my brother. You hold on. [CHARLES JEFFERSON *exits, the shadows fade from the walls, the lights come back up.* STEPP *walks over to* FOSTER.]

STEPP: How come you try to shame me like that in front of the brother?

FOSTER: A man talks and don't say nothin', I figure that man shames himself. He don't need nobody do it to him.

STEPP: I was just tryin' to hip the brother to the basic precepts of revolutionary consciousness.

FOSTER: You was just tryin' to hip the brother to the basic precepts of your mouth. He don't need no advice from you about revolutionary consciousness.

STEPP: You heard him askin' me all those questions.

FOSTER: [*Rises.*] He was just waitin' for you to get unpuffed. He never seen a man so much in love with his own mouth before.

STEPP: How come you're talkin' to me like this?

FOSTER: How come you make me talk to you like this? How come you don't know no better than to stand there talkin', shootin' off your mouth, when you should be thinkin' 'bout Charles Jefferson? [*Crosses to center.*]

STEPP: I was thinking about Charles Jefferson. That's what I was talkin' about.

FOSTER: Shit. You was talkin' about yourself. [*Crosses to body bag.*] You was all puffed up and talkin' about yourself. Charles Jefferson's hangin' on the end of his tore-up blanket and you is the wind blowin' the body back and forth like it had no meanin' to it.

STEPP: [*Crosses to center.*] Now wait a minute. You know me better than that.

FOSTER: I don't know nothin' about you, 'cept maybe you is always forgettin' and forgivin', and pretendin' and walkin' around with a mouthful of shit you done copied down from some book. If you ain't willin' to do nothin' 'bout what you believe in, then it's just shit comin' outa your mouth, and I ain't interested in that. I ain't interested in what you're gonna do when you get outa here, I wanna know what you is gonna do here! I ain't interested in hearin' you talk no more about over-pigs and under-pigs and any other kind of pigs. I wanna know what you is gonna do here, right here and right now! That's what I'm waitin' on. Charles Jefferson got some justice coming to him and it ain't comin' out of your mouth. [HURSPOOL, *sweating and naked to the waist, enters right no. 3 entrance, crosses to center bench for his shirt.*] I'm waitin' on you, Willy. [STEPP *crosses to left bench.* FOSTER *holds out the shirt to* HURSPOOL.] Here's your shirt, Hurspool. Didn't know you played handball.

HURSPOOL: [*Sits down on center bench.*] Thought I'd play some ball take my mind off everything.

FOSTER: What's on your mind, brother Hurspool?

HURSPOOL: They shoulda known how he was. They shouldn't of put him in that holdin' cell like that, alone.

FOSTER: I guess maybe the only ones that really cared about Charles Jefferson was us—you, me, brother Willy, here.

HURSPOOL: Some of the brothers sayin' it was Lloyd that put the knife in his mattress.

FOSTER: That right?

HURSPOOL: You see the way he grabbed him 'round the head like that, like he was fixin' to pull his head off or somethin'? You can't tell what a man like that is gonna set himself to do.

FOSTER: You sayin' Lloyd planted that knife, or you just reportin' what some of the brothers was sayin'?

HURSPOOL: I don't know no more than you boys, but seems to me a man like that wants to prove himself to the rest of the pigs, you can't tell what he's gonna do. He gets it into his head the only way they gonna trust him bein' black is to do somethin'. Maybe a couple of them got together and made him do it. That makes sense now, don't it?

FOSTER: Yeah, that makes sense. [*Turning to* STEPP] Wouldn't you say that makes sense, brother Willy? [STEPP *stares at* FOSTER *for a moment and then just turns away and lowers his head.* HURSPOOL *grows increasingly apprenhensive.*] Course the only trouble with that was that it wasn't Lloyd that found the knife. It was Rollock.

HURSPOOL: Sure it was, but you know how they work it. The pig that plants the knife ain't never the one that finds it. That way there ain't no suspicion on him. He lets the other man do it. I been thinkin' 'bout that all day and that's what makes the most sense to me. It gotta be the new man. He's the one got somethin' to prove.

FOSTER: You been thinkin' 'bout that all day, Hurspool?

HURSPOOL: That's right.

FOSTER: [*To* STEPP] You think brother Hurspool here has come up with the right answer, brother Willy?

STEPP: [*With great reluctance, his voice almost inaudible*] No.

FOSTER: What's that, brother Willy? I didn't hear you.

STEPP: No.

FOSTER: [*Crossing up to right center bench*] Maybe you oughtta do some more thinkin', brother Hurspool. [SMILING MAN *enters and stands by body bag staring at* HURSPOOL. *Every time* HURSPOOL *smiles or attempts to laugh off a question,* SMILING MAN *replies in kind, mimicking him.*]

HURSPOOL: I don't know no more than you boys do. I'm just tryin' to do some figurin', same as you. [*Pause.*] How do you boys figure it? [*There is a long interval of silence.* HURSPOOL *looks from one to the other.*] Maybe I oughtta nose around. See if any of the guards been sayin' somethin'. [*He makes an attempt to stand, but* FOSTER *pushes him down again.*]

FOSTER: Why don't you give yourself a chance to get cool, brother Hurspool? Don't forget you is all sweated up. [*The silence has almost become palpable.*]

HURSPOOL: There's been some talk I may be transferred to the guards' latrine. You boys hear anything about that?

FOSTER: No, I didn't. [*To* STEPP] You hear anything about that?

STEPP: No.

FOSTER: [*To* HURSPOOL] That's a good job.

HURSPOOL: So far all's it is is talk, but the guy that's there is supposed to have made parole. They let him out I may get it.

FOSTER: That right?

HURSPOOL: Yeah, that's right.

FOSTER: [*Crossing down; to* STEPP] You hear enough of this shit, or you wanna hear some more?

HURSPOOL: What you boys talkin' about?

STEPP: [*Crosses to left of* HURSPOOL] Why did you do that to Charles Jefferson, Hurspool?

HURSPOOL: [*Standing up and crossing down center*] I ain't done nothin' to Charles Jefferson! What I want to do anythin' to Charles Jefferson for? I like him same as you. You know that. [FOSTER *has picked up dumbbells and is moving in on* HURSPOOL. SMILING MAN *moves in to* HURSPOOL's *right. From offstage right we hear* DI SANTIS *calling,* "Hurspool." FOSTER *breaks down left to bench.* SMILING MAN *moves to below body bag.* HURSPOOL *moves to up right of center.* DI SANTIS *enters right no. 3 entrance to right of* HURSPOOL.]

DI SANTIS: I got some good news for you, Hurspool. Sergeant Coyne's been looking through your jacket and he figures you got enough clean time to get transferred. You're taking DeVegas' place in the guards' latrine. You want that job?

HURSPOOL: Yes sir. I was just tellin' the boys 'bout that position opening up. [SMILING MAN *laughs and* DI-

SANTIS *immediately becomes wary of the situation. There is a note of suspicion in his voice now when he speaks to* HURSPOOL.]

DI SANTIS: Oh, yeah? You been talkin' it over with the boys here?

HURSPOOL: I wasn't talkin' 'bout nothin', just talk that's all.

DI SANTIS: Just talk, huh?

HURSPOOL: Yes, sir, that's right, just talk, passin' the time.

DI SANTIS: [*Looks at* HURSPOOL *for a few long moments, and then decides to put by his suspicion.*] Tell you what you do, Hurspool. Why don't you go up to your cell now and clear out your stuff. [SMILING MAN *laughs again, this time more openly.* DI SANTIS *looks at* SMILING MAN *and then at* FOSTER, *whose face is lined with a small bitter smile.*]

HURSPOOL: I didn't know I was gonna be moved outa my cell.

SMILING MAN: Shit.

DI SANTIS: [*Too occupied with* SMILING MAN *and* FOSTER *to reply to* HURSPOOL] What's going on here? You boys still havin' a little laugh about somethin'? Come on, what's the joke? Come on.

STEPP: [*Sitting, center bench*] There ain't no joke, Mr. Di Santis.

DI SANTIS: That's right, there ain't no joke. [*Turning to* HURSPOOL] What have you been talking about, Hurspool?

HURSPOOL: Nothin', Mr. Di Santis. I ain't been talkin' 'bout nothin'.

DI SANTIS: Nothin' with nothin', huh? [*To the* OTHERS] Lemme tell you boys somethin', maybe you understand me, maybe you don't. [DI SANTIS *begins speaking confidently, but in time his speech becomes agonized, disjointed. He paces right to left as he*

speaks.] You think you got somethin' figured out here,
but you don't. Not by a long shot, you don't. I mean
you're in a prison, you know. It's not like being outside. There is a difference. There is a big difference.
Now sometimes things happen in here that wouldn't
happen on the outside. Okay, so maybe that's the way
things are, maybe there's no help for it. I don't know.
You got a friend, and that friend means something to
you because maybe for the first time in your life you
run into someone who gives a shit about you, sees
something in you . . . things that nobody else would
ever bother looking for . . . and then some con, some
con who wasn't fit to polish his shoes, kills him . . .
in a few seconds just . . . just . . . so you wanna do
somethin' about it. Maybe you think it's right at the
time because nobody just does somethin' he thinks
is wrong, nobody just wakes up in the morning and
thinks he's gonna do something that's wrong . . . but
it turns out that way, and it keeps goin' like it's not
gonna end, and it should end because . . . um . . .
because thinking about it, or maybe talkin' it over
with someone you respect, you ain't so sure about it
anymore. Maybe you'd even like for things to be
different . . . go back to what it was . . . but you can't
make it any different because it's too late. It's just . . .
um . . . too late. So you might be sorry and it's too
late. You understand what I'm saying? [*At end of
speech he is between the two benches.*]

STEPP: [*Rises.*] Yeah, we understand all right. Now
why don't you just leave us alone, Mr. Di Santis? Just
take your friend here and leave us alone.

DI SANTIS: [*His gaze on* FOSTER] All right. Let's just
leave it at that.

HURSPOOL: [*Crossing right*] I'll just get started movin'
my stuff. [DI SANTIS *starts to exit with* HURSPOOL.]

FOSTER: About Jefferson, Mr. Di Santis . . .

DI SANTIS: [*Stops at center.*] Yeah?

FOSTER: Fuck you! [*For a long moment* DI SANTIS *just stares at* FOSTER.]

HURSPOOL: [*Anxious now to be gone*] I'll just get started then, Mr. Di Santis.

DI SANTIS: [*Still staring at* FOSTER] Started doin' what, Hurspool?

HURSPOOL: Movin' my stuff.

DI SANTIS: [*Slowly turning to* HURSPOOL] Movin' your stuff where, Hurspool?

HURSPOOL: Outta my cell, Mr. Di Santis. Outta my cell!

DI SANTIS: Oh, you don't have to do that now. I don't know what I was thinkin' about before. You just sit down here and enjoy yourself. This is your recreation hour. I'm gonna get somebody else to move your stuff.

HURSPOOL: Let me move my stuff, Mr. Di Santis. Please.

DI SANTIS: Now you just stay here and enjoy yourself in the sun. I'm gonna get somebody else to move your stuff. You get back to your cell you're gonna be all moved out. [DI SANTIS *exits right no. 1 exit.* HURSPOOL *looks into the face of each of the* MEN. SMILING MAN *begins walkin' toward him.*]

SMILING MAN: For a job. He kill Charles Jefferson for a transfer and a job.

HURSPOOL: [*Suddenly shouting out*] The man give me no choice! Before Mr. Di Santis there was Mr. Lester, and before Mr. Lester there was Mr. Monte, and before Mr. Monte . . . the man give me no choice. Used to tell Mr. Monte I wasn't gonna do nothin' for him. Used to draw myself up like one bad nigger and just stand over him and say I wasn't gonna do nothin' for him. He'd just laugh and say there wasn't a nigger born he couldn't do what he was fixin' to do with. He'd just say he had his ways. Mr. Monte come into my cell when I was gone and tear everythin' up, everythin' I did he find a way to make wrong, always takin' away whatever I had, writin' me up for disciplinary reports, not lettin' nobody visit with me, breakin' the packages I got so's the food was all spread out with glass. That's what Mr. Monte called "light treatment." "You don't learn to adjust, Hurspool, why we just naturally got to progress onto the next plateau." [*He grows angry with his remembrance.*] Shit, I wasn't scared of nothin'. I coulda tore his head off 'fore he had a chance to open his mouth. I was twenty-five years old! [*Turning to* FOSTER] You tough boy, Bobby Foster? You and Smilin' Man tough-ass black nigger? Tell you what they used to have up in the doctor's office: plain old barber's chair only it was plugged into the wall socket. They had it fixed up like an electric chair with a metal band they put around your head so's the doctor could give you what they called electro-shock therapy. Why you wasn't actin' right, you was sick. "You sick, boy? You need a little therapy to get you straight again." They tied me in that barber chair and they pulled my hands down real good with leather straps and that doctor plugged in the electricity and he just raised that switch up and down and up and down. "You my man, nigger? You my man, nigger?" Four times comin' and goin' in that room. All that screamin' and nobody listenin', a whole prison full of people and nobody listenin'. "Yes, sir, I'm your man." And they give me a pack of cigarettes, and marked down on the sheet they don't have to give me no more medical treatment 'cause I was cured. [*Turning to* STEPP] Tell you what I did after that, Mr. Stepp, 'cause you is a heavy thinker. They say to me, "What's happenin' in that cell block? What's that nigger sleeps next to you sayin'?" And I told them, and they was pleased with that. Yes, sir, they was so pleased they let me be for a whole month before they say to me . . . [HURSPOOL *spits on the floor.*] . . . "I just spit on the floor and I want you to go clean it up." [HURSPOOL *sinks to his*

knees and begins cleaning up the spit with his hand.]
I say to myself maybe if I go clean that floor they
gonna leave me be for another whole month, and I
go clean it fast as I can. I say, "Yes, sir, I'm sure
gonna get to that spit right now." [*Stopping his motions and looking blankly forward*] Pretty soon there
ain't no names. They just uniforms they put in the
cell with me. They want me to talk to them about
uniforms, shit, there ain't no harm in talkin' to them
about uniforms. Ain't nothin' attached to nothin', no
faces, nothin', nothin', nothin'. [*Looking up*] The
man gimme a good job now cleanin' out his toilet.
[*Slowly lowering his head*] Seems like I been waitin'
a lifetime for a nice job like that. [*For a long moment* FOSTER *stares at the crumpled form of* HUR-
SPOOL, *and then he slowly walks forward.* STEPP
grabs his arm.]

STEPP: You wanna off this mother you got all the time
in the world, 'cause he ain't got no place to go, but
once you do him you ain't got no more time either.

FOSTER: Take your hand off me, Willy.

STEPP: What's important to you? Your rep? You gonna
do somethin' 'cause Smilin' Man and the rest of them
expect you to do somethin'? They ain't had a thought
in their head since they were born. I'm tryin' to explain somethin' to you because you're my brother. I
don't give a shit about this motherfucker. But you
kill him you're makin' the same mistake the brothers
in Africa did.

FOSTER: I don't wanna hear you talk about Africa no
more! All these years listen' to you feedin' yourself
dreams and more dreams about Africa till there ain't
nothin' left in your head but a bunch of pictures in
a dream.

STEPP: You don't know what you're talking about,
Bobby.

FOSTER: That's what you turned your Africa into, that's
what you turned your revolution into . . .

STEPP: You never read anything, you never try to understand.

FOSTER: And that's what you turned yourself into! Nothin' but a bunch of pictures in a dream with nothin' there to live on. I ain't gonna kill this man, but not for your reasons—because I look at him and I see what he is, and I can't. Because that has to do with feeling and you don't feel anything anymore. [*Pointing to* HURSPOOL] What do you feel when you look at him, Willy? Somethin' ya kill or you don't kill for a cause?

STEPP: Yeah, baby, that's right, for a cause. That's why you kill people, for a cause! If I thought killing this motherfucker would serve a purpose, I woulda offed him in two seconds. I wouldn't have stood around like you did waitin' for permission.

FOSTER: That's because nothin' exists for you, Willy, outside your causes. No one. Not me. Not Charles Jefferson. No one.

STEPP: You wanna survive in here you gotta believe in somethin' beside people. You gotta believe in somethin' more important than people. People come and people go. People get beaten to death in the Adjustment Center. People hang themselves on torn-up blankets.

FOSTER: No names, no faces, just uniforms, huh Willie?

STEPP: That's why I'm gonna get outa this prison. That's why I'm gonna get outa whatever prison they got built for me, and I'm gonna see to it they answer to me, to Charles Jefferson, and to every man whose life they've destroyed.

FOSTER: What kind of goddamn revolutionist are you, Willy? The only use you got for people is when they're dead. Then you can come into the yard and stand on their bodies and make a speech. Well, you can't do anything for people when they're dead. They need you when they're alive! Charles Jefferson

needed you when he was alive—he needed you—
and all you ever gave him was a speech!

STEPP: And what did you give him?

FOSTER: Nothin'. He was my friend, and I gave him
what he always got outa his life—nothin'. [FOSTER,
his eyes clouded with tears, stands motionless, as DI
SANTIS *enters, right no. 1 entrance, and crosses up to
left of body bag.* SMILING MAN *crosses up to center
bench, picks up* HURSPOOL's *shirt, which he throws
angrily to* FOSTER *and exits right no. 1 exit.* FOSTER
drops the shirt in HURSPOOL's *lap and with a look at*
DI SANTIS *moves to exit down left no. 1 exit.* DI SANTIS
takes a violent swing at the body bag with his club.
FOSTER *stops below left bench and turns to* DI SANTIS.]

DI SANTIS: [*Walking over to right of* HURSPOOL] You
boys still talking? Surprises me to find a mustang like
you still talking, Foster. Thing like that can ruin your
rep. I guess maybe somewhere along the line you
got domesticated without anybody noticing it. Well,
that's good, Foster. I guess that's all a prison's supposed to do—make a man like you serviceable. Now
a man's a real mustang, you can't put a harness on
him, you can't make him plow the ground, you can't
do anything with him. So whatta ya do? You find a
way of helping that man in spite of himself. You put
that man in the Adjustment Center and you ride his
back and you whip his sides till the foam starts comin'
outa his mouth. You dig your spurs in till his legs
start bendin' and his belly starts draggin' on the
ground. [FOSTER's *hands begin opening and closing as
his anger mounts.* STEPP *watches with growing appre-
hension, fearful that* FOSTER *will give way to sudden
violence. He moves between* FOSTER *and* DI SANTIS,
trying to nudge FOSTER *away.*]

STEPP: Come on, man, let's go. You know this mother
ain't right no more. [FOSTER *pushes* STEPP *out of the
way and stands there confronting* DI SANTIS.]

DI SANTIS: Now I'll tell you the truth, Foster, when we get a guy like that down in the Adjustment Center we never know what's gonna happen. Some of them mustangs sag down on their knees the first night. They get locked up in that concrete room, all alone, cold, wet, the light burning day and night so they can't sleep, tryin' to take a drink of water outa a cup smeared round the rim with little moist pieces of shit, vomiting their insides up. And then there are some that don't go the first night, or the second night, or the first week or the tenth week. They go on for months and months, and then they catch a little germ and they get sick and they die. The guard opens the cell one morning and there he is, curled up in the corner of the floor like some fuckin' marigold somebody forgot to take care of. [DI SANTIS *lifts* HURSPOOL *to his feet.*] But that ain't gonna happen to my man, here. He's what we like to call domesticated. [*As* FOSTER *suddenly moves to strike* DI SANTIS, HURSPOOL *lashes out and, with a single hand, grabs* DI SANTIS *about the throat and begins strangling him.* DI SANTIS *tries to strike* HURSPOOL *with his club, but* HURSPOOL *grabs his wrist. When* DI SANTIS *finally drops his club, trying to wrench* HURSPOOL's *hand away,* HURSPOOL *begins choking him with both hands.* FOSTER *and* STEPP *are motionless, transfixed.* HURSPOOL *slowly sinks to the ground, the dead body of* DI SANTIS *still in his arms.*]

HURSPOOL: Why don't you boys go over to the handball court? [*Both* FOSTER *and* STEPP *seem unable to move.* HURSPOOL's *voice has taken on a cold, authoritative edge.*] Go on over to the handball court and leave me be! This ain't got nothin' to do with you no more. Go on! This is between me and this man. We gonna sit here awhile by ourselves, but we gonna come up with somethin'. Yes, sir, we gonna come up with somethin' we gotta sit here a thousand years.

[*To* DI SANTIS] Ain't that right, my man? Ain't that right? [STEPP *pulls* FOSTER *away and they exit, left no. 3 exit.* HURSPOOL *touches* DI SANTIS' *face, stroking the hair out of his eyes.*] You my man. Ain't you my sweet man?

LIGHTS FADE AND OUT

Cold Storage

A Play in Two Acts

For Alice

Cold Storage by Ronald Ribman, originally presented by The American Place Theatre in New York City on April 6, 1977, opened on Broadway at the Lyceum Theatre December 29, 1977. The play was produced by Claire Nichtern and Ashton Springer in association with Irene Miller; directed by Frank Corsaro; set and costume design by Karl Eigsti; lighting by William Mintzer; production stage manager, Clint Jakeman.

CAST

(In Order of Appearance)

RICHARD LANDAU . . . . *Len Cariou*
MISS MADURGA . . . . *Ruth Rivera*
JOSEPH PARMIGIAN . . . . *Martin Balsam*

ACT I

A hospital roof garden in New York City

ACT II

The roof garden, early evening the same day

ACT I

A hospital roof garden in New York City. A number of tables and chairs are placed about the roof, along with a scattering of artificial bushes and plants. In the appointments of the roof garden and in the architecture of the building itself there is a quiet Beaux Arts elegance.

ON RISE: *This June day is pleasant.* RICHARD LANDAU, *a man in his mid-forties, dressed in pajamas and a rather handsome-looking robe, sits downstage in a wheelchair. His eyes are shut and in his hand he holds a candy bar. As he sits there, motionless for the moment, it is difficult to tell if he is asleep or simply lost in his own thoughts. Several yards behind him a nurse,* MISS MADURGA, *sits by herself, reading an issue of* VOGUE *magazine.* MISS MADURGA *is young, slender, and attractive—a woman who obviously takes care of her physical appearance. For some moments there is silence on the roof, a silence broken only by the occasional turning of a magazine page, and then* JOSEPH PARMIGIAN *wheels himself onto the roof garden and into this almost motionless tableau.* PARMIGIAN *is a man in his mid-sixties. Over his robe and pajamas he has spread a small blanket on his lap. The nurse, busy with her magazine, scarcely seems to notice his arrival.* PARMIGIAN *glances at her for a second as she turns a page and then moves his wheelchair downstage, coming to a stop near* LANDAU. *When he sees that* LANDAU's *eyes are closed and there is no possibility for conversation, he*

287

lets out a little cry of disgust and turns away, his fingers impatiently drumming on the arm of the wheelchair. For some seconds silence returns again, and then LANDAU *begins making small sounds of agitation, his face contorting into an angry grimace. As* PARMIGIAN *stares at him,* LANDAU *raises the candy bar in his hand and begins to crush it under great tension.*

PARMIGIAN: You're squashing it. [LANDAU *doesn't seem to hear.*] You're squashing it!

LANDAU: [*His eyes blinking open*] What?

PARMIGIAN: If you don't want it, give it to me. [LANDAU *looks down at the candy bar, realizing perhaps for the first time what he has done.*] There's no point squashing something just because you don't want it. [PARMIGIAN *wheels himself over to* LANDAU *and, taking the candy bar out of his hands, begins unwrapping it.*] That fat Puerto Rican your private-duty nurse?

LANDAU: What fat Puerto Rican?

PARMIGIAN: [*Without turning his head, angrily gesturing over his shoulder with his thumb at* MISS MADURGA] That! That! What other fat Puerto Rican is there out here?

LANDAU: Yes, she's my private-duty nurse, but I hardly think she's fat.

PARMIGIAN: Is that so? Is that your evaluation, Mr. What-ever-your-name-is?

LANDAU: Richard Landau.

PARMIGIAN: Well, let me tell you something, Mr. Richard Landau. They're all fat, and the longer you stay here the fatter they get. [*Takes a bite out of the candy bar, makes a sour face, and tosses it back into* LANDAU's *lap.*] Keep your candy. It's stale.

LANDAU: Miss Madurga is from Honduras, not Puerto Rico.

PARMIGIAN: Is that what she told you? Honduras, huh? Honduras?

LANDAU: Yes.

PARMIGIAN: And you believed that?

LANDAU: Yes, I believed that. Why shouldn't I?

PARMIGIAN: Because she's a liar. She used to be my private-duty nurse before I was forced to let her go because of her overweight problem, and she told me she was from Guatemala. Guatemala! [*Turning his head and shouting back at* MISS MADURGA] Fat chance Guatemala! [*The* NURSE *momentarily lowers her magazine, exchanges a glance with* PARMIGIAN, *and then returns to her reading.*] They're never from Puerto Rico, you see. They're always from Honduras, or Guatemala, or Panama, or Ecuador, or Tierra del Fuego. No matter where they tell you they're from, it's never Puerto Rico. They just don't want to admit it.

LANDAU: Why wouldn't they want to admit it?

PARMIGIAN: Because it's not classy enough for them . . . because they're so used to giving us cock and bull stories they don't know what the truth is anymore— how do I know? I caught one of them walking around in a sari with a spot between her eyes and a diamond sticking out of her nose. She was telling all the patients she was from Ceylon, or Borneo, or someplace. She even had a bagful of tea leaves to prove it. The only flaw in her disguise was that every time she wheeled me in for my cobalt treatment I could see a half-finished banana sticking out of her cleavage. You ever see anyone from Ceylon walking around with a half-finished banana sticking out of her cleavage?

LANDAU: I really don't know what they walk around with in Ceylon. I've never been there.

PARMIGIAN: Well, neither have I. Who the hell's ever been to Ceylon? But I can tell you one thing: their national fruit sure ain't no banana! You want some advice, Landau? No matter how weak you get, don't let them know it. You can't throw the covers off the bed, tell them you feel as strong as a bull elephant.

The first sign of weakness they see in you, the truth goes out the window. You'll never hear it again. A five-hundred-ton meteorite hits you in the head, they'll tell you a chip of paint fell off the goddamn ceiling. Bastards! [MISS MADURGA *puts her magazine down and stands up. Although she moves silently, and* PARMIGIAN *appears not to be looking in her direction, she's hardly gotten to her feet before he's aware of it. He speaks without turning his head to face her.*] Going in for a little smoke, Miss Madurga? You don't have to hide in the broom closet with the rest of them. We know all the doctors and nurses are smoking in the broom closet.

MISS MADURGA: [*Walking over to them*] I'm just going in to get something to eat, Mr. Parmigian. I haven't had my lunch yet. [*Turning to her patient*] Can I get you anything before I go, Mr. Landau?

LANDAU: No, I'm fine, thank you.

PARMIGIAN: You can get me something.

MISS MADURGA: What would you like, Mr. Parmigian?

PARMIGIAN: Sixty thousand dollars so I can pay my hospital bill for the week.

MISS MADURGA: Just try to rest, Mr. Parmigian. It doesn't help getting yourself excited all the time.

PARMIGIAN: You call this excitement, being wheeled onto a hospital roof to sit in the sun? I'll tell you what excitement is. It's being alive! It's shacking up in an Armenian brothel and feeling the fleas crawling around on the bed!

MISS MADURGA: Is that what you really want?

PARMIGIAN: Yes! Fleas! I want fleas!

MISS MADURGA: [*To* LANDAU] As you can see, Mr. Parmigian and I go back a long way.

PARMIGIAN: Yeah, six months. If you stay alive in this hospital six months, that's a long way. You become an antiquity, a pyramid of longevity.

MISS MADURGA: [*Continuing with* LANDAU] Last winter

we read all five cantos of William Spenser's *Faerie Queene* together.

PARMIGIAN: Edmund Spenser!

MISS MADURGA: Yes, of course, Edmund Spenser. [*She rests her hand gently on* PARMIGIAN'*s shoulder for a moment, and then starts to exit.*] I'll be back in time to take you down for your appointment, Mr. Landau.

PARMIGIAN: [*Shouting after her*] It's grotesque reading the entire *Faerie Queene,* all *seven* books, and still calling him William Spenser! [*She pauses for a moment, turns around to look at him, and then exits.*] Hypocrites! Liars!

LANDAU: She seemed genuinely concerned about you.

PARMIGIAN: Oh yeah? Well, let me tell you something. I don't need their genuine concern. All I want is the truth. You come from Puerto Rico, I don't wanna see you walking around with a diamond sticking outa your nose. You're smoking Marlboros in the broom closet, I don't wanna see you sticking up "No Smoking" signs in the corridors. No more hypocrisy! No more lies!

LANDAU: Sometimes people lie just to be kind.

PARMIGIAN: [*Looking at* LANDAU *silently for a second*] Jesus, you really say things like that all the time?

LANDAU: I'm sorry. I didn't mean to sound insensitive.

PARMIGIAN: Banal.

LANDAU: All right. Banal, for whatever difference it makes. [LANDAU *stares down at the candy bar in his lap, and slowly begins rewrapping it.* PARMIGIAN *watches him for a few moments.*]

PARMIGIAN: What are you saving it for? Halloween? I told you it's stale.

LANDAU: I'll throw it away later. The nurse gave it to me. There's no garbage can out here.

PARMIGIAN: [*Reaching over and taking the candy bar out of* LANDAU'*s hands*] Don't throw it away later. [*Tosses it backward over his shoulder.*] Throw it away now.

LANDAU: [*Watching the candy bar clunk to the floor*] I could have done that.

PARMIGIAN: Yeah, but you didn't.

LANDAU: Because it's not very neat.

PARMIGIAN: Who cares? What are you in here for anyway?

LANDAU: Exploratory surgery.

PARMIGIAN: Oh yeah? What are they exploring for? Cancer? [*For some reason this strikes* PARMIGIAN *as terribly funny, and he breaks out in a paroxysm of laughter.*]

LANDAU: It was just a shadow on an Xray of my stomach, a few cells they weren't quite sure about.

PARMIGIAN: Sure.

LANDAU: Really. Just a small twinge. I don't even feel it anymore.

PARMIGIAN: Whatta ya working on, Mr. Landau?

LANDAU: I don't understand.

PARMIGIAN: Sure you understand. What are you working on? An ulcer? [PARMIGIAN *begins to laugh uncontrollably again.*] Is that what you're working on for yourself? An ulcer? You know what I thought I had? A tickle in the throat. Honest to God, that's what I thought I had. I came through the front door and I told them I had a tickle in the throat! [*The laughter stops as suddenly as it began.*] Take my word for it. On this floor it's never a twinge in the stomach. It's never a tickle in the throat. You got what I got.

LANDAU: What's that?

PARMIGIAN: The big C. You're going down for the big count, same as me, Mr. Landau, Mr. Richard Landau.

LANDAU: I told you I'm just here for an exploratory.

PARMIGIAN: Sure. And you're all dressed up. You look terrific in your Bloomingdale pajamas. You look . . . spiffy. You know what I weighed six months ago? Two hundred twenty pounds. I looked spiffy, too. I was the King Kong of the fruit and vegetable business. I had a pair of fists like two ham hocks. Now I can't even find them anymore. I tell 'em my clothing doesn't fit me anymore, they tell me the hospital laundry must be stretching them out. Can you believe such a pack of crap? The hospital laundry is stretching them out? You'd have to be some kind of a goddamn moron to believe something like that. What did you used to do for a living?

LANDAU: I didn't *used to* do anything for a living, Mr. Parmigian. I'm still doing it. I'm an investment adviser in fine art.

PARMIGIAN: Oh yeah? What the hell's an investment adviser in fine art?

LANDAU: I recommend purchases in fine art to investors interested in capital appreciation. I generally handle accounts in European glass and Chinese ceramics.

PARMIGIAN: Hey, that's terrific. That's really terrific. You got any recommendations for long-term growth? [PARMIGIAN *begins another round of uncontrollable laughter at his own joke, laughter that ends in a series of bad coughs.*]

LANDAU: Are you all right, Mr. Parmigian? Mr. Parmigian? [*When* PARMIGIAN *doesn't answer him,* LANDAU *stands out of his wheelchair.*] I'll get a nurse. I'll be right back.

PARMIGIAN: [*Grabbing his arm*] Don't bother.

LANDAU: Are you sure you don't want me to get you somebody?

PARMIGIAN: Yes, I'm sure! I'm sure! It only hurts when I try and stay alive. When I make jokes and try and stay alive. Listen, as long as you're up, you wanna do me a favor?

LANDAU: If I can, yes.

PARMIGIAN: Don't worry. It's just a little favor. It's not going to put you out much.

LANDAU: What do you want me to do?

PARMIGIAN: Get behind my wheelchair and push me off the roof.

LANDAU: What?

PARMIGIAN: Get behind my wheelchair and push me off the roof. I'd do it myself only I don't have the guts.

LANDAU: I really don't think you ought to joke about something like that, Mr. Parmigian.

PARMIGIAN: You think it's a joke? [*Releasing the brake on the wheelchair*] Look, off with the brake, off with everything. I'm ready to roll. Come on, be a sport before one of them comes out here with her morphine needle and the glucose bottle.

LANDAU: No . . . how can you ask somebody . . .

PARMIGIAN: You do it now you'll be just in time for the six o'clock news. [*Using his fingers to form an imaginary headline*] "Incredible shrinking Armenian and his wheelchair splatter to death on the pavement in front of Hope Memorial. Cancerous dealer in fine art sole witness to bizarre tragedy." Listen, you'll be famous for five or six minutes.

LANDAU: I have no desire to be famous at the cost of somebody else's life. Now, please, just let me put the brake . . . [*As he moves his hand toward the brake,* PARMIGIAN *slaps it away.*]

PARMIGIAN: All right. Why should I expect something for nothing. I'll make it interesting for you. As soon as you push me over I'll go into a triple somersault, a full layout, fold up like a jackknife, and do a terrific swan right through the entrance awning. You live another six months you won't see something like that again. Come on, whatta ya say?

LANDAU: I'm not going to listen to this. I don't know whether you're joking with me or not, but I'm not going to listen to this.

PARMIGIAN: All right, I'll do it myself. The railing is weak, half the screws are out. A couple of good smashes into it and over I go. [*Starts to wheel himself forward.* LANDAU *grabs his chair.*]

LANDAU: No!

PARMIGIAN: Take your hand off my chair!

LANDAU: No, I'm not going to take my hand off your chair!

PARMIGIAN: You take your hand off my chair or I'll bite it off! Do you understand me? I'll bite it off!

LANDAU: You're not going to bite anything off!

PARMIGIAN: I'm warning you, Landau! My teeth are rotten! I'll give you an infection they won't heal up with a million units of penicillin!

LANDAU: [*Putting on* PARMIGIAN's *brake*] You just stay where you are! You understand me? Just stay where you are.

PARMIGIAN: [*Suddenly losing all fight in him*] All right. You win. I give up. I don't have the energy to fight with anybody.

LANDAU: I'm going to sit down again. You just stay where you are. Right where you are. [LANDAU *sits down again in his wheelchair, keeping a wary eye on* PARMIGIAN.]

PARMIGIAN: I want a Dr. Pepper. Go inside and get me a Dr. Pepper, I'm thirsty.

LANDAU: Not now.

PARMIGIAN: What's the matter? It disturbs you?

LANDAU: Seeing somebody try to take their own life? Yes, it disturbs me. Nobody has the right to do something like that.

PARMIGIAN: Why not? Whose life is it?

LANDAU: That's not the point. The point is that . . . Look, they're always coming up with something.

PARMIGIAN: They're coming up with nothing.

LANDAU: Don't say that, because that's not true. They're making fantastic progress all the time. Every day you read about something new. Just last Sunday there was an article in the *Times* about how cockroaches can't get cancer.

PARMIGIAN: That's wonderful news if you're a cockroach.

LANDAU: That's not the point. If they can't give cockroaches cancer, maybe they can find out what it is that prevents cancer.

PARMIGIAN: You want to know what prevents cancer? Death! Death prevents cancer.

LANDAU: Well, with that attitude you might as well just give up.

PARMIGIAN: I have. Push me off the roof.

LANDAU: Look, I can't handle this kind of thing right now! I just . . . [*Catching himself, and then offering up an innocuous remark in hope of ending the conversation*] You're just depressed. Tomorrow you won't feel so depressed, you'll be glad you're still alive.

PARMIGIAN: No, I won't.

LANDAU: Yes, you will, believe me.

PARMIGIAN: No, I won't, and why should I believe you?

LANDAU: Because people survive! They go on! They live. Because nobody tries to commit suicide unless he's depressed.

PARMIGIAN: I happen to be in a very good mood at the present moment, Mr. Landau, or hadn't you noticed?

LANDAU: I don't call this being in a very good mood.

PARMIGIAN: Why not? The sun is shining, the grass is coming up, the dogs are peeing all over the sidewalk. Why shouldn't I be in a very good mood?

LANDAU: You just tried to commit suicide.

PARMIGIAN: That's the best time to commit suicide, when you're in a good mood. I've tried to commit suicide three times this month, and never once was I in a bad mood.

LANDAU: You know what I think, Mr. Parmigian? I think you just enjoy the idea of committing suicide. I think if I put my hand on your wheelchair to push you off the roof, you wouldn't let me. You'd find a reason for wanting to stay alive.

PARMIGIAN: Who knows? Maybe when I got to the edge I would change my mind. You want to give it a try? You never know.

[*For some long moments they stare silently at each other as if the measure of something was being taken.*]

LANDAU: Why do you insist on involving me with this? Why don't you do it yourself if you're so determined to do it?

PARMIGIAN: So the tune changes a little bit. Now you're willing to watch if you don't have to participate.

LANDAU: I didn't say that.

PARMIGIAN: I thought that was what you were saying.

LANDAU: No.

PARMIGIAN: My mistake. [*Pause.*] To tell you the truth, the reason I asked you is that I need someone to make the decision for me. I don't have the courage myself. What I said before about not having any guts is true, literal. They took out my bladder, shaved off my prostate, hooked up my large intestine to my urinary tract, and tied my bowels to my hipbone. See . . . [*Momentarily lifting up his blanket as if to expose his operations.* LANDAU *looks away.*] Now my urine flows with my blood, and when I shake my leg my liver drips prostatic fluid on my shoes. And that's the good news. You want to hear the bad news? Last week I ran outa Blue Cross. My wife tells me not to worry because I have a prosperous fruit and vegetable business in the Village. She's going to take care of my bills down to the last tangerine. That's what I'm going to leave her. These people with their X-ray machines, and their cobalt machines, and their knives and operating rooms, are going to take everything, and my wife, for thirty years of work and love, is going to be left with a tangerine. That's what I dream about at night when they give me the morphine . . . floating over the rainbow on a shrinking carpet of tangerines.

LANDAU: I'm sorry. It must be a terrible thing watching your estate being destroyed by an illness.

PARMIGIAN: It's not an estate. It's a fruit and vegetable business.

LANDAU: Yes, of course. That's what I meant.

PARMIGIAN: You believed that?

LANDAU: Believed what?

PARMIGIAN: That I dream about floating over the rainbow on a carpet of tangerines.

LANDAU: Yes, if you say so, why not?

PARMIGIAN: Because it's a lie. Well, maybe it's not a lie, maybe it's a distortion. Actually, it's not so much a distortion as a lie—a lying distortion. That's probably the best that can be said about it. You see what state I'm in, Landau? I have no perspective. You want to know what I really dream about? Filth! Absolute filth! I pretend to myself I dream about my wife, my family, my estate, but the truth is I dream about absolute filth. A man with a shred of decency left in him wouldn't tell dreams like mine to the Marquis de Sade.

LANDAU: Fortunately, nobody's under any compulsion to tell his dreams to anyone.

PARMIGIAN: You're one hundred percent right.

LANDAU: If they're medicating you with narcotics, there's no point in holding yourself responsible for your dreams.

PARMIGIAN: You are absolutely correct. No point at all. [*Pause.*] I'll tell you what, Landau. You tell me your filthy dreams and I'll tell you mine.

LANDAU: I have no dreams that would interest anybody.

PARMIGIAN: You'd be surprised at what interests me. The closer I get to death, the more everything interests me. Dreams other people throw out with the garbage I can spend a whole day living on.

LANDAU: I have no dreams . . . of interest to anybody.

PARMIGIAN: What an absolutely marvelous quality of surface veneer you have, Mr. Landau.

LANDAU: If you're interested in surface veneer, perhaps I might show you something in a nineteenth-century Chinese lacquer box. You might find it interesting to see how coat upon coat of lacquer can be laid down until the box itself may be removed leaving nothing behind but the form and the lacquer—the black, brilliant, slightly poisonous lacquer. [*Pause.*] I'm sorry to disappoint you, Mr. Parmigian, but there's nothing in me you're going to be able to live on. I've got nothing to give you.

PARMIGIAN: Nothing?

LANDAU: Nothing.

PARMIGIAN: All right, I'll accept that lie. There's no point in being too pushy the first ten minutes you meet somebody. First you should break the ice, so I'll give you an ice breaker, a riddle. What's shaped like a big green football with four legs and a tail?

LANDAU: How outrageous you are.

PARMIGIAN: That's not the answer.

LANDAU: I don't know the answer.

PARMIGIAN: Perhaps you'd like to think about it?

LANDAU: There would be no point in thinking about it. I don't know the answer.

PARMIGIAN: A watermelon. The answer is a watermelon.

LANDAU: A watermelon does not have four legs and a tail.

PARMIGIAN: I lied. [*For some moments the* TWO MEN *stare silently at each other.*] Now I'll give you the whole filthy truth. I have a . . . dream . . . for want of a better word let's call it a dream . . . a kind of recurrent dream that night by night progresses further and further, pulling me down into it—an effect undoubtedly caused by the narcotic. In this . . . dream, I am shacking up with a queen. [LANDAU *reacts slightly to the word "queen."*] Not that kind of queen.

A real queen. With a tiara on her head. She walks
around in a silk gown with her breasts almost hanging out, and we spend our time figuring out ways
to poison her husband, the king. That surprises you,
doesn't it? You think because I own a fruit and
vegetable store my imagination's limited to blue-
berries and cauliflower heads.

LANDAU: I don't know what your imagination's limited
to.

PARMIGIAN: Sure you do. That's the way the mind
works. You want to be the hero of the story you've
got to look like Don Juan and Robert Redford. You
got a little defect, a pimple on your ass, and you're
out of the running, nobody wants to know you. Well,
let me tell you something. That's the same kind of
thinking we're counting on to take out the king. In
this dream, this recurrent dream that progresses night
by night, the poor bastard suffers from the same delusion everybody else does. He takes one look at me
and as far as he's concerned I'm invisible. The music's
playing, and they're waltzing around in a ballroom
four thousand yards long, and I'm leaning up against
a marble pillar like a shriveled imitation of Richard
the Third—and I'm invisible. In the exalted circles
of his imperial brain, I don't exist. Well, good, okay,
because one of these nights that poor bastard's going
to be licking the sour cream off his silver spoon and
his exalted head's gonna come crashing down into
the borsch.

LANDAU: You enjoy that?

PARMIGIAN: Enjoy what?

LANDAU: Being the hero of your own dreams.

PARMIGIAN: Sure, why not? Who else should be the
hero of my dreams? Listen, maybe it's not sour cream
at all but a charlotte russe. How's that? Suppose it
turns out to be a poisonous maraschino cherry? A
single cough as the juice trickles down his throat,
whipped cream along the corners of his mouth . . .

and farewell, King . . . [*Noticing a strange look on* LANDAU's *face*] What's the matter?

LANDAU: You're talking about killing someone.

PARMIGIAN: Let me tell you about her bedroom. Heavy red damask curtains that shut out the light of day, a hundred pinpricks of flame from a hundred candles glowing in little dishes of leaves and flowers made of filigree and gold; and she moves about the room, her reflection in the glass of a dozen smoky mirrors, the small silk butterflies on her gown making dark fluttered shadows on her perfect skin. [PARMIGIAN *has lost himself in his vision, and only slowly acknowledges* LANDAU's *presence.*] Kill someone? I tell you, my friend, I would poison half the world to kiss a certain milk-blue vein on her breast.

LANDAU: In your dream.

PARMIGIAN: Yes, of course, in my dream. Only a madman would conceive of that awake. [*Raising his hand to his jaw and letting out a small cry of pain*] Ow! Ow! My teeth are rotting. They make my teeth ache in that lousy castle with their whipped creams, their cordials, their sugared strudels. Ow! Ow! [*Shaking a tooth back and forth.*]

LANDAU: You ought to see a dentist. They must have a dentist in this hospital.

PARMIGIAN: I don't need a dentist in the hospital. I need a dentist in the castle. [*Continuing to shake the tooth until he pulls it out*] No blood. You see that? No blood at all. Dry as a dried out well. [*Rotating the tooth in his fingers*] God, look at this tooth. A thousand facets, and every facet a filling. How many cows have we munched together? How many chickens? How many loaves of white bread? It nourished me for a lifetime, Landau, and now there's not so much as a spot of blood left in me to nourish it. Well . . . [*Throwing the tooth backwards over his head*] So much for philosophy. What's the matter?

LANDAU: Nothing. It's just strange seeing something that's a part of you being thrown away like that. Everything so disposable, so damn disposable.

PARMIGIAN: It's just a tooth.

LANDAU: It's still part of you . . . was part of you. Almost obscene; almost terrifying, really.

PARMIGIAN: What is?

LANDAU: A hundred dirty little jugs of oil wiped over in a hundred dirty little restaurants, and then one day you wipe away the restaurants and the people, and it's all so disposable. [*Standing up as if suddenly reminded of something.*]

PARMIGIAN: What are you standing up for?

LANDAU: I have an appointment. I . . . I have to go down to the X-ray room some time this afternoon. I have to swallow something and then they're going to X-ray it.

PARMIGIAN: That's a terrific test. You'll like it a lot.

LANDAU: You had that test?

PARMIGIAN: Oh, sure. That's one of the best procedures in this hospital. That's where they wheel you in with your Bloomingdale pajamas, and when they're finished they take your pajamas away and send them to the cleaners to stretch.

LANDAU: I'll be home in a few days. Time enough to finish the boiled meat in the refrigerator, time enough to have a few friends over for dinner.

PARMIGIAN: Oh yeah, that's right. You're just in for an exploratory. I forgot. Tell me something, Landau. You seem to be in pretty good physical shape. You do something?

LANDAU: I play squash a couple of afternoons a week, and on the weekends some tennis if I can get away.

PARMIGIAN: That's probably a big help to your whole cardiovascular system—all that movement in your Adidas sneakers.

LANDAU: Pumas.

PARMIGIAN: Listen, your cardiovascular system stays in

good shape there's no reason why you couldn't go on living until this time next year.

LANDAU: I wish you'd stop doing that.

PARMIGIAN: Doing what?

LANDAU: Implying that there's something terminal about me.

PARMIGIAN: Was that what I was doing?

LANDAU: Yes! You know perfectly well that that's . . . oh, never mind. It doesn't make any difference.

PARMIGIAN: Tell me something, Landau. You a married man?

LANDAU: Yes.

PARMIGIAN: You got any children?

LANDAU: Yes, I have two girls.

PARMIGIAN: Where do you go with your family for the summer? The end of Long Island? The Catskills?

LANDAU: Nantucket. We used to rent a house in East Hampton, but it got too . . .

PARMIGIAN: [*Interrupting him*] Crowded, so you went off to Nantucket. What do you do in Nantucket? Entertain the art world and walk along the beach?

LANDAU: We get in a lot of riding. We bought some bikes.

PARMIGIAN: Ah . . . ten-speed Fujis.

LANDAU: Peugeots.

PARMIGIAN: And you get in twenty miles of pedaling with your wife every Monday, Wednesday, and Friday.

LANDAU: Weekends . . . and mostly with the kids. . . . My wife prefers . . .

PARMIGIAN: [*Interrupting him again*] Sunbathing . . . in a bikini.

LANDAU: Sunbathing in whatever she wears! You make it sound so mindless.

PARMIGIAN: Do I?

LANDAU: Yes, you do. And I don't particularly like it.

PARMIGIAN: If you're interested, I'll tell you everything there is to know about your relations with your wife.

LANDAU: You know nothing of my wife—not the way she boils the children's eggs, or removes the fishbones from their fish . . . nothing!

PARMIGIAN: It doesn't matter. Your wife is forty years old, maybe. She doesn't weigh any more now than when she was nineteen. When she puts on a bathing suit she's a knockout, except for the small varicose veins which you noticed just popped to the surface behind her knees last summer.

LANDAU: I think you'd better just stop right there, Mr. Parmigian.

PARMIGIAN: Why? The veins bother you?

LANDAU: Hearing you talk about my wife bothers me, that's all.

PARMIGIAN: It annoys you she spends a couple of hundred dollars more a year on clothing than you like, but when she walks outa Bonwit Teller she looks like a million bucks, and when she stops by the office and bends over your desk she gives half the art department the hots, and that's just the way you like it. . . .

LANDAU: [*Suddenly putting both his hands on the back of* PARMIGIAN's *wheelchair*] That's enough!

PARMIGIAN: If you don't like what I'm saying, go ahead and push me off the roof! [LANDAU *instantly lets go of the wheelchair*.] You're a pretty violent man, Mr. Landau.

LANDAU: I'm not a violent man. You just irritated me, that's all. I've never done a violent thing in my life. I hate . . . violence. [*Walking away and staring outward at the city*] Ugly city of gas and gasoline. City where they plant a few scraggly trees so everybody can pretend he's living back in a forest. [*Turning to* PARMIGIAN] You know why these trees never grow into anything? Why they always cut them down? Because nothing is allowed to interfere with the power cables beneath the street. What has grown beautiful on the surface must not offend the thrust of power below the surface. That's when the city comes. One morning in my sleep I hear power saws—buzz, buzz—men with uniforms, hands like brown leather. "Why are you cutting down those trees?" "Mind your own business, Jack! Stick your head back in your window, Jack!" A week later they're back again. Six holes the size of a dog's grave are dug, and they plant the replacements—trees no thicker than a broomstick. For thirty years a tree is allowed to live, cut into by children with penknives, shit on by dogs, backed into by cars, allowed to grow into something of dignity and value—to be replaced by a broomstick? There is no replacement! What is killed is killed forever!

PARMIGIAN: Listen, it doesn't pay to get irritated. You'll probably be back on the squash court in two or three weeks.

LANDAU: You think so?

PARMIGIAN: No.

LANDAU: What the devil's the matter with you?

PARMIGIAN: That's pretty obvious, isn't it?

LANDAU: I'm not talking about that. You don't seem to give an ounce of thought to what you're saying. I don't know you ten minutes and you got the gall to talk to me as if you've known me for ten years. You don't know anything about me, my family, or my wife.

PARMIGIAN: That's right.

LANDAU: You bet that's right. So let's just knock it off.

PARMIGIAN: I apologize.

LANDAU: [*Sitting down again*] All right. Let's just forget it.

PARMIGIAN: I can see you're a very private person.

LANDAU: All right. All right. Let's just forget it.

PARMIGIAN: [*After some moments of silence*] Landau?

LANDAU: What?

PARMIGIAN: Are you of the Hebrew persuasion?

LANDAU: Yes, I'm Jewish. What about it?

PARMIGIAN: Nothing.

LANDAU: Then why did you bring it up?

PARMIGIAN: I just wanted you to know . . . some of my best friends are Jewish.

LANDAU: [*Staring at him*] That's . . . wonderful. That's just . . . beautiful.

PARMIGIAN: To tell you the truth I'm beginning to lose my friends.

LANDAU: I wonder why.

PARMIGIAN: Don't wonder why! You'll find out. At the beginning you get a lot of friends dropping in . . . two, three dozen of them a day . . . and then after a while it drops off. They don't come around anymore. You're lucky to get a handful of drooping flowers once a month. You know what those miserable drooping flowers remind me of?

LANDAU: [*Closing his eyes and resting his fingers against them*] No. But I have a feeling you're going to tell me.

PARMIGIAN: A vision I used to have when I was a young man. It was a vision of immortal ripeness, a summer's day when time stopped and everything was frozen into its exact moment of perfection. The peaches were hanging perfectly on every tree, every blade of grass was perfectly formed into a little tiny green spear. . . . I was a grasshopper setting out for a day of love through an endless field of strawberries. . . . [PARMIGIAN *just breaks off without finishing.*]

LANDAU: [*Opening his eyes*] And then what?

PARMIGIAN: And then what? Time began. The grasshopper took a big leap and got hit with a spray of DDT.

LANDAU: If you're that interested in frozen perfection, Mr. Parmigian, maybe you ought to visit the deep freeze at Food City.

PARMIGIAN: Ah, you're coming back to life: a little sarcasm, a little insensitivity. Maybe you'll understand what I'm trying to tell you as well. You married your wife as I married my wife, expecting eternal perfection.

LANDAU: That's not why I married my wife.

PARMIGIAN: Wasn't it?

LANDAU: No. What you're talking about is a parody of love, some kind of grotesque parody.

PARMIGIAN: Then why is it the veins in the back of her legs are beginning to bother you?

LANDAU: They don't bother me! What bothers me is a man who talks about love and perfection and obviously understands neither. You're in love, Mr. Parmigian, you don't stand around examining someone for physical deterioration.

PARMIGIAN: I do. You see what Time is, Landau? Everyman's Launcelot reaches Everyman's Lady in the Lake only to find out that she's turned into Mother Cabrini.

LANDAU: Maybe your wife looks like Mother Cabrini, but not mine.

PARMIGIAN: My wife's a saint, that's why she looks the way she does. But that's not here or there, either. The point is that Everyman, you, me, Don Quixote, Everyman, spends his life in a fevered quest for the unattainable, the object desired beyond belief: The Lady in the Lake, the Holy Grail, the Moon Goddess on the Mountain, whatever you wish; but even as we get there, even as the object of our quest is finally in our hand, at that ultimate moment of exaltation, what happens? The object diminishes, it turns meaningless in front of us, it disappears in our hand like a crystal of snow. Don't you find that odd, Landau? Don't you find that very odd?

LANDAU: I don't find it anything. I never really thought about it.

PARMIGIAN: No great quests in your life?

LANDAU: No.

PARMIGIAN: No great adventures?

LANDAU: I buy art for people interested in capital appreciation. Twice a week if I can get away I play squash. Mornings I drink my coffee, afternoons I bite into a sandwich. That's my great adventure.

PARMIGIAN: Oh, what a great liar you are. Death is knocking like a recruiting officer on the front door, and you still persist in lying to yourself.

LANDAU: I've never lied to myself about anything.

PARMIGIAN: Bullshit. It's time to stop fencing with me, Landau. It's time for you to spread your filthy dream out in front of me like a moth-eaten Moroccan carpet!

LANDAU: I don't have any filthy dreams, and even if I did I don't see how you could be interested in sexual perversions in the condition you're in.

PARMIGIAN: [*His voice gradually rising with fanatical zeal*] I'm not talking about sexual perversions. I wouldn't give two cents for the pathetically harmless sexual imaginings of your Jewish brain. What I'm talking about is the will-o'-the-wisp you've been pursuing all your life, the lodestone, the magnetic star that pulls you and all of us through all the years of our life, attracts us though we hate it; that's the real pornography of our brain, the one common central lie that sits at the heart of all our lives, distorting it, corrupting it, deforming it! It is this lie, and this lie alone, that is the enduring filth of our lives!

LANDAU: [*Grown equally excited*] What lie? What lie are you talking about?

PARMIGIAN: [*Suddenly calm*] I haven't got the faintest idea. I thought you might know. You're Jewish.

LANDAU: What has that got to do with anything?

PARMIGIAN: Everybody knows Jews are filled with secrets, all kinds of oriental cabala nobody knows anything about.

LANDAU: That's garbage! Absolute garbage!

PARMIGIAN: You deny it?

LANDAU: Yes, of course I deny it!

PARMIGIAN: Naturally, of course. I can see I made a

mistake with you. I should have passed myself off as a Jew, then we'd be having a different sort of discussion out here. We wouldn't be engaged in pleasant chitchat. We'd be talking about the mysteries of the universe, things of importance that have been kept secret for five thousand years. Unfortunately, we're never going to be discussing this because I revealed myself to you as an Arab!

LANDAU: I thought you were from Armenia? You said you were from Armenia!

PARMIGIAN: That's close enough to being an Arab! And while we're on the subject of Arabs, let me tell you the only ones in the world that really understand Jews are those with Arabian blood in them like me! There's something flowing through Arabian blood that lets us understand Jews!

LANDAU: What? Camel dung? What are you talking about? The only thing flowing through blood is blood cells!

PARMIGIAN: You don't believe in racial memories? You think after five thousand years of Arabs and Jews living together the secrets of one don't flow in the blood of the other?

LANDAU: There are no secrets! There's nothing there to flow!

PARMIGIAN: Don't tell me what flows and what doesn't flow! You've got a secret! Every Jew's got a secret! Why don't you do yourself a favor and get the filthy thing off your chest once and for all? Look at it this way: sooner or later you're going to spill your guts out here, everybody does; maybe you'll call in a rabbi and what do you think he's going to do with what you tell him? He's gonna tell it to his wife, and inside of two seconds it's going to be all over the congregation. You won't be able to eat a piece of matzoh without having half a dozen bearded faces staring at you. With me you get a guarantee. Where I'm going nobody brings messages back from.

LANDAU: What is that? A guarantee? You're going to give me a guarantee?

PARMIGIAN: Absolutely. I know my customers. You buy the suit you get a guarantee and two pairs of pants.

LANDAU: What the hell is that supposed to mean?

PARMIGIAN: With a Jew you give him a guarantee; if you were a Puerto Rican I'd give you a bunch of dominoes.

LANDAU: What an incredibly bigoted thing that is to say!

PARMIGIAN: You think I'm a bigot?

LANDAU: Yes, I think you're a bigot! Yes!

PARMIGIAN: Where do you get the nerve to accuse me of being a bigot? Let me tell you something. I happen to be a member of the American Civil Liberties Union. You can't be a bigot and be a member of the American Civil Liberties Union.

LANDAU: Then don't talk that way! I wasn't out here five minutes before you were making comments about my nurse because she's from Puerto Rico according to you, and then you're making anti-Semitic statements to me about being a Jew and needing a guarantee, and then you're back on the Puerto Ricans with their dominoes!

PARMIGIAN: That's what they do. They play dominoes. What's the matter? You don't see them on the street playing dominoes?

LANDAU: That's not what I'm talking about. It's the implications of what you're saying. I'm a Jew, so I need a guarantee. What is that supposed to mean? A Jew is tight-fisted with his money? He's different than anybody else? You know, I don't believe I'm having this conversation! I don't believe I've gotten myself involved in a conversation like this!

PARMIGIAN: What makes you so touchy?

LANDAU: I'm not touchy!

PARMIGIAN: Listen, Landau, take my word for it. You're

touchy. It's very difficult holding a pleasant conversation with you.

LANDAU: Then stop making those kind of remarks! I've heard them all before.

PARMIGIAN: Oh yeah? Where was that?

LANDAU: What difference does it make where? It doesn't make any difference where!

PARMIGIAN: What's the matter? That's another secret, too? I never met a man with so many secrets. Talking to you is like talking to a sphinx: the tongue sits in the mouth without a word while the feet are being eaten up with the sand.

LANDAU: I'd like to see that card.

PARMIGIAN: What card?

LANDAU: The one from the American Civil Liberties Union.

PARMIGIAN: What's the matter? You don't think I'm a member of the American Civil Liberties Union? Let me tell you something. I marched in three separate peace marches! I was there when the draft cards were burned! I was there when it took real courage to stand up for what you believed in!

LANDAU: Just let me see the card.

PARMIGIAN: I was singing "Blowing in the Wind," and the FBI was taking pictures!

LANDAU: Just let me see the card.

PARMIGIAN: You want to see the card?

LANDAU: Yes! Yes! I want to see the card!

PARMIGIAN: Then I will show it to you, mister, mister dealer in fine arts for investment purposes. I've got it right here in my pajama pocket because I can't leave my wallet in my room because of the Puerto Ricans. [*Pulling out his wallet and irately flipping through a stack of cards*] You want a card? I will show you a card! [*Pulls out a card and tosses it into* LANDAU'*s lap.*] There's a membership card! [LANDAU *picks it up.*] Now what do you have to say for yourself?

LANDAU: This is a membership card in the B'nai B'rith.

PARMIGIAN: So what? I'm a member of that, too. You want cards? I'll show you cards. [*Begins wildly tossing cards at* LANDAU.] Here's one from the Police Athletic League. And here's one from the March of Dimes and Ralph Nader and the Japanese Dragon Society, and a credit card from what's left of Abercrombie and Fitch. . . .

LANDAU: [*Being inundated with cards*] Never mind! Never mind!

PARMIGIAN: [*Continuing with all the zeal of the truly offended man*] And a membership card from the time I worked in the International Ladies' Garment Workers!

LANDAU: I said never mind! Forget it!

PARMIGIAN: You want cards? I got cards! Don't you tell me what I belong to. I was a member of the American Indian Society when they couldn't sell a blanket by a railroad station! You come into my room I'll show you a real Navajo blanket hanging from the wall!

LANDAU: All right. All right.

PARMIGIAN: I happen to have a personal letter from Sacco and Vanzetti!

LANDAU: All right!

PARMIGIAN: I had a correspondence with the Rosenbergs! [LANDAU *tries to hand everything back to him.*] Watch out for my urine bag! I don't want to sit here like an old man with stains on his leg!

LANDAU: What are you doing with a B'nai B'rith card?

PARMIGIAN: Why shouldn't I have a B'nai B'rith card? I support everything! Everything has a right to live.

LANDAU: [*Standing*] Not everything. [*Walks over to the edge and stares outward.*]

PARMIGIAN: What's the matter now? You remembered another appointment?

LANDAU: No.

PARMIGIAN: I touched another nerve?

LANDAU: You touched nothing.

PARMIGIAN: Then why are you in and out of your chair, Jack-in-the-Box?

LANDAU: I just don't like sitting in it, that's all.

PARMIGIAN: Why not? It's a terrific-looking chair.

LANDAU: Look, maybe it's a terrific-looking chair to you, but it's not a terrific-looking chair to me. I . . . I don't like the feeling of being tied down to it.

PARMIGIAN: So who's tying you down to it? Just because your nurse put you in a wheelchair doesn't mean you have to sit in it. It's just a hospital regulation to wheel you around from place to place so you can get used to being a cripple.

LANDAU: There's a surgical supply store across the street. The cab left me out in front of it yesterday. A whole window full of trusses, artificial arms and legs, perfect plastic arms and legs hanging in the window, stacked up on little shelves like pieces of cordwood.

PARMIGIAN: Let me tell you something. A good truss is a terrific thing. [*Throwing back his blanket*] I can show you a truss here . . .

LANDAU: Never mind! I don't want to see it.

PARMIGIAN: What's the matter, Mr. Landau? You don't like broken things? Let me tell you, everything gets broken. Nothing stays in one piece forever. Not even a grasshopper sitting on a strawberry.

LANDAU: A good piece of ceramic does; a good piece of porcelain with a fine underglaze. I picked up a pair of Kwan Yin figures made out of blanc de chine at an estate auction last month. They were absolutely perfect, without that slightly green color you see so often in even the best of white porcelain. The man I bought them for wanted to know if he could drill a small hole through the bottom so he could run an electric cord up through it. He thought they would make a fine pair of lamps.

PARMIGIAN: So what did you tell him?

LANDAU: [*After a long moment of silence*] I told him he could do what he wanted with them. [*There's another long moment of silence before* PARMIGIAN *answers.*]

PARMIGIAN: Well . . . sometimes you need a good lamp in the house.

LANDAU: [*Spinning around to face* PARMIGIAN] Not out of Kwan Yin figures! Not out of two hundred years of . . . of . . .

PARMIGIAN: Perfection?

LANDAU: Yes. Perfection.

PARMIGIAN: Everything ends up being made into something else. When I first got married, I had an orange crate. You know what I made it into? A coffee table. It was also a doghouse because the dog used to creep in from the side and sleep in it. [LANDAU *walks away in annoyance.* PARMIGIAN *watches him pace around a bit before coming to a halt in front of the flower box.*]

PARMIGIAN: You like that? That's the spring garden. It's also the winter, summer, fall garden, because they never take it out of there.

LANDAU: It almost looks alive . . . until you touch it.

PARMIGIAN: It's better than alive. It's plastic. You dust it off every once in a while you'd think you were in the Garden of Eden.

LANDAU: How unpleasant a forgery feels when you expected life.

PARMIGIAN: Or you could sit here and look out and imagine you're on a big sailing ship. You want to be a navigator, Landau? Forget about your pots and pans, and I'll make you into a navigator. You see that building over there? That's the North Star. I say that's the North Star because you never want to look up for the real North Star, because that's where the sea gulls are. I was sitting right here with an ice-cream cone and one of them went right on it. He took off from the East River and made a direct hit from forty thousand feet.

LANDAU: That what you do? Sit here all the time?

PARMIGIAN: Why should I sit here all the time? I've got a busy schedule for myself. Before breakfast I sit in my room. After breakfast I sit by the nurses' station. There's also another spot you can sit. The dayroom. There's a woman in the dayroom who sits there with a pack of cards. She's a bridge player waiting for three customers who can sit up straight in a chair. In my frank opinion the statistical probability of this happening is from nil to nothing, but this woman is a survivor from the Titanic or the Hudson River Day Line—whichever one—the story is never clear from her. If you want, I'll introduce you.

LANDAU: No, thank you.

PARMIGIAN: That's a smart move on your part because two months ago she spilled a bottle of Pepsi-Cola on the table and made a big mess for herself: the napkin was stuck to the table, the cards were stuck to the cards—it was a big mess. She spent all morning crying about it, but you can't play with cards like that.

LANDAU: That's your busy schedule?

PARMIGIAN: I get them on the rounds, too.

LANDAU: What rounds? What are you talking about?

PARMIGIAN: The old doctors come around with the young doctors every day, and if your case has some interest for them, they stand around your bed making suggestions. I'll tell you one thing, Landau: make yourself interesting the night before they make up the schedule. Make sure they put you down on the list! Don't let them pass you by! [*Glancing backward to make sure they are alone*] You know what I got? A PDR. You know what a PDR is? [LANDAU *shakes his head.*] A PDR is a Physician's Desk Reference. I bought it from an intern for five dollars. You know what a PDR has? It lists all the reactions to the drugs. So what I do when they give me a drug is I develop a new reaction, a reaction they can't find in the PDR. This makes my case interesting. [MISS MADURGA *enters.*]

MISS MADURGA: They should be ready for you now in X ray, Mr. Landau.

LANDAU: All right. Thank you. [LANDAU *begins walking toward the exit.*]

MISS MADURGA: I'll take you down in your chair, Mr. Landau. [LANDAU *hesitates for a moment, and then returns to his wheelchair. As she starts to wheel him out, she remembers something—an ice-cream sandwich she bought in a machine. She takes it out of her pocket and hands it to* PARMIGIAN, *who wordlessly takes it.*] I had it left over from lunch. I don't know why I bought it.

PARMIGIAN: [*Looking up from the ice cream to* LANDAU] Have a good afternoon, Landau. [*As the* NURSE *begins to wheel* LANDAU *out,* PARMIGIAN *shouts after him.*] Remember what I said to you! Be interesting! [LANDAU *looks back at* PARMIGIAN, *and the two men stare at each other until* LANDAU *exits.* PARMIGIAN *looks down at the ice-cream sandwich in his hand, and speaks softly to himself.*] Be interesting.

LIGHTS FADE OUT

ACT II

The roof garden. Early evening the same day.

ON RISE: PARMIGIAN, *in his wheelchair, leafs through a newspaper.* LANDAU, *seated now in a nearby lounge chair, stares mutely down at his hands. For some moments, as* PARMIGIAN *studies the TV section, all is silence.*

PARMIGIAN: Everything's a rerun. Eight o'clock is a rerun, nine o'clock is a rerun, the Movie of the Week is a rerun. June is a month filled with contempt.

LANDAU: How can you watch that junk?

PARMIGIAN: That's my weakness, Landau. Everything interests me. Even junk.

LANDAU: What happened to all your reading? I thought you used to read all the time.

PARMIGIAN: I read everything already. Shakespeare, Spenser, Chaucer, Marlowe, Gunga Din. If you want to know the truth, I'm the only person in the world who ever read *The Faerie Queene* twice. The second time was a rerun. You want the newspaper?

LANDAU: No, thank you.

PARMIGIAN: You should read the newspaper. Keep up an interest in world events. [*Throws the newspaper away on the floor.*] It's better than staring down at candy wrappers or your fingernails. What are you looking for down there? A hangnail?

LANDAU: [*Putting on a pair of reading glasses*] I was just thinking about something, that's all.

317

PARMIGIAN: Don't think. It's a waste of time. Whatever
there is in this world to think about has already been
thought about. [LANDAU *opens up a leather attaché
case and begins studying a folder full of papers.*] You
know what Spengler said after he got done thinking
about *The Decline of the West*? "I got a headache."
The same thing was said by Hegel. The same thing
was said by Schopenhauer. The same thing was said
by all of them with the exception of Plato. With him
it was a slightly different story. He got a wet behind
from sitting too much in a cave. What happened with
your X rays?

LANDAU: Nothing. It was inconclusive.

PARMIGIAN: And you expected results. Let me tell you
something. In this hospital there are no results.
Everything is always inconclusive. Even the food is
inconclusive. It looked like a piece of veal on my
plate tonight, but when I pushed away the gravy it
looked like a piece of pork, except when I took a
bite of it, it tasted like turkey. So what was it?

LANDAU: Well, what did you order? You must have
ordered something.

PARMIGIAN: Ice cream.

LANDAU: I mean for the main course.

PARMIGIAN: That's what I ordered for the main course.
Ice cream.

LANDAU: You can't live on ice cream, Mr. Parmigian.

PARMIGIAN: Sure you can live on ice cream. There was
once a famous emperor who lived on nothing but ice
cream. That's what he was called, the Emperor of
Ice Cream. Except for an occasional rotten tooth, he
was doing okay for himself.

LANDAU: [*Matter-of-factly, as he makes a note on one
of his pages*] Nobody lives on ice cream.

PARMIGIAN: [*Suddenly, almost inexplicably, reacting
violently*] Don't tell me nobody lives on ice cream!
If you want to live on ice cream, you can live on ice
cream! For your information there happens to be a

tribe of savages in Borneo that lives on nothing but sweet potatoes! If you can live on sweet potatoes, you can live on ice cream. And when I am finished with the ice cream, if all I can eat is chocolate mousse, then I am going to live on chocolate mousse! [PARMIGIAN's *outburst results in an embarrassed silence for both* MEN.] You want to hear something interesting? During the war I worked for a man who used to wear a white apron and had eyes like a lizard. He taught me everything there was to know about the fruit and vegetable business, and now, for the last three days, I can't remember what the rest of his face looks like. [LANDAU *remains occupied with his work, refusing to be pulled into conversation.*] What are you working on there?

LANDAU: Some items coming up for sale in an estate auction.

PARMIGIAN: What interests you?

LANDAU: Some nineteenth-century glass, and some Japanese bronzes.

PARMIGIAN: What else interests you?

LANDAU: I might put in a bid on some Chéret lithos.

PARMIGIAN: Who's Chéret?

LANDAU: He made posters . . . a contemporary of Toulouse-Lautrec.

PARMIGIAN: You got anything going for you in the twentieth century, Landau?

LANDAU: Not in this auction.

PARMIGIAN: Besides this auction.

LANDAU: [*Suddenly stops shuffling through his papers, and sits still.*] Besides this auction I don't know what you mean, Mr. Parmigian.

PARMIGIAN: Why is it, Landau, I always get the feeling you know exactly what I mean, but you're always telling me you don't know what I mean? [LANDAU *removes his glasses and looks up, as if he might say something.*] You like cuckoo clocks, Landau?

LANDAU: Not particularly. Why do you ask me that?

PARMIGIAN: I used to have a German cuckoo clock. It kept terrific time, except after a while the cuckoo stopped coming out.

LANDAU: So?

PARMIGIAN: So what?

LANDAU: So what is the point?

PARMIGIAN: What point? There is no point. I just wanted to tell you what happened to my cuckoo clock. [LANDAU, *slightly irritated, stares at him for a moment, and then puts his glasses back on again, and returns to work.*] You ever make a mistake with what you're doing, Landau?

LANDAU: Everybody makes mistakes.

PARMIGIAN: What was your biggest mistake?

LANDAU: I don't remember offhand. I'm really rather busy here, Mr. Parmigian.

PARMIGIAN: You don't remember your biggest mistake?

LANDAU: I bought an engraving by Pieter Brueghel that turned out to have been done by Van der Heyden.

PARMIGIAN: Van der Heyden. That sounds like a big mistake.

LANDAU: It was.

PARMIGIAN: I made a big mistake like that once. I thought it was going to be a big summer for pomegranates. I bought two hundred pomegranates and a hundred and six of them rotted.

LANDAU: Pomegranates? How can you talk about pomegranates when I'm talking to you about Pieter Brueghel.

PARMIGIAN: Why not? What's the difference? A mistake is a mistake.

LANDAU: There's no difference in your mind between an engraving by Pieter Brueghel and a bunch of pomegranates?

PARMIGIAN: Sure there's a difference. One's a painter, and the other's a pomegranate.

LANDAU: And that's the difference?

PARMIGIAN: That's right. That's the difference.

LANDAU: I'm not going to argue this. [*Returning to his work*]

PARMIGIAN: What's the matter? I don't have enough culture for you? Let me tell you something. There was a great culture in Armenia when the Jews in Egypt didn't know how to put up a ten-foot pyramid! When the Greeks were walking around without underwear, they were making rugs in Armenia with a thousand knots to the inch!

LANDAU: That has nothing to do with the difference between a Brueghel and a pomegranate! We were talking about Brueghel and pomegranates!

PARMIGIAN: I know what we were talking about!

LANDAU: Then what is your point? What is your point, Mr. Parmigian?

PARMIGIAN: What are you getting your eyes all clouded up for? You look like you got a thunderstorm in your face.

LANDAU: I want to know your point! What is your point?

PARMIGIAN: My point is that when you consider a cuckoo clock that keeps time without a cuckoo, when you can work all those years for a man who walked around with a white apron and had eyes like a lizard and still can't remember his face, when *you* can make a mistake with a painting, and *I* can make a mistake with a hundred and six pomegranates . . . [PARMIGIAN, *his voice reaching a crescendo of intensity, suddenly comes to an abrupt stop.*]

LANDAU: Yes? What?

PARMIGIAN: I don't know. I forgot the point. There was a point, but I forgot what it was.

LANDAU: Then what are you yelling about? How can you scream about everything with such conviction when you don't even know the point of what you're talking about?

PARMIGIAN: Because I know something that nobody else in the world knows.

LANDAU: What? What do you know?

PARMIGIAN: I know the secret of the universe! The same secret the Jewish rabbis were working on in their secret cabalas for the last five thousand years!

LANDAU: What secret? And don't start in with the Jews again. I've heard enough about Jews from Gentiles to last me ten lifetimes.

PARMIGIAN: What have you heard?

LANDAU: Never mind what I've heard. Just stick to the point. What secret of the universe?

PARMIGIAN: *The* secret of the universe! *The* secret! The one and only secret worth a damn! It came to me one summer night when I was alone in the store. My last customer, a midget, had just left and I was staring down at a hundred and six rotten plantains. You know what a plantain is? It's a big banana.

LANDAU: I know what a plantain is . . . and I thought it was a hundred and six pomegranates. That's what you were talking about before, wasn't it? Pomegranates!

PARMIGIAN: The pomegranates were from the year before. This time it was plantains, a hundred and six of them. Staring down, looking at that rotten fruit, I asked myself what is the purpose behind creating fruit whose only reason for existence is to rot? That's when I heard the voice. The voice said to me, "You're missing the point, Parmigian. The point is, there is no point! And while you're at it you ought to stop by the hospital and check out that tickle in your throat." And that, my friend, my Jewish friend, is the secret of the universe. There is no point! I, Joseph Parmigian, have solved the problem five thousand rabbis with five thousand beards working five thousand years couldn't solve—there is no point! [*For a long moment there is silence between the two* MEN, *and then* PARMIGIAN *sticks his hand into his robe pocket and withdraws a piece of cake neatly wrapped in a napkin. With great precision he care-*

fully folds back each of the four corners of the napkin, exposing the cake] You want a piece of hospital rum cake? It's made without rum.

LANDAU: [*Ignoring the offer*] There is a point to things in this world. Just because you haven't found it doesn't mean it isn't there.

PARMIGIAN: [*Biting into his cake*] Good. Good. Maybe you'll tell me what it is?

LANDAU: I don't have to tell you. All you have to do is look around you.

PARMIGIAN: [*Idly looking around*] Where should I look?

LANDAU: Not under your wheelchair, Mr. Parmigian. There's a sky over your head, a universe. You look at it and then tell me there's no point to it.

PARMIGIAN: [*Staring at the sky for some moments*] There's no point to it.

LANDAU: Forget it. I don't have the time for this. [*Trying to return to his work.*]

PARMIGIAN: Sure you have the time. You got at least six months. You want to see some real action, Landau? Look under my wheelchair. There's an ant carrying off a dead roach. And there comes his buddy. He's going to help him carry off the roach, and later the both of them are going to come back and finish off the crumbs from the rum cake.

LANDAU: You turn everything into meaninglessness, don't you?

PARMIGIAN: Don't overestimate me, Landau. Some days I can't even turn my wheelchair. I want to come out here I have to sit by my door, waiting for some jerk to come along and give me a push. And sometimes they even forget I'm out here. It rains and I sit out here screaming my head off for half an hour and nobody hears me. So I sit here waiting . . . waiting for what? A push inside? No, not a push inside. I am waiting for something . . . something!

LANDAU: [*Speaking to himself, almost as if it just slipped out*] The courage to die.

PARMIGIAN: [*Turning to him*] What did you say?

LANDAU: It's unimportant. I was thinking of something else . . . someone else.

PARMIGIAN: Don't tell me it's unimportant. You said something. What was it?

LANDAU: I said you were probably waiting for the courage to die. I'm sorry. I didn't mean it the way it sounded.

PARMIGIAN: Don't be sorry. It's a good observation. "Waiting for the courage to die." It shows a brain with a lot of perception. Unfortunately, that's not what I'm waiting for. What time is it now on your five-hundred-dollar Rolex?

LANDAU: A quarter after seven.

PARMIGIAN: You know what happens in another fifteen minutes? The midget I told you about with a mustache and a Brooks Brothers suit comes into my store. The beginning of every week he comes in for an artichoke and a little plastic bag of dried-up oriental mushrooms. For six years I waited for him to tell me what kind of a dish it is he makes from an artichoke and a bag of dried-up oriental mushrooms.

LANDAU: Why don't you ask him? If you're so interested why don't you just ask him?

PARMIGIAN: Because that's what he's waiting for! Why should I give him the satisfaction? He stands there by the cash register with a crooked smile and a little leather Gucci briefcase in his hand . . . sometimes with a cigar, too, puffing smoke rings big as a garbage can cover. What happened to your private-duty nurse?

LANDAU: She left at four o'clock.

PARMIGIAN: She's coming back tomorrow?

LANDAU: No. I won't need a private-duty nurse until after the exploratory.

PARMIGIAN: Ask for the same one.

LANDAU: Why? What difference does it make?

PARMIGIAN: You know what a toad looks like, Landau? You don't get that one back, they'll give you a toad.

LANDAU: I thought you didn't like her. You said she was too fat.

PARMIGIAN: [*Answering with some difficulty*] She used to sit on the edge of my bed, reading to me in a thin dress with the sunlight coming through . . . driving me crazy. [*Looking directly at* LANDAU] Now she got engaged to a man who eats plantains, and her dress is as thick as a rubber sheet. [*Noticing a change of expression on* LANDAU's *face*] What's the matter, Mr. Landau. You don't think I have a penis anymore? I'll give you a surprise. I got a penis! In spite of all the operations, and the cutting, and the needles, and the twisting around, I got a penis. And when it comes time for me to leave this hospital, I'm going out like a knight from the *Faerie Queene*—with everything I got sticking straight up in the air! [*The lights on the roof garden come on automatically.*] That's the warning light. It comes on automatically. Impending darkness sensed without benefit of human intelligence. [PARMIGIAN *seems to have a little trouble breathing now.*] In half an hour the new tenants of this place arrive. Four hundred thousand mosquitoes from New Jersey—my visitors for the evening. They're crossing the Hudson right now.

LANDAU: Why don't you give yourself a break, Mr. Parmigian? You look exhausted.

PARMIGIAN: You getting any visitors tonight?

LANDAU: No. My wife'll be here tomorrow with the children.

PARMIGIAN: What about your parents? Your friends from the world of ceramics and cut glass?

LANDAU: I'm not expecting any visitors.

PARMIGIAN: You're a smart man, Landau. A man without expectations. A realist. You know what happens to friends? They vanish like a row of chicken hawks taking off from a branch. They used to come around with flowers . . . they bought them in the subway, but a flower's a flower . . . they used to come around in the afternoon, in the evening. Then when the ultimate prognosis was made, they could hardly wait to get out of here. Two seconds in the room and they'd start fidgeting, looking at the ceiling, looking at the walls. I'd lie there looking at what? A tiny ant, once, that had climbed eighteen stories up from the street just to frizzle to death on the radiator. And then they'd leave, rushing out into the street with their hangman faces, disappearing into the traffic like a puff of smoke.

LANDAU: People do for us what they can.

PARMIGIAN: That's a brilliant perception, Landau. You know what I'm going to do with it as soon as I leave this roof? I'm going to write it down in my book of Great Sayings of the Western World.

LANDAU: It doesn't help anything being unpleasant, Mr. Parmigian.

PARMIGIAN: Another great saying from the man without expectations. For your information everything in this hospital is improved by being unpleasant. You know what a semiprivate room is when you're pleasant? It's four in a room. You know what a semiprivate room is when you're unpleasant? It's yourself in a room!

LANDAU: And that's what you like? Being alone?

PARMIGIAN: Sure, that's what I like. Now I don't have to listen to people with appendectomies, people with prostatectomies, people with stones, and nose jobs, and one with a pacemaker in his heart buzzing away with atomic energy at four in the morning. Now I can concentrate totally on my disease. I can devote my entire thought process to my disease—which happens to be the emperor of disease! The emperor!

LANDAU: If that's the way you feel, why do you work out such a busy social schedule for yourself: nine o'clock by the nurses' station, ten o'clock hustling back into bed to catch the doctors on their rounds, eleven o'clock out here? That's a little bit inconsistent, isn't it?

PARMIGIAN: One thing has nothing to do with the other. It's a matter of respect.

LANDAU: What respect? What are you talking about?

PARMIGIAN: The emperor of disease does not share a room with a nose job and a bunch of kidney stones!

LANDAU: I didn't realize there was such a hierarchy of disease.

PARMIGIAN: There's a hierarchy with everything in this world. You start off with an ameba and you end up with a tuna fish.

LANDAU: What about a whale?

PARMIGIAN: What about a whale?

LANDAU: Well, a whale's bigger than a tuna fish. If you're going to create hierarchies for yourself, why not end up with a whale?

PARMIGIAN: Because a whale's a jerk compared to a tuna fish!

LANDAU: And what about human beings? Or don't they count?

PARMIGIAN: I'll tell you about human beings. A human being is an even bigger jerk than a whale. In my book the tuna fish is number one! It never gets cancer and it makes a terrific salad!

LANDAU: Well, if that's going to be the measure of everything for you, you ought to consider the cockroach. That never comes down with cancer, either!

PARMIGIAN: Then that's what's on top of the world: the cockroach and the tuna fish! What's the matter? You think I'm trying to make a joke? You think I'm trying to amuse you? I have no time for stupidity! One million years from today when the last cancer cell has wiped out the last human being, and they visit us from outer space, you know what they're going to see? A cockroach and a tuna fish riding the BMT subway down to Wall Street!

LANDAU: And this is what you spend your entire thought process on? The circles of the world bounded by a cancer cell; the horizon no bigger than the back of a cockroach?

PARMIGIAN: Why do you make yourself such an absurd person, Landau? Do you think I would spend my entire thought process on a question an imbecile could answer for himself in two seconds? No, my friend, my dear Richard Landau, I am devoting my entire thought process to one question, and one question alone: What am I waiting for? What is it I am waiting for? I am like a man in a dark passageway, a man who has heard a door open somewhere, and now waits to see what is coming . . . something silent coming.

LANDAU: Maybe it's the rest of the ants coming to pick up the rum cake you dropped all over the floor.

PARMIGIAN: Five thousand years of cabalistic training and that's the answer you give me? A bunch of ants coming to pick up a piece of rum cake?

LANDAU: [*Suddenly, surprisingly angered*] I don't have any answers to give you! I don't have any answers to give anyone! Five thousand years of cabalistic training? Well, I haven't had any cabalistic training! Not five thousand years! Not two thousand years! Nothing! You understand that? Nothing! I am not a college graduate! I am not a high school graduate! I didn't even have a chance to . . . [LANDAU, *realizing that he has momentarily lost control of himself, comes to an abrupt halt.*]

PARMIGIAN: To what?

LANDAU: [*Standing up*] Nothing that concerns you. I don't know why you keep bringing this up. For a man who sees no point to the universe, you have a pretty strange interest in mysticism.

PARMIGIAN: Jewish mysticism.

LANDAU: All right, Jewish mysticism.

PARMIGIAN: I keep bringing this up because you're a

Jew, and every Jew has an understanding of mysticism.

LANDAU: From what? Where am I supposed to get this understanding? I'm not a scholar. I'm not a rabbi.

PARMIGIAN: From the bones. It comes from the bones.

LANDAU: Nothing comes from the bones! How can you have read everything you say you've read, how can you talk about Hegel and Schopenhauer, and having found the secret of the universe, and still believe in such garbage? Bones? It's inbred in the bones? Well, let me tell you something. I've heard that kind of garbage before!

PARMIGIAN: Where was that?

LANDAU: Wherever you'd like it to be! Spain! France! Germany! In the back of a restaurant in Madrid! Wherever!

PARMIGIAN: What were you doing in back of a restaurant in Madrid?

LANDAU: I don't know why I said that. It doesn't mean anything to me.

PARMIGIAN: You were in all those places?

LANDAU: No place. I was no place.

PARMIGIAN: What were you doing in all those places? [*There is a certain manner in* PARMIGIAN'*s speech and expression that brings* LANDAU *to a halt. For some moments he stares at* PARMIGIAN.]

LANDAU: You're not interested in mysticism at all.

PARMIGIAN: Tell me about all those places, Landau.

LANDAU: It's just something to talk about, just something else to talk about, isn't it?

PARMIGIAN: Tell me about Madrid, Landau. Tell me about the restaurant in Madrid.

LANDAU: Tell you about anything that isn't silence is what you mean! You're interested in anything that isn't silence! It doesn't matter what it is, does it, Mr. Parmigian? It's all the same to you: the cabala, ants, reruns on the television, anything, everything, as long as it isn't silence. [LANDAU *gathers up his belongings.*]

PARMIGIAN: Where are you going?

LANDAU: I'm going inside.

PARMIGIAN: What for? There's nothing inside.

LANDAU: There's nothing outside either, Mr. Parmigian.

PARMIGIAN: [As LANDAU starts to exit] Landau! Don't leave me out here. Stay with me a little while. You don't have to talk. You don't have to say anything to me. Please. I don't want to be alone. I . . . I can't be alone no more.

LANDAU: Then go inside. You've got a whole floor full of people to feed yourself on.

PARMIGIAN: Who? The woman who sits in the dayroom, shuffling her cards? The rest of them who lie in their rooms, staring at the ceiling, dying with the spit running out of their mouths and a thousand tubes in their body? Who, Landau? Who?

LANDAU: I don't know.

PARMIGIAN: Stay with me, Landau, for a little while, for a little while and then I won't bother you no more. [LANDAU slowly sets his attaché case down.] I know what I am, but I also know what dying is. I'm being left alone here. I'm watching a world filled with things, with people, with a million adventures, slowly shutting me out, putting me aside, separating me from themselves. A little less attention every day, a little longer to answer the bell when you ring it. And the mind's not stupid. It sees what's happening . . . it sees. . . . But it thinks it's going to go on living forever, no matter what the body tells it, no matter what it hears the doctors tell it—the truth is a lie it won't believe. You'd tell it yourself, but you don't have the heart. And when death comes—what? It must be a big surprise. The mind must be stunned with surprise. It was just on the point of making new worlds for itself, just on the point of telling me this roof garden is a *Bounty* from which I will never mutiny, a Garden of Eden from which I will never be thrown out. Give it the whole universe and it wouldn't have enough room, or put it in a little box and watch it make worlds within worlds, little worlds without end. How such a thing could die, I don't know. [*For a moment there is silence between the two men as* PARMIGIAN *stares blankly forward, and* LANDAU *is lost in his own thoughts.*] What do you think about, Landau? When I ask you what you are thinking of and you tell me you are thinking of something else, or nothing?

LANDAU: Nothing.

PARMIGIAN: What does nothing look like?

LANDAU: Things . . . different things . . . a room . . . if there was sunlight in the room . . . a dresser . . . a chair. . . . A man I once met in a police station in Portugal . . . a man who wanted me to remember his name, and I can't anymore. I don't think I was eight years old.

PARMIGIAN: What were you doing in a police station?

LANDAU: My father was there somewhere. The war had broken out that day . . . or some other day . . . and we went around. . . . I think it was just the two of us because I don't remember my mother or sister going with us into any of those buildings . . . embassies . . . maybe they were embassies because the floors were marble . . . white marble . . . rosy marble . . . so we had the day together, my father and I . . . I didn't do that too often with him . . . it was nice being alone with him . . . I must have liked that . . . I must have. [*Pause.*] I'm sorry. You asked me something?

PARMIGIAN: I asked you what you were doing in a police station in Portugal.

LANDAU: They were deporting some of the German Jews. I know that now because I read a lot about it, and I've written a lot of letters about it. You see, I have a file. In my dresser at home I keep a file about that. [*Pause.*] That man in the police station kept talking and talking.

PARMIGIAN: About what? [LANDAU *just looks blankly at him.*] About what, Landau?

LANDAU: I had some candy. My father had given me some candy and the man was hungry and he wanted it. He kept offering me things . . . things he had in his pockets. I finally gave him the candy for some money, or something else, something else that wasn't money.

PARMIGIAN: He must have made a strong impression on you to remember him so many years.

LANDAU: He was nothing to me! Just another Jew waiting to be sent away like the rest of them. They had him handcuffed to a chair, and he kept telling me how stupid it was, how he could lift up the chair and just walk out of the building with it if he wanted to. He had a thousand different escape plans if only he wasn't handcuffed. I was alone with him and I was so frightened, and I couldn't leave the room because my father had told me to stay there. I was not allowed to even get out of my chair. And the man's screaming and pulling and pulling on the handcuff, and his wrist is bleeding, and it's an old handcuff, or they didn't close it properly, and it opens up—and he is free. Free to escape. For one awful moment in his life, free of them. And he rubs his wrist and, sitting very quietly now in the chair, snaps the handcuff shut again. [*Shutting an imaginary handcuff on his wrist.*]

PARMIGIAN: I don't understand.

LANDAU: Can't you? Can't you understand how a man could be more afraid of making a futile attempt to escape than of anything they could do to him if he tried? Well, it doesn't matter.

PARMIGIAN: Why do you always say that? This doesn't matter. That doesn't matter. It's important that people understand each other.

LANDAU: They understand each other. It just never makes any difference.

PARMIGIAN: So tell me, and we'll see if it makes a difference.

LANDAU: [*Studying him for a moment before answering*] He didn't want to be humiliated again, not laughed at again, not made a joke of again. Can you understand that? Really understand that? How a man could say to himself, "Better to take one final train ride to hell, than live another day in Europe; better to let it all end than have to listen one more time to Europe's murderers coming down a thousand dirty Jewish alleys?"

PARMIGIAN: I can understand that.

LANDAU: No . . . no . . . I will not let you say that . . . you cannot say that . . . no.

PARMIGIAN: Where are your parents that don't come to the hospital, Landau? Your sister?

LANDAU: They walked down an alley and they went away. I kept trying to run after them, but the stones were wet or slippery, and I couldn't keep my balance, and they were around the corner and they were gone —it was like the dog. My father had a dog and the dog got too big to be kept in the city, so we left him with a farmer, and the dog ran after the car, down the road, trying to catch up to us in the car . . . trying, trying so hard not to be left behind . . . but they were gone, gone like all the rest of them, the man in the police station . . . all gone away. I did a lot of research about this . . . about what they were doing with the German nationals they deported, and I have a file. In my dresser . . . I keep a file . . . about that. [*Drawing himself up in a chair next to* PARMIGIAN] You know I've been doing something very interesting since April. There was some Chinese cloisonné work on auction in this apartment on Park Avenue, this old apartment, but I wasn't there more than a few seconds before I realized that this apartment had the exact same layout as the apartment my parents rented in Munich. I had a difficult time keeping track of the auction. There were a lot of bids I wanted to enter, but it seemed to get so warm in the living room, and there was a hall, and I wanted to go down the hall. I felt embarrassed getting up; I was representing clients and there's a certain responsibility, but I went down the hall and stood by the kitchen . . . and it was as if I could remember my mother doing the dishes in the kitchen, and my father in the dining room, sitting at the table with his books, studying, wearing that great heavy sweater of his—I always thought one day I'd have that sweater. I can't tell you what a feeling came over me standing there in this woman's apartment. My hands were trembling, I couldn't stop them, and inside me there was such a sense of overwhelming joy, my whole body felt alive again because this was all something new, I had remembered something that wasn't there before, something that was lost . . . a table filled with medical books! My father was in medical school then because they were medical books he was studying! When we lived in Munich my father was in medical school! And I walked over to the table and I could see him sitting there . . . months later . . . years later . . . maybe another apartment . . . his hands covered by a cloth because somebody had broken his hands. . . . Did the Nazis break his hands? Did they break his hands under a brewer's cart? But the bedroom was wrong. It wasn't where my bedroom was, so . . . so what I've been doing that's very interesting since April is that I've been trying to figure out where my bedroom was. [*Standing up and walking a few feet away.*]

PARMIGIAN: Why didn't they send you back to Germany, Landau? Why your family and not you?

LANDAU: My father found a man . . . Luis Boscan. And for money—I guess everything my father had left—he took care of me. His wife used to tell me that they would have taken my sister, too, but my mother was afraid to let her go . . . she was just a baby . . . it was a choice . . . it wasn't a matter of money . . . my mother made a choice. I . . . um . . . Anyway, they were nice people. I still write to them. Sometimes they write to me. They like to tell me about the time they met my father, where it was, what the day was like, what he was wearing; they always seem to find something new, some little detail . . . I . . . [*Suddenly grown angry*] I don't like talking about the Boscans. My life is a history of the Boscans! Their sons, and the businesses their sons went into! Their daughters and who they married! Their grandchildren! My life has a history that has nothing to do with the Boscans! It had a beginning! It had people in it! It had . . . It had . . . What did it have? What? I would sit by a window thinking the day would come when my father would walk around the corner of that alley again . . . my mother, my sister . . . my sister . . . oh, God. How many years did I sit by that window wishing they had saved her instead of me! Waiting! Waiting! Just like the rest of them. Waiting for passports that never arrived, waiting for boats that would take us out of there, waiting at the embassies, the British, the American, waiting to reach invisible people, diplomats who could save anyone, if only you could touch them— but you couldn't, because they hid themselves down corridors no refugee could enter, behind doors no Jew could open! A world died trying to touch these faceless people who had no pity, while I sat by a window—waiting!

PARMIGIAN: And later?

LANDAU: And later there was no later! Not for them. Not for me.

PARMIGIAN: No, Landau, that's not true. For you there was a later, and later you must have felt happy you were alive.

LANDAU: Is that what you think?

PARMIGIAN: I would have felt that way.

LANDAU: Yes. You would have. Anything to stay alive. In talking to you I am very aware of that.

PARMIGIAN: And what's wrong in wanting to stay alive?

LANDAU: Nothing. For you, nothing.

PARMIGIAN: And for you? What's wrong in wanting to stay alive, for you?

LANDAU: I don't want to talk about this.

PARMIGIAN: Why not? Because your parents threw you clear of a whirlpool that was sucking them down, and you don't know why you're happy you're alive?

LANDAU: No! Because being happy I'm alive doesn't mean anything to me! How can you be happy you're alive when you don't know who you are? When you have no yesterday, no past? When the only ground you have to stand on is the memory of what you were, and it's not there anymore? He's killed everything, cut off every link to what I was, so that even when I do remember I can never be sure it's true. He's killed, and He's killed, and I have no way back.

PARMIGIAN: Who's He, Landau?

LANDAU: You know Him. You sit in your chair waiting, and you know Him. You die in a concentration camp and His hand reaches into your mouth for the gold teeth and you know Him. A handcuff falls off your wrist and you think you can escape until His fingers snap it shut again, and you know Him.

PARMIGIAN: There is no Him, Landau, just us.

LANDAU: How glib you are. I listened to you all afternoon going on and on as if you knew something that was worth all those words, and all I could think about was how every sound I make is unpleasant to me, how much I've grown to hate the sound of my own voice. I'm tired of being a man. Tired of putting on my clothes in the morning. Tired of taking them off at night. Tired of turning on the gas to broil a piece of meat and standing there with the match in my hand, watching it burn down till it scorches my fingers, forgetting what it was I came there to do. [*Looking directly at* PARMIGIAN] And nothing of this has anything to do with you.

PARMIGIAN: That's absolutely true. That's why you should talk to me. I can give you a hundred percent objective opinion. That's what every Jew needs. A one hundred percent objective opinion from Armenia.

LANDAU: I don't need any opinions from you or anyone else.

PARMIGIAN: Excuse me, Landau. In my opinion I never met anyone who needed more opinions than you do. You remind me of a man with a club foot who tells everybody he's got a ballet slipper on his foot. Which reminds me of something in my dream with the King of Bavaria and his wife. In the dream for some strange reason I have turned myself into a hunchback. I walk around with a big hump on my back. What do you think about this?

LANDAU: Nothing!

PARMIGIAN: Another "nothing" from the master of "nothing." What's the matter, Landau, don't you see the similarity between our two cases? You with your club foot and me with my hump?

LANDAU: What similarity? There's no similarity! You just invented that! You just gave yourself a hump on the back when you decided to give me a club foot! You never dreamed you were a humpback until you decided I had a club foot! [LANDAU *turns away from him.*]

PARMIGIAN: Landau?

LANDAU: What?

PARMIGIAN: You came out a winner. You came out a big winner.

LANDAU: Why? Because I survived? Is that what makes me a big winner?

PARMIGIAN: You not only survived, Landau, you triumphed! A boy with no education turns himself into a man who can almost tell the difference between a Van der Heyden, whatever that is, and a Pieter Brueghel. A boy dropped down in the middle of Portugal alone ends up in America with a wife, two

children, and a ten-speed bike. This is a triumph,
Landau. A triumph!

LANDAU: It doesn't feel like a triumph.

PARMIGIAN: That's because nothing we ever do feels like
a triumph, because the mind's a piece of garbage. It's
never happy with what we do for it. I once took my
mind down to Barbados for two weeks, and you
know what it said to me? "You should have taken us
to Jamaica!" So don't wait around for thanks from
it. I'll let you in on a little secret. The real reason
Adam and Eve got thrown out of the Garden of
Eden had nothing to do with a piece of fruit, because
there's nothing wrong with a piece of fruit, it's a good
laxative. What it was was that God finally got tired
waiting around for thanks from the human brain. He
said, "If I have to wait around for thanks, I'm going
to die of old age. So screw it, and while I'm thinking
about it, screw them!"

LANDAU: I thought you didn't believe in God.

PARMIGIAN: When did I say that?

LANDAU: A few minutes ago, right after you got done
talking about pomegranates or plantains or whatever
it was.

PARMIGIAN: Who remembers what I said a few minutes
ago? Why do you live in the past? The past is a
bunch of junk, too. Yesterday you were worried
about the varicose veins in your wife's leg, today she
bought herself a new bottle of perfume. Concentrate
on the perfume. There's a new world coming in every
twenty-two seconds.

LANDAU: You really believe that?

PARMIGIAN: Absolutely. Right now in a laboratory
under the mountains of Zurich there's a man with
one eye working on a new cure for cancer. It won't
work, but that's what's happening in the present.

LANDAU: Not my present, Mr. Parmigian.

PARMIGIAN: What is your present? A man tied to a chair

in a Portuguese police station, talking to an eight-year-old boy?

LANDAU: That's right! That's my present! You think it helps anything listening to you reduce everything to an absurdity?

PARMIGIAN: And you? You think it helps anything listening to you reduce everything to a tragedy?

LANDAU: My God! What do you think it was? Don't you think it was a tragedy?

PARMIGIAN: No. It was worse than a tragedy. A tragedy doesn't even begin to get at it. It was a monument, Landau. A monument! Compared to what happened to you, Oedipus putting out his eyes was a minor occurrence.

LANDAU: And this is what I am supposed to forget?

PARMIGIAN: You can't walk around with a monument, Landau. It's enough to walk around with a club foot.

LANDAU: Leave me alone, Mr. Parmigian. I don't want to discuss this with you.

PARMIGIAN: Who do you want to discuss this with? A psychiatrist? You got a psychiatrist, Landau? Don't bother answering me. I can see from the way you twitch around in a chair you must have worn out a hundred leather couches already. You know what you can do for fifty dollars an hour? You can visit five massage parlors and have a terrific time.

LANDAU: Stop it! Talking to you . . . trying to talk to you . . . and listening to this . . . it's . . . it's . . .

PARMIGIAN: Absurd? It's absurd, Landau?

LANDAU: It's humiliating!

PARMIGIAN: Of course it's humiliating. You know why it's humiliating? Because no matter how many times you try to explain it to yourself, your wife, your psychiatrist, the man on the bus with the pince-nez on his nose, it comes out a diminishment. Real suffering, Landau, real suffering is a catastrophe without language. It's a dinosaur egg big as a moon which cracks open with a two-inch chicken inside of it. Don't you think I know this?

LANDAU: I don't know what you know. You turn everything into an absurdity. [*Sitting down.*]

PARMIGIAN: Only suffering. Only suffering. Look around you. Don't you notice something peculiar? Here is a terrific roof garden for the patients, but where are the patients? Why don't the patients use this terrific roof garden? You want an answer? They don't use this terrific roof garden because they know I'm out here. Inside is a dayroom with a woman sitting alone in it. Nobody will go in. They will walk by it because they know she's in it. When we're forced into the same room to watch a television show, you know what the entrance looks like? A bunch of leopards meeting for the first time in the jungle: a little nod of the head, a little acknowledgment that somebody might be alive besides ourselves, and that's it. At night you can hear the silence in the separate rooms like a dozen crystal chandeliers waiting to explode.

LANDAU: Then why talk to me? If that's what happens around here, why talk to me?

PARMIGIAN: Because you're a little bit of a fooler, Landau. A little bit of a trickster. When I saw Miss Latin America wheel you out here, I thought it was a hundred and seventy pounds of fresh meat arriving. There was a big skirmish in the hall for you, a collision of crutches and glucose bottles. They should have known you've been in the refrigerator for thirty-five years. That's why you don't care what happens to you with your exploratory, that's why you can sit out here and everything I say to you, "It's nothing." "It's not important." "It doesn't matter." I got a dazzling truth for you. You never got out of that police station alive! You're not waiting for a death sentence here, because you're still waiting for a death sentence from the time you were eight years old!

Well, it's not going to happen! The judge is never coming back into the room, the jury fell asleep in the jury box, the executioner died with his victims, so as far as anybody cares you can get up and walk out!

LANDAU: How do you walk out of what's in your mind? How do you get up and walk out of what's in your mind?

PARMIGIAN: [*After working* LANDAU *up to a fevered pitch, the accusatory tone suddenly drops completely out of* PARMIGIAN'*s voice.*] Who knows? I'm not a psychiatrist. This analysis is from a movie I once saw with Ingrid Bergman and Gregory Peck. She got him all worked up to a big climax with an orchestra in the background, and there was a tremendous breakthrough. You got a breakthrough like that, Landau? [*They stare at each other for a few moments, and then* LANDAU *begins to laugh, a strange laugh that twists his mouth into a wry self-deprecating kind of contortion. He covers his mouth with his hands as if trying to hide the sound.*] You laughing? Is that what your laughing sounds like?

LANDAU: [*Lowering his hands*] Oh, God.

PARMIGIAN: It's a joke, huh? A joke?

LANDAU: A very sad joke . . . pain into absurdity, memory into counterfeit.

PARMIGIAN: That's the thing. In this universe that's the only thing we got for a joke. With an orchestra, without an orchestra, it's still a watermelon with four legs. What we want from it is not coming. [*Looking down at the floor*] What's coming here is an ant after a piece of rum cake.

LANDAU: His name was Reischmann! The man in the police station, his name was Reischmann!

PARMIGIAN: Good for you. You remembered his name. You saved him from oblivion.

LANDAU: He gave me a glass paperweight. A millefiore glass paperweight. It couldn't have been very good.

341

We never learned to make good glass paperweights in Germany.

PARMIGIAN: And you saved it all the days of your childhood, huh, Landau?

LANDAU: No. Somewhere along the line I lost it. Somewhere here, somewhere there. I'd like to remember it all very clearly: every blow, every hurt in every eye, the humiliation my father must have known cleaning dishes in a hundred dirty little restaurants so we could survive—and all that's really there are bits and pieces . . . a piece of glass you keep for a while and then you lose it or you throw it away, a Passover table set with crystal and lace, the strands of my sister's hair when she was all dressed up and proud.

PARMIGIAN: When I think of bits and pieces I think of a 1933 Buick I once had with a hundred and six patches on every tire.

LANDAU: [*Lost in his own thoughts*] I do some photography work now. It's a nice hobby. Summers I take pictures of the kids on the beach . . . birthdays and anniversaries, holidays when my wife's family comes over for dinner . . . and the pictures fill pages, and the pages fill albums, and one album sits stacked on another. . . .

PARMIGIAN: You know, it would amaze you what you could do with a good patch. The patches on this 1933 Buick were so good that when the tires disintegrated the patches kept rolling for another hundred and seventy-two miles. They ran over a state trooper who was giving a speeding ticket to a nun that looked like a penguin. [LANDAU, *again, begins to laugh, an explosive, almost mechanical laugh, that gradually grows real.*] That's it, my friend, laugh a little bit, and while you're laughing I'll wait a little bit longer with you. I'll give the man working with one eye in the Zurich laboratory another month.

LANDAU: It probably won't make any difference. The Swiss never save anything but themselves.

PARMIGIAN: Even their cheese is full of holes.

LANDAU: He's probably an incompetent, the man in the laboratory.

PARMIGIAN: Absolutely. Worse than incompetent. How else do you think he lost his eye? [*For some moments,* BOTH MEN *laugh, sharing their private joke, and then* LANDAU *wipes his eyes, stands up, and reaches for his attaché case.*]

LANDAU: I'm going inside now, Mr. Parmigian. [*Walks toward the exit.*]

PARMIGIAN: Will you take me inside with you?

LANDAU: [*Turning and looking at* PARMIGIAN's *upturned face for a moment.*] Yes. [*As* LANDAU *touches the back of* PARMIGIAN's *wheelchair,* PARMIGIAN *reaches down and releases the brake.*]

PARMIGIAN: Look, off with the brake, off with everything, and I'm ready to roll. [*Pause.*] Landau?

LANDAU: Yes?

PARMIGIAN: I'll meet you out here tomorrow?

LANDAU: All right.

PARMIGIAN: Landau?

LANDAU: Yes?

PARMIGIAN: I promise you a very interesting day.

LIGHTS DIM AND OUT AS THEY EXIT

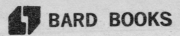 **BARD BOOKS**

the classics, poetry, drama and distinguished modern fiction

FICTION

ACT OF DARKNESS John Peale Bishop	10827	1.25
ALL HALLOW'S EVE Charles Williams	11213	1.45
ANAIS NIN READER Ed., Philip K. Jason	33624	2.50
THE AWAKENING Kate Chopin	38760	1.95
THE BENEFACTOR Susan Sontag	11221	1.45
BETRAYED BY RITA HAYWORTH Manuel Puig	36020	2.25
BILLIARDS AT HALF-PAST NINE Heinrich Böll	32730	1.95
CALL IT SLEEP Henry Roth	37549	2.25
THE CASE HISTORY OF COMRADE V. James Park Sloan	15362	1.65
CATALOGUE George Milburn	33084	1.95
THE CLOWN Heinrich Böll	37523	2.25
A COOL MILLION and THE DREAM LIFE **OF BALSO SNELL** Nathanael West	15115	1.65
DANGLING MAN Saul Bellow	24463	1.65
EDWIN MULLHOUSE Steven Millhauser	37952	2.50
THE EYE OF THE HEART Barbara Howes, Ed.	20883	2.25
THE FAMILY OF PASCUAL DUARTE Camilo José Cela	11247	1.45
GABRIELA, CLOVE AND CINNAMON Jorge Amado	18275	1.95
THE GALLERY John Horne Burns	33357	2.25
A GENEROUS MAN Reynolds Price	15123	1.65
GOING NOWHERE Alvin Greenberg	15081	1.65
THE GREEN HOUSE Mario Vargas Llosa	15099	1.65
HERMAPHRODEITY Alan Friedman	16865	2.45
HOPSCOTCH Julio Cortázar	36731	2.95
HUNGER Knut Hamsun	26864	1.75
HOUSE OF ALL NATIONS Christina Stead	18895	2.45

SUN CITY Tove Jansson	32318	1.95
THE LANGUAGE OF CATS AND OTHER STORIES Spencer Hoist	14381	1.65
THE LAST DAYS OF LOUISIANA RED Ishmael Reed	35451	2.25
LEAF STORM AND OTHER STORIES Gabriel García Márquez	36816	1.95
LESBIAN BODY Monique Wittig	31062	1.75
LES GUERILLERES Monique Willig	14373	1.65
A LONG AND HAPPY LIFE Reynolds Price	17053	1.65
LUCIFER WITH A BOOK John Horne Burns	33340	2.25
THE MAGNIFICENT AMBERSONS Booth Tarkington	17236	1.50
THE MAN WHO LOVED CHILDREN Christina Stead	40618	2.50
THE MAN WHO WAS NOT WITH IT Herbert Gold	19356	1.65
THE MAZE MAKER Michael Ayrton	23648	1.65
A MEETING BY THE RIVER Christopher Isherwood	37945	1.95
MYSTERIES Knut Hamsun	25221	1.95
NABOKOV'S DOZEN Vladimir Nabokov	15354	1.65
NO ONE WRITES TO THE COLONEL AND OTHER STORIES Gabriel García Márquez	32748	1.75
ONE HUNDRED YEARS OF SOLITUDE Gabriel García Márquez	34033	2.25
OUR TOWN Thornton Wilder	26674	1.25
PARTIES Carl Van Vechten	32631	1.95
PNIN Vladimir Nabokov	40600	1.95
PRATER VIOLET Christopher Isherwood	36269	1.95
REAL PEOPLE Alison Lurie	23747	1.65
THE RECOGNITIONS William Gaddis	18572	2.65
SLAVE Isaac Singer	26377	1.95
A SMUGGLER'S BIBLE Joseph McElroy	33589	2.50
STUDS LONIGAN TRILOGY James T. Farrell	31955	2.75
SUMMERING Joanne Greenberg	17798	1.65
62: A MODEL KIT Julio Cortázar	17558	1.65
THREE BY HANDKE Peter Handke	32458	2.25
THE VICTIM Saul Bellow	24273	1.75
WHAT HAPPENS NEXT? Gilbert Rogin	17806	1.65

BARD BOOKS

DISTINGUISHED DRAMA

ARMS AND THE MAN George Bernard Shaw	01628	.60
CANDIDE Lillian Hellman	12211	1.65
THE CHANGING ROOM, HOME, THE CONTRACTOR: THREE PLAYS David Storey	22772	2.45
A HISTORY OF THE AMERICAN FILM Christopher Durang	39271	1.95
EDWARD II Christopher Marlowe	18648	.75
EQUUS Peter Shaffer	24828	1.75
THE FANTASTICKS Tom Jones and Harvey Schmidt	22129	1.65
GHOSTS Henrik Ibsen	22152	.95
HEDDA GABLER Henrik Ibsen	24620	.95
THE INSPECTOR GENERAL Nikolai Gogol	28878	.95
THE IMPORTANCE OF BEING EARNEST Oscar Wilde	37473	1.25
THE LOWER DEPTHS Maxim Gorky	18630	.75
MISS JULIE August Strindberg	36855	.95
OUR TOWN Thornton Wilder	26674	1.25
THE PLAYBOY OF THE WESTERN WORLD John Millington Synge	22046	.95
THE CHERRY ORCHARD Anton Chekhov	36848	.95
THE SEA GULL Anton Chekhov	24638	.95
THE SHADOW BOX Michael Cristofer	36913	1.95
THREE PLAYS BY THORNTON WILDER Thornton Wilder	27623	2.25
UNCLE VANYA Anton Chekhov	18663	.75
THE WILD DUCK Henrik Ibsen	23093	.95
WOYZECK Georg Büchner	10751	1.25

Where better paperbacks are sold, or directly from the publisher. Include 25¢ per copy for mailing; allow three weeks for delivery.

Avon Books, Mail Order Dept.
250 West 55th Street, New York, N. Y. 10019

BDD 6-78